# Entertaining 101

BETH LE MANACH

### BETH LE MANACH

# Entertaining 101

## 101 Recipes Every Host Should Know How to Make

**DK | Penguin Random House**

**Publisher** Mike Sanders
**Art & Design Director** William Thomas
**Editorial Director** Ann Barton
**Senior Editor** Olivia Peluso
**Senior Designer** Jessica Lee
**Photographer** Ed Rudolph
**Food Stylist** Marah Abel
**Prop Stylist** Jennifer Barguiarena
**Recipe Tester** Ben Weiner
**Copyeditor** Hannah Matuszak
**Proofreaders** Christina Guthrie & Mira S. Park
**Indexer** Beverlee Day

First American Edition, 2025
Published in the United States by DK Publishing
1745 Broadway, 20th Floor, New York, NY 10019

The authorized representative in the EEA is Dorling Kindersley
Verlag GmbH. Arnulfstr. 124, 80636 Munich, Germany

A catalog record for this book
is available from the Library of Congress.
ISBN 978-0-5938-4484-7

DK books are available at special discounts when purchased
in bulk for sales promotions, premiums, fund-raising, or
educational use. For details, contact SpecialSales@dk.com

Printed and bound in China

**www.dk.com**

MIX
Paper | Supporting
responsible forestry
FSC™ C018179

This book was made with Forest
Stewardship Council™ certified
paper – one small step in DK's
commitment to a sustainable future.
Learn more at
www.dk.com/uk/information/sustainability

# DEDICATION

To my daughters: May you find that one thing in life that makes
your heart sing and throw your whole soul into it.

And to my husband, who has always pushed me to do the same.

# CONTENTS

# INTRODUCTION
## An Entertainer is Born

My love for entertaining began when I was twelve. My parents were consummate entertainers, and our home in Fairfield, Connecticut, was always filled with friends and relatives, eating, drinking, and dancing long after the kids went to bed.

These parties were more than just food and drink offered up to the hungry hordes; they were sensory experiences. Ones I can easily call up in my mind forty years later. My father is a "jack of all creative trades," and my mother has always been a woman of refined tastes, so together they were a dynamic duo. They created an environment for their guests that centered on just the right amount of candlelight, music, and decorations. At Christmastime, there was a soaring seven-foot Christmas tree in the living room, with freshly picked evergreens, pine cones, and berries decorating every surface. Easter meant willow baskets filled with springtime bulbs and large flowering branches. But even our cozy Sunday-night dinners were held in the dining room, with homemade meals and candles decorating the table. My parents were masters at setting a scene. "If the candles are lit, it feels like fine dining—even if we're eating hamburgers," my father would always say.

I think this is why the parties went on so long: Guests felt nurtured and cared for in my parents' home. As kids, my siblings and I were included in these celebrations, too. Never relegated to the basement or kiddie table, we were integrated with the adults because that's where the fun was happening! There was always a lap to sit on, a funny story to listen to, or a game of charades to play.

My parents knew how much I loved to bake, so they would let me make the occasional fruit tart or batch of Christmas cookies, despite the mess I left in their kitchen. They encouraged my sister Meg and me to participate in these events, and if we weren't making something for the party, we were serving the food my parents had made. They would present us with freshly ironed aprons, place a serving platter in one hand and a stack of napkins in the other, and send us out into a crowded living room. There, we were met with lots of *oohs* and *ahs* as their guests would make a big fuss over whatever we were offering. Which, of course, just made us want to do it again and again.

In this house, I learned the value of a hot hors d'oeuvre, a beautifully set table, and the spirit of true

hospitality—which often meant extending a holiday invitation to anyone who had nowhere to go. There was always room at my parents' table for just a few more guests, and their invitations were coveted.

When Meg and I moved into our first apartment, we sought to recreate this hospitality. While our friends were hosting balcony keggers with chips and dips, we scraped together whatever money we had to throw sit-down dinner parties because, well, that's what Mom and Dad always did. Dinner may have been a simple shrimp pasta and a $7 bottle of wine, but the table was set, the candles were lit, and there was always a homemade dessert or two. These parties made our friends feel special and a little bit more "grown-up" than we probably had the right to feel. But it *meant* something to everyone, and soon our invitations were coveted, too.

In 1997, I met my French husband, Philippe. He took me to France to meet his family, and I realized that my high school French wasn't cut out for much, except coloring at the kiddie table or helping in the kitchen.

It was there in the French kitchen that my heart skipped a beat. Philippe's mother and sisters-in-law moved through the kitchen in complete unison, a type of choreography that can only be achieved through years of cooking together. I must have looked so out of place as I stood there mesmerized at the scene: homemade vinaigrettes whisked up with a splash of this and a drizzle of that, special machines that looked like coffee makers spinning away to keep the beurre blanc sauce warm, and oysters cracked open with the flip of a wrist. A new world of food and hospitality opened up to me, one I couldn't stop thinking about. As the years wore on and the trips to France became more frequent, I couldn't wait to get back home to Los Angeles to impress my husband with re-creations of his favorite childhood dishes.

In 2000, Philippe and I were married, and in 2008, we bought our first house. We wanted a little house on a big lot, an oasis in the urban sprawl of Los Angeles. But we were outbid on just about every property we saw. Suddenly, a neglected bank-owned gem crossed our path: It was a 1949 cottage on a big lot, but it was just the diamond in the rough we'd dreamed of. It didn't have a dining room, but hey, it was Southern California—we'd dine outside!

We went to work fixing it up, creating two outdoor dining rooms for hosting large groups of family and friends. The crown jewel of all this work was a formal French vegetable garden, inspired by the one we had seen at the Château de Villandry, a castle in the Loire Valley known for its magnificent gardens. It would serve as the setting and inspiration for so many of our parties and my Franglais style of cooking.

At this time, I was working in video production for an LA-based digital media company. The company received a grant from YouTube to launch a lifestyle channel, and they were in need of cooking content—fast and cheap. I volunteered to share a few of the party menus I had been serving up in our new house and invited the crew over to shoot a few of them.

As the videos aired, a funny thing happened: I was surprised to find that a lot of this "easy entertaining advice" was new to people. I quickly realized that there was a whole generation of young adults who didn't grow up in homes with parents who entertained or even cooked from scratch, for that matter.

I saw an opportunity to provide recipes, menus, and game plans that would take the stress out of entertaining and make it easy and fun! I somehow convinced my boss at the time to let me create a spin-off YouTube channel, and in 2012, Entertaining with Beth (EWB) was born.

Over the last thirteen years of building my brand on YouTube, I've realized that the sweet spot for most beginners is recipes that look and taste great but also offer a practical twist or a killer tip that saves you time, money, or your own sanity! Because let's face it, whipping up your favorite weeknight meal is one thing, but add a few guests to the mix and it becomes "cooking theater," which is a whole other ball game.

I've become close to my followers, and it feels like we're a big group of pen pals exchanging ideas and tips on our shared passions of cooking and entertaining. Many of them began watching my videos as students living at home, but now they have homes of their own. I love hearing about their adventures (and misadventures!) in entertaining. I've also found that the same perennial questions always pop up: "What's a great egg bake I can make for Christmas morning?" (Puffy Egg Bake on page 169) or "What's an easy dinner idea I can serve to impress my visiting in-laws?" (Frenzy-Free Chicken Pot Pie on page 114). They have questions about hosting book clubs, baby showers, Easter Sundays, Mother's Days, and more—and I love providing the answers!

I'm determined to make entertaining easier because I have seen how much joy it can add to our lives. So, I've taken it upon myself to compile the top 101 recipes I believe everyone should know how to make to be able to entertain our friends and family without losing our minds in the process! It's my hope that this book will be the answer to all of your entertaining questions, a true manual for the beginner or an easier approach for the seasoned host.

# A FEW GROUND RULES

If you are new to entertaining, welcome! This book was written for you. Beginners hold a special place in my heart because twenty-five years ago, that was me. Entertaining can strike fear in any of us because it's one step beyond cooking for ourselves—it's cooking for (*gulp*) an audience.

This is why I'm including a few ground rules before you begin to help calm your nerves and ensure things go smoothly. That way, you can concentrate on the job at hand: feeding your guests while also having a good time!

## Don't Overdo the Guest List

Start small and work your way up. If you are a true beginner, start by hosting four guests. Ideally, they should be a group of close friends, another couple you know well (if you're hosting with a significant other), or a few "love-you-no-matter-what" family members. It always lessens the stress if you don't feel the need to impress.

Once you feel more comfortable, work up to six guests, then eight, then ten or more. But do not, for any reason, start at ten guests unless you have a death wish. Or never plan on entertaining again. Because this is what will happen. The stress at that level will create a frazzled host who is so traumatized by the experience that they'll never want to do it again. And why does this happen so often? It's the Guest Factor at play.

## The Guest Factor

There's something funny that happens when you're planning a party. There's the version in your head of how you *think* things will go and then there's the reality of what *actually happens*.

It reminds me of a college internship I had, where I had to assist a fashion designer backstage at a fashion show. The designer didn't have enough shoes for all the models, but he assured me that the girls could share the shoes: "When they come off the catwalk, they will just trade shoes, and all will be well." Well, obviously that didn't happen. Why? Because what *wasn't* anticipated was the chaos. The frenzy that ensued backstage as the girls looked for their "shared shoes." All the shoes ended up in a big heap in the middle of the dressing room, with the leggy models grabbing mismatched shoes while yelling obscenities at each other. Yeah, it was not a good look.

I think back to this scene anytime a beginner entertainer is thinking through their "run of show" for the party they are planning. It often goes something like this: *I'll get the rice started and then put the roast in the oven. Meanwhile, I'll reheat the sauce, pop the bread in the toaster, and boil the water for the string beans . . .* This is where I feel a bit like Simon Cowell from *American Idol* dying to blurt out, "Let me stop you right there."

Because what the "uninitiated" don't factor in are the guests! Yes, *there will be guests* who will cozy up to you in the kitchen right when you are about to spring into action. Seeing you alone in the kitchen feels like an enticing invitation for a private little chitchat. They will feel the need to "keep you company," peppering you with questions about your new job, your new haircut, or the date sitting out in the living room. Added to this are the newly arriving guests, with coats to take, flowers to put in vases, or apologies to accept about being stuck in traffic.

All this distraction can derail even the most seasoned host and get things off course. So, *don't* invite too many guests to begin with or plan a meal that involves too much active cooking. Your guests have come to visit with you, so you'll need to make yourself available! Learn more about how to handle these sticky situations in the Well, That's Awkward section on page 26.

## Prep Wisely

If it can be helped, do not shop, prep, and cook on the same day. You'll be too exhausted and frazzled! If you can, it's better to shop a day or two before you cook.

For larger parties like Thanksgiving or Christmas, you can purchase all the shelf-stable items like broths, spices, and canned goods a full week in advance.

## Remember Self-Care

Entertaining can be a lot of work; between the shopping, cooking, and cleaning, you can easily find yourself utterly exhausted before the party has even begun.

You don't want to be so tired that you can't muster up enough strength to be a gracious host. There comes a point when it's "pencils down, people," and the work must come to a screeching halt so you can concentrate on getting *yourself* ready.

My motto is always "leave an hour for a shower" before guests arrive. It will settle your nerves and keep you feeling your best!

## Invite a "Bestie"

If you are hosting more than four guests, be sure to designate a good friend who can be "called into service" at a moment's notice to help mix drinks, clear plates, or serve dessert. Even the most well-meaning cohost can get sidetracked socializing, so it's better to pick someone who is not hosting the party with you. They'll be more available to help.

## Think It Through

When planning a menu, balance the prep with many things you can make ahead of time and only one or two things you need to make on the day of. You don't want to be cooking five dishes on the day of your party! It's much better to balance it out. See the section starting on page 249 for my suggested menus that employ this strategy.

## Serve Family Style

This is something I learned from my French in-laws. They place all the food on large platters, set them in the center of the table, and let everyone pass the platters and serve themselves. This is less stressful for you because it means you don't have to plate everyone's dinner in the kitchen, restaurant style. It also allows your guests to take only what they want, which cuts down on food waste because you can wrap up the leftovers, unlike food left on someone's plate.

When I started doing this, I found it also made for a friendlier, more jovial table. Just be sure your platters aren't so big that they are too hard to pass! In that case, set up a buffet.

## Embrace the Mishaps

Accidents do happen! There will always be something that may not go as planned: a menu that turns out to be too complicated, an antisocial guest who won't get off their phone, or a weather event that can't be helped. I have had plenty of roasts that were undercooked, a turkey breast that flew off a sheet pan, and too many failed desserts to name. But my mistakes have not only made me a better cook—they have also provided years of laughter for my family and friends. I hope any of your own little mishaps will do the same for you!

# ENTERTAINING ESSENTIALS

It can be tempting to rush out and buy something new every time you throw a party: a turkey platter for Thanksgiving, a punch bowl for a holiday open house, or a tortilla warmer for taco night. I'll confess, these are real items I have fallen prey to getting myself. But when you purchase these kinds of items, you might end up using them only once before they litter up your garage!

Instead, I recommend investing in an "entertaining wardrobe" of classic pieces that can be used time and time again. Then, you can limit new purchases to some lovely fresh flowers.

## Creating an Acquired Look

The secret to forming a collection of tabletop items that you will cherish forever is to build one that has a little bit of soul to it. Something will always feel a bit off for you and your guests if your table looks like everything is straight out of a mail-order catalog. And let's face it, that's an expensive way to go, too!

Instead, mix and match new and old things, handmade and manufactured items, thrift store finds and family heirlooms. That way, you'll have a collection that looks acquired because, well, it is! This approach will also add more warmth and personality to your parties. It has a funny way of making your guests feel at home without knowing why they feel that way.

## The Cast of Six Characters

Before we get into specifics of actual pieces, let's talk about materials.

A collection is best built when all the pieces in it, the "cast of characters," relate to one another. They should feel like they belong on the same planet. That way, when you bring them together in various combinations, you and your guests will experience a sense of harmony around the table.

My favorite pieces for entertaining are ones made from natural materials like clay, wood, stone, or metal. They are timeless and will always be in style. Collections are meant to be acquired over a long period of time. If you collect too many trendy pieces, you may be doing yourself a disservice, as they could feel dated and out of place in twenty years.

This cast of characters is meant to last the test of time.

**1 POTTERY AND CERAMICS:** Even if it is purchased new, pottery instantly adds a human touch to any table. Look for pieces with slight irregularities that don't have cookie-cutter, uniform shapes. This will sell the idea that they could be handmade, even if they're not. You'll get the most versatility out of earth tones, like cream, gray, beige, or sage. *Cost Plus World Market, Crate & Barrel, Anthropologie, and Target are all good sources for affordable pottery and ceramic pieces.*

**2 WOOD PIECES:** I love entertaining with wood, especially outdoors. Weathered pieces with a nice patina will add texture to your collection. Antique bread and cutting boards or vintage pizza peels are great used as serving platters or as cheese or breakfast boards. Large wooden bowls can be used for serving summer salads or chilled pasta. You can also line them with napkins when serving breads, muffins, or chips. *You can find wonderful wooden pieces at flea markets or on Etsy or eBay.*

**3** **NATURAL WOVEN PIECES:** Concentrate on a variety of materials like willow, rattan, bamboo, or water hyacinth. I collect small baskets in varying weaves for serving breads, muffins, or scones. Larger serving baskets work well for displaying bottles or glasses on a bar, and shallow baskets with handles are great for presenting crudité platters or for setting out plates, napkins, and cutlery on a buffet. *Look for affordable woven pieces at Cost Plus World Market, Target, or Crate & Barrel. Or source vintage baskets at thrift and antique stores or yard sales.*

**4** **TERRA-COTTA:** Mexican, Spanish, or Portuguese terra-cotta is great for summer garden parties or fall gatherings like Thanksgiving. Look for bowls, platters, or covered casserole dishes in interesting shapes. Terra-cotta works well for serving hearty dishes like roast chicken or summery appetizers like guacamole or bruschetta. *You can find a variety of great terra-cotta on Amazon or Etsy.*

**5** **METALS:** Metal pieces will add a little sparkle to your table, especially if you are using a lot of natural materials in earth tones. You can incorporate silver serving pieces and flatware, antique wire racks for serving muffins, brass candlesticks, or pewter gravy boats. *Look for affordable metal pieces at flea markets, thrift stores, and antique malls or on eBay.*

**6** **GLASS:** Glass has a wonderful reflective quality that adds warmth and interest in both outdoor and indoor settings under the glow of candlelight. Look for etched glass or faceted designs that will catch the light. Glass with a slight green or blue tint (as in recycled or Mexican glass) is also pretty. Or go with organic-shaped or bubbled glass that looks handblown and artisan. *Craft fairs and home shops are great places to look for interesting glass. But so are 99 cent stores and thrift stores!*

## The Essentials

As you look to build out your essentials, try to keep these pieces within the cast-of-character framework. For example, you may like the aesthetic of chargers under plates. They can be made of wood, metal, or basketry, but all three will look good under a white plate. The ideas below are a wish list but by no means a starting point (to start your collection, see the checklist on page 21).

- **WHITE PLATES:** These are the most useful and versatile. They also help make your food pop. You can always bring in more color with napkins, flower arrangements, and other table accessories. Go for creamy white instead of bright white; it will be warmer and feel more inviting. Bring greater interest to white plates by using ones with scalloped edges, pierced details, or gold-ribbon edges. *Crate & Barrel, Cost Plus World Market, Target, and Williams Sonoma are great sources.*

- **SERVING PLATTERS:** Invest in all-white serving platters in various sizes. That way, they'll always coordinate when you bring them together on a buffet. *Crate & Barrel, Cost Plus World Market, Target, and Williams Sonoma are great sources.*

- **SERVING PIECES:** Serving spoons, forks, and tongs are always underestimated. They are the jewelry of the table; when hosting a buffet with several dishes, you could need up to six or eight sets. Invest in vintage pieces to get a better quality for a lower price. *Etsy and eBay are great sources for these.*

- **GLASSWARE:** The most useful glasses to invest in are all-purpose wine glasses; highball, lowball, or all-occasion tumblers; and champagne flutes and champagne coupes. Champagne coupes aren't the most practical for serving champagne, since they splash easily and don't keep champagne as cold as flutes do, but I use them for serving fancy desserts, ice creams, or chilled starters. A few carafes in varying heights also come in handy for water, mixers, and juice. Or, at the very least, you can use recycled French lemonade bottles! (The kind that have the swing-top metal clasps with ceramic stoppers. You can find them in better grocery stores or online.) Buy the lemonade and then save the bottles to use later as carafes. *You can find good-quality glassware at Crate & Barrel, Cost Plus World Market, Williams Sonoma, and Amazon.*

- **NAPKINS AND TABLECLOTHS:** Choose linen or cotton textiles in solid colors that will look nice for multiple events. For example, robin's-egg blue is beautiful against terra-cotta for a summer outdoor party and equally pretty against white plates for an indoor Easter brunch. The most useful colors are plain white linen with a hemstitched edge (a classic for holidays), pastel light blue or dusty rose for spring occasions, blue-and-white stripes for summer, and earth tones like sage, gray, or beige for fall. *Look to places like Crate & Barrel, Cost Plus World Market, Williams Sonoma, and Etsy for beautiful high-quality linens.*

- **FLATWARE:** I'd recommend investing in two sets of twelve-place settings: a dressy set (silver-plated or vintage silver) for holidays and a casual set for brunches and BBQs. *For modern flatware sets, look to Crate & Barrel and Williams Sonoma; for anything vintage, shop on Etsy or scour flea markets and antique malls.*

- **SIGNATURE PIECES:** Invest in a few whimsical items that coordinate with your collection but also serve as conversation pieces. This could be a vintage gravy boat with an interesting shape, an ironstone tureen with a fun decorative top, or a dainty candy dish for cookies, crackers, or other finger foods. These pieces are the punctuation marks on a collection already filled with personality. *Look to craft fairs, flea markets, Etsy, and even Amazon for signature pieces.*

## The Entertaining with Beth "Starter Kit"

When you're just beginning your collection, follow this checklist and consider it an "entertaining starter kit." Start with basic white and with a small number of settings, since you won't be entertaining for ten guests right off the bat. Increase quantities of napkins and glasses by two to three pieces to account for stains and possible breakage. This collection will grow as you grow, and it's fun to build upon it as the years roll on.

- ❏ 8 off-white plates, in textured ceramic or pottery
- ❏ 8 off-white dessert/salad plates, in textured ceramic or pottery
- ❏ 8 off-white soup bowls, in textured ceramic or pottery
- ❏ All-occasion flatware for 8, with a transitional design that can be dressed up or down
- ❏ 12 all-purpose wine glasses
- ❏ 12 champagne flutes
- ❏ 12 all-purpose tumblers
- ❏ 12 high-quality white linen napkins
- ❏ 1 wooden salad bowl
- ❏ 1 set of vintage salad servers
- ❏ 1 set of vintage candlesticks
- ❏ 3 white platters, in small, medium, and large sizes
- ❏ 3 sets of vintage serving pieces for platters
- ❏ 1 glass carafe
- ❏ 12 mugs, in textured ceramic or pottery
- ❏ 1 vintage breadbasket
- ❏ 1 pretty glass cake stand
- ❏ 1 vintage pie/cake server
- ❏ 3 to 4 small bud vases for your table

This starter kit is just that: a place to start. As you grow as a host, you can build upon your collection and have fun with it! Following is a guide to widen your collection as money (and space!) allow. I "lived with" my starter kit for many years while Philippe and I were in an apartment. Frankly, we didn't have the space for much more, and saving for a house took all of our resources. But a few years into owning a home, we had more space, threw bigger parties, and started to widen out the starter kit. These were the items I chose to add next.

## As Space and Resources Allow

- ❏ Increase your 8-piece setting to 12.
- ❏ Add more colors and textures for napkins. Add a tablecloth or two.
- ❏ Add more platters. The more guests you include, the more recipes you will make and the more platters you will need.
- ❏ Add some specialty glasses like martini glasses, margarita glasses, and punch bowls.
- ❏ Add a few more baskets and some terra-cotta platters, bowls, and plates for greater visual interest in your collection of white plates.
- ❏ Look for fun signature items like gravy boats, candy dishes, or wine coasters.

# HOW TO USE THIS BOOK

### The Recipes

This book includes 101 recipes that I believe everyone should know how to make. They span all occasions and seasons. For ease of use, they are separated by course, from drinks to desserts.

The recipes serve either four, six, or eight or more guests. I structured it this way so that beginners starting with four guests can easily follow the recipe and not have to figure out how to cut it down. It's always mentally easier to double a recipe than to reduce it.

Before setting out, read through the entire recipe, including the notes. Recipes are like driving directions: It's helpful to know where you're headed before you zoom out of the driveway. The notes section will also help you execute a tip before it's too late to take advantage of it.

### Notes

Each recipe includes helpful notes to ensure you get the best results. These are the tips I often impart in my videos: the dos and don'ts, what happens if you decide to take a shortcut or go rogue. I've included these mostly because I've made these mistakes, too, and I don't want you to suffer the same fate!

### Make-Ahead Game Plans

Entertaining is all about organization. Without it, the whole thing falls apart, leaving you in a heap of frustration! To help alleviate the stress, each recipe includes a game plan for how to break down the prep and, if possible, make a portion of the recipe ahead of time.

### Pairs Well With

Recipes also include suggestions for other recipes to pair with them for easy menu planning. These could be appetizers that would go well together or a dessert that would be great following a main course. However, if you'd rather leave the menu planning to me, skip ahead to page 249.

### Menu Plans

It can be stressful to think through a full menu. Which dishes pair well together? How should you consider the prep? You don't want to pick five or six recipes that are *all* heavy lifters! It's better to balance them out. Pair recipes that require active cooking with others you can make ahead of time. Mix dishes that can go into the oven as soon as the guests arrive with a few things you can just "set and forget." This will make your party prep run a lot smoother.

I know menu planning takes some thinking through. But not to worry, I've done all this work for you! All you have to do is follow the plan. Starting on page 249, I've created menus for eight occasions using the recipes from this book. Each one includes five or six recipes, along with the seasons they are best suited for (you don't want to be shopping for white peaches in December!) and how many guests they serve.

Each menu also includes a game plan outlining how to manage the prep. It includes things you can do a few days before along with the tasks that need to be done an hour or so before guests arrive.

## Tools of the Trade

I don't feel the need to own a pan for every purpose, mostly because I don't have a ton of storage in my kitchen. But there are a few key pieces that are worth the investment and will prove helpful for the recipes in this book. Drumroll, please . . . !

### COOKING EQUIPMENT

- 5-quart (4.7 L) Dutch oven
- Cast-iron skillet: 10-inch (25 cm) or 12-inch (30 cm) (Lodge pre-seasoned skillets are the best for the quality and price)
- Skillet set: 8-inch (20 cm), 10-inch (25 cm), and 12-inch (30 cm). Make the 12-inch (30 cm) skillet nonstick.
- Small and medium saucepans (if you can swing it, All-Clad is always worth the investment)
- Heavy-bottom roasting pan (again, All-Clad is worth the money)
- Grill pan or outdoor BBQ
- Oven-safe three-piece casserole set: small, medium, and large
- Blender
- 7-cup (1.7 L) food processor
- Large wooden cutting board
- Utensils: nonstick tongs, a medium wire whisk, a rubber whisk, and a nonstick spatula
- A knife block with a set of knives or, at the very least, a chef's knife, a bread knife, and a paring knife
- Digital meat thermometer
- Potato peeler (OXO brand is my favorite)
- Potato ricer (OXO brand)
- Mandoline (OXO brand)

- Garlic press (Rösle brand is my favorite)
- Fine-mesh sieve

### BAKING EQUIPMENT

- Heavy-duty half-sheet pan (Nordic Ware brand is my favorite)
- 12-cup (2.8 L) Bundt pan (Nordic Ware or Wilton brand)
- 9-inch (23 cm) nonstick metal pie plate
- Two 9-inch (23 cm) nonstick cake pans
- 9½ × 5½ × 2½-inch (24 × 14 × 6.5 cm) loaf pan
- 9-inch (23 cm) springform pan
- Standard muffin pan
- 9½ × 2-inch (24 × 5 cm) deep-dish, nonstick, removable-bottom quiche/tart pan
- 9-inch (23 cm) square baking pan
- A set of mixing bowls (Pyrex is always a good choice)
- Electric mixer (hand mixer or standing mixer)
- Measuring cups, measuring pitchers (2-cup/480 ml and 4-cup/960 ml Pyrex pitchers are the most useful), and measuring spoons
- Utensils: a wooden spoon, a rubber spatula, and a metal offset spatula
- French-style wooden rolling pin
- 16-inch (41 cm) pastry bag and tips (Wilton brand is my preferred choice)
- Metal biscuit cutter set
- Assorted cookie cutters

## A WORD ABOUT INGREDIENTS

The following ingredients are the ones I use most often in my recipes. This section will make your shopping easier and, most importantly, ensure you get the same results as I do.

- **Baking Spray:** I prefer PAM baking spray with flour.

- **Butter:** I use salted American butter for all my recipes. Land O'Lakes is my favorite brand. I find that salted butter in the US is more flavorful than "salty," and your baked goods will thank you for it. Outside the US, use unsalted butter and add an additional ⅛ teaspoon (a large pinch) of kosher salt to the recipe.

- **Chocolate:** I prefer Ghirardelli or Nestlé.

- **Dairy:** All recipes call for whole milk, full-fat sour cream, full-fat cheese, or full-fat yogurt. You'll get the best flavor and texture that way.

- **Flour:** All recipes call for all-purpose flour.

- **Parchment Paper:** Is essential for baking cookies, scones, and biscuits that slide off without burnt bottoms. I buy mine precut on Amazon to avoid the frustration of having to measure and cut it each time.

- **Salt:** Kosher salt for cooking and baking and fleur de sel for finishing.

- **Sugar:** Granulated sugar will ensure lighter, more delicate cakes, muffins, and scones. Domino or C&H Sugar are my preferences. Organic sugars are coarser and may not have similar results.

- **Tomato Paste:** I always buy tomato paste in the tube; it's sweeter and has more flavor than the kind that comes in a can. Mutti is my favorite brand.

- **Turbinado Sugar:** Also known as Sugar in the Raw. I keep it on hand for topping scones and muffins; it creates a nice crackly crunch.

- **Vanilla Extract:** Always use pure vanilla extract—nothing imitation. You'll get the best flavor that way.

# WELL, THAT'S AWKWARD

Entertaining is not without its awkward moments, and when these situations arise, it's helpful for newcomers to have a guide for how to handle them. Here's how I've learned to navigate these scenarios.

## Guests Who Bring Uninvited Guests

In this situation, the damage is already done as soon as you've discovered the infraction. So, there's no use trying to undo it. All you can do is make everyone feel as comfortable as possible. Blurt out something like, "Oh, the more the merrier. Welcome, Fred! I'm so glad you could join us!" Then, welcome everyone in, serve them drinks, and make introductions. Once they're distracted, slip off to add another place setting to the table.

## Guests Who Arrive Late

I usually allow an hour and a half for cocktails and appetizers, which is a sort of padding for any latecomers. Personally, I believe that if someone is an hour and a half late for dinner, it's more impolite to keep the other guests waiting than to start without the latecomer. So, proceed as planned. You can bet the latecomer will not be late to your house again when they walk into a dinner already being served.

## Guests Who Don't Mingle or Contribute to the Conversation

Oh, the introverts! Bless their fragile hearts. As the host, you are in the best position to take care of them and jumpstart the conversation. Find someone who the "non-mingler" might have something in common with: This can be a common interest or something as basic as the part of town they live in. For example, you could start that conversation by saying, "Steve, tell us about that Alaskan fishing trip you went on last summer! Bob [the non-mingler] loves fishing, and I'm sure he'd like to hear all about it." It works best to pair someone with a lot to say

with someone interested in listening. It's a win-win situation because Steve now has a captive audience for his fishing stories and Bob is "mingling with Steve" without having to put that much effort into it.

## Guests Who Won't Get Off Their Phones

I know the tendency is to look the other way, but I say: Chat them up instead. And not in a "How's work going?" type of way because that won't release their death grip on their device, since you'll only get a shrug or a mumbled response. Your questions need to be really specific and all about them to get them to release. Start with something like, "Jane, tell me more about your nightmare boss! How's she treating you these days?" This prompt includes two key elements: One, it's all about Jane, so she's interested, and two, it's worthy of a good rant, which will distract her long enough to forget about her phone.

## Guests Who Latch Onto You Like a Baby Koala

The best way to untether these folks is to put them into service. These types of guests make excellent helpers, since it channels their nervous energy into feeling useful. Assign jobs that allow them the opportunity to mingle with the other guests. A few of my favorite prompts include "Greg, would you mind passing this cheese platter around? No one seems to be taking any of it," and "I see Greta's glass is empty. Would you mind topping her off?" In both situations, you've given Greg two opportunities to engage: one with the larger group and another that's more one-on-one. He'll connect with one of them and be off to the races.

## Guests Who Start Heated Discussions About Religion or Politics

This is always a fun one. If this happens and you are between courses, it's the perfect opportunity to jump up and say, "Oh, wait until you try this chocolate cake. It's insane!" At which point, you turn to the headstrong person and say, "Sebastien, would you help me get dessert ready?" Once you're in the kitchen, say something like, "I'm sorry that conversation wasn't going well. Susan is really passionate about that subject, so it's probably best not to bring it up again." Then, the next morning, call Susan and apologize for Sebastien, basically saying the same thing. That way, you won't have to worry about this happening again if these people find themselves together at another one of your parties.

## Guests Who Neglect to Share Food Allergies and Special Diets

The best cure for this is a well-stocked pantry. For vegetarians, I always keep pasta and jarred pesto on hand; that's a quick and easy dinner you can whip up if your beef tenderloin isn't going to fly. For vegans or those with gluten allergies, I keep a box of vegetable broth in the pantry and Trader Joe's frozen rice blends, frozen peas, and frozen spinach in the freezer. With these ingredients, you can put together a quick and easy soup. Season it with a splash of tamari sauce and toasted sesame oil and you're done.

## Guests Who Break Something

There's no use exclaiming "Oh no, that was a wedding present from my late Aunt Millie!" even if it was. It will just make an awkward situation worse. Something I always say is "Oh, don't even worry about it! I bought that at a yard sale years ago for just a few bucks!" or "I needed to clear things out, and you just helped me!" That always softens the blow and gets a laugh. And it can apply to just about anything in your house!

## Guests Who Won't Leave Once the Party Is Over

If you have tried everything and they are still not getting the hint, try this. Wait for a lull in the conversation, like after someone has told a funny story and the laughing winds down to a soft sigh. This is your time to strike! *Do not delay*, or you'll have to wait for another lull in the conversation. Then say this: "Well, this has been so much fun! I'm so glad you all could make it." (Rarely will you have to continue to this next part: "We need to do this again soon!") They usually get the hint and get up to collect their coats.

If this doesn't work, and you have kids, try this: Get them changed into their PJs and then parade them around the living room to say goodnight to everybody. Most often, your guests will get the picture.

If those two options don't do the trick, then unfortunately, desperate times call for desperate measures, and you'll need to consider the nuclear option: the dishes. Start by clearing away the dessert plates and ask folks to do the same. (This is key because it gets them out of their seats and onto their feet and it breaks up any conversations that have gone on for far too long.) They'll follow you into the kitchen, where you can ask them to help you scrape the plates, organize the dishes, and sort any linens. All of a sudden, you'll hear a few yawns, followed by "Oh yes, it is getting late. We really should go." Unless, of course, your guests are French: Then, they *will help you do all the dishes* and sit back down again. And if your husband is also French, he'll offer them another glass of wine and you'll have to start this process all over again.

Now that you have all the bases covered, it's time to flip through these pages and dream of your next gathering! Just remember to plan, organize, have fun, and repeat. You've got this!

# DRINKS

# DIY BLOODY MARY BAR

A lazy Sunday brunch calls for Bloody Marys. In keeping with the vibe, you can set up a DIY Bloody Mary bar to make serving them even easier. All you have to do is whip up a pitcher of Bloody Mary mix the night before and then set it out with the vodka and assorted garnishes and let your guests serve themselves. Not only will this put less stress on the host, but it will also loosen everyone up as they chat about which garnishes they like best. Classics include a leafy celery stalk, green olives, and lemon wedges. But the trend in Bloody Marys these days is "more is more," and loading up the garnishes to such a degree that they become the main attraction is all the rage! Offer a variety of garnishes that deliver different flavor sensations from briny to cooling; see my favorites below.

*SERVES 4 (Makes about 5½ cups/1.3 L)*

## BLOODY MARY MIX

44 ounces (1.3 L) pure tomato
  juice

1 tablespoon (15 ml) lemon juice
  (from about ½ lemon)

1 tablespoon (15 ml) prepared
  horseradish

1 tablespoon (15 ml) pickle juice,
  from the jar

1 teaspoon (5 ml) Worcestershire
  sauce

½ teaspoon (2.5 ml) celery seed

¼ teaspoon (1.25 ml) garlic
  powder

¼ teaspoon (1.25 ml) Tabasco
  sauce

Freshly cracked black pepper, to
  taste

One 750 ml bottle Grey Goose
  vodka (see Note 1)

Ice cubes, for serving

## RIM SALT

1 tablespoon (18 g) kosher salt

1 teaspoon (5 ml) celery seed
  (see Note 2)

1 to 2 lemon wedges (in case
  guests want seconds)

## MUST-HAVE GARNISHES
(see Note 3)

Lemon wedges (cooling)

Celery stalks with leaves
  (cooling)

Pickle spears (briny)

Pitted green olives (briny)

4-inch (10 cm) bamboo
  toothpicks with knots for
  holding garnishes (see
  Note 4)

## OPTIONAL GARNISHES

Baby corn (cooling)

Caper berries (briny)

Parsley (cooling)

Pepperoncini (spicy)

Roasted shrimp (from Roasted
  Shrimp Cocktail on page 54;
  cooling)

Swiss cheese cubes (cooling)

Tabasco sauce (spicy)

## NOTES

1. Most guests will use only 1 to 2 ounces (30 to 60 ml) of vodka per drink, but it's always nice to have a well-stocked bar for next time. When building a home bar, I say always spring for the good stuff.

2. I like celery seed instead of celery salt. It will balance the rim flavor and prevent it from being too salty.

3. The garnishes provide a balance of flavor; they each bring spicy, briny, or cooling sensations. It's best to have a mix of garnishes that tick these boxes. I usually don't add too many spicy things, since the mix already has a nice spicy kick!

4. The little knot on the bamboo pick latches on nicely to the rim of the glass, which will keep the garnishes upright. You can find bamboo picks at Cost Plus World Market, at BevMo!, or online.

1. **Make the mix:** Fill a 47-ounce (1.4 L) pitcher with the tomato juice, lemon juice, horseradish, pickle juice, Worcestershire sauce, celery seed, garlic powder, Tabasco sauce, and black pepper. Whisk to combine. Keep refrigerated until ready to serve.

2. **Make the rim salt:** Mix the salt and celery seed on a small plate or saucer. Create a small slit in the middle of a lemon wedge so it fits on the rim of a tall glass. Rub the rim with the lemon to wet it and then place the rim in the salt mixture, pressing the glass slightly so the salt coats the rim.

3. To serve, place a few ice cubes in a glass. Add 1 to 2 ounces (30 to 60 ml) vodka. Place the celery stalk and pickle spear in the glass, standing upright, and then pour in the mix. Garnish with a lemon wedge on the rim and a few olives on a bamboo toothpick. Add additional garnishes as desired.

4. To create a DIY Bloody Mary bar, set out the pitcher of mix, the vodka, an ice bucket filled with ice, the toothpicks, and all the garnishes laid out in small bowls. Have guests serve themselves.

### MAKE-AHEAD GAME PLAN

One day ahead, mix the Bloody Mary mix. Refrigerate until ready to serve.

### PAIRS WELL WITH

Ham, Leek, and Gruyère Strata (page 195)
Puffy Egg Bake (page 169)

# SWEET AND SPICED MULLED CIDER

When I was growing up in Connecticut, early October meant apple cider. We'd bring home large jugs of it after a day spent "apple picking." To be honest, we never did the actual picking; we just ran into the little farm stand to pick up bags of apples that *someone else* had picked. The apple cider sold at this farm stand is still the best I've ever had. I've spent years in Los Angeles, pining away for it every fall. Not "apple juice" or "hard cider," but *real* apple cider! So, imagine my surprise a few years back when I saw that Trader Joe's was selling apple cider, made from apples picked in Connecticut no less! Apple cider is great on its own, but hot apple cider sweetened with honey and flavored with spices is even better. Serve this in the fall with my Connecticut Christmas Bread (page 199) or while taking a pause from all your holiday baking. It's a delicious drink that warms the body and soul!

*SERVES 4* (Makes 8 cups/1.9 L)

64 ounces (1.89 L) apple cider

15 whole allspice berries

4 cinnamon sticks

4 star anise

Two 2-inch-long (5 cm) orange peels, made with a potato peeler

1 teaspoon (5 ml) whole cloves

½ teaspoon (2.5 ml) honey

### GARNISH

4 cinnamon sticks

4 clementine slices

4 star anise

1. Heat the apple cider in a Dutch oven over high heat for 3 to 4 minutes.

2. Add the allspice berries, cinnamon sticks, star anise, orange peels, cloves, and honey.

3. Simmer over medium-high heat until the apple cider is flavored with the spices, about 15 minutes. The flavors will become more pronounced and sweeter the longer it simmers.

4. Just before serving (to avoid any choking hazards), remove the spices with a fine-mesh strainer while simmering the cider to keep it warm.

5. Ladle the cider into mugs and then add the garnishes on top.

**MAKE-AHEAD GAME PLAN**
Up to one day ahead, make the cider. Strain out the spices, cover, and refrigerate. Reheat when ready to serve.

**PAIRS WELL WITH**
Connecticut Christmas Bread (page 199)

All-Occasion Cut Sugar Cookies (page 221)

# STRAWBERRY MARGARITA SMOOTHIES

Margaritas fall into two camps: frozen or on the rocks. Personally, I've never been a fan of either. The frozen variety always feels like sipping a snow cone, and the on-the-rocks alternative is usually too strong for my taste. Enter my margarita mash-up: a margarita smoothie. They are dangerously delicious because they go down smooth and easy! The simplest way to get the best flavor and texture is to use frozen strawberries and allow them to thaw in the refrigerator for a few hours before serving. This makes a perfectly chilled drink that isn't too frozen or too slushy, either. It also ensures the best flavor when strawberries are out of season. Blend these up with a fistful of fresh mint, and they're the perfect drink to kick off a summer party!

*SERVES 4* (Makes 4 cups/960 ml)

24 ounces (680 g) frozen sliced strawberries, thawed in the refrigerator for 4 hours (see Note 1)

1 cup (240 ml) tequila blanco (see Note 2)

¼ cup (60 ml) Cointreau (see Note 3)

¼ cup (60 ml) fresh lime juice (from 2 or 3 limes)

⅓ cup (80 ml) fresh mint leaves

1 to 2 tablespoons (15 to 30 ml) agave syrup

## GARNISH

1 tablespoon (18 g) kosher salt

1 teaspoon (5 ml) lime zest

2 limes

4 fresh mint sprigs

## NOTES

1. You can use fresh strawberries if they're in season; add a few ice cubes before blending for the "smoothie effect."

2. This is also known as silver tequila. It has a fresh taste with notes of agave and citrus, which is ideal for margaritas.

3. Triple sec is the traditional orange liqueur for margaritas, but I prefer the more subtle, less alcoholic flavor of Cointreau.

1. **Make the garnishes:** Mix the salt and lime zest on a small plate or saucer. Slice one lime into four wheels; cut a small slit into each wheel. Slice the other lime into four wedges; cut a slit into the center of each wedge.

2. Place the strawberries and any juice from the bag and the tequila, Cointreau, lime juice, mint leaves, and 1 tablespoon (15 ml) agave syrup in a blender. Blend on high until completely pureed and smooth, about 1 minute.

3. Taste and add another 1 tablespoon (15 ml) agave syrup if you would like it sweeter.

4. Rub a lime wedge along the rim of each cocktail glass. Dip each glass upside down into the salt-lime mixture, coating the rim.

5. Pour the smoothies into the glasses. To garnish, insert a mint sprig into the center of each lime wheel. Then, attach a wheel to each glass and serve immediately.

## MAKE-AHEAD GAME PLAN

- Four hours before serving, place the frozen strawberries in the refrigerator.
- Two hours before, slice the limes, cover, and refrigerate.
- One hour before, prep the salt/zest mixture. Cover with plastic wrap and leave at room temperature.

## PAIRS WELL WITH

Leave-It-Chunky Guacamole (page 73)

Better BBQ Chicken (page 133) or Fall-Off-the-Bone Sticky Ribs (page 117)

# WHITE WINE SANGRIA

In the heat of the summer, this sangria is a fabulous way to greet your guests. Not only is it light and refreshing thanks to the crisp white wine and a splash of lime sparkling water, but it also looks beautiful with the fruit and herbs dancing in the glass! Just holding one in your hand has the power to cool you down immediately. Garnish with fresh thyme and a few skewered melon balls to set the tone for a garden-fresh dinner party! Use a clear glass pitcher and wide mouth goblets to make the most of the brightly colored fruit.

*SERVES 6 TO 8* *(Makes 4 cups/945ml)*

Two 750 ml bottles sauvignon blanc or pinot grigio, chilled (see Note 1)

⅓ cup (80 ml) peach schnapps

1 tablespoon (15 ml) agave syrup

10 frozen peach slices (see Note 2)

6 to 8 cantaloupe balls, made with a melon baller

Ten ¼-inch-thick (6 mm) Granny Smith apple slices (from ½ apple)

1 to 2 fresh thyme sprigs

### FOR SERVING

One 42.3-ounce (1.25 L) bottle lime-flavored sparkling water

6 to 8 fresh thyme sprigs

8 honeydew melon balls, made with a melon baller

8 cantaloupe balls, made with a melon baller

Six to eight 4-inch (10 cm) bamboo toothpicks with knots (see Note 3)

### NOTES

1. Use a light, crisp wine. Stay away from chardonnay; it's too heavy for sangria.

2. Frozen peaches have three benefits: There's no cutting and pitting needed; they are always ripe and flavorful; and they keep the sangria chilled without watering it down with ice cubes. My preferred brand is Dole.

3. The little knot on the bamboo pick latches on nicely to the rim of the glass, which will keep the garnishes upright. You can find bamboo picks at Cost Plus World Market, at BevMo!, or online.

1. Pour the wine, schnapps, and agave syrup into a 64-ounce (1.89 L) pitcher. Stir to combine.

2. Add the fruit to the pitcher from heaviest to lightest: peach slices, cantaloupe balls, and then apple slices. This creates visual layers in the pitcher. Then, add the thyme.

3. Transfer to the refrigerator and keep chilled for 1 to 2 hours before serving (not longer, since the apples will begin to brown).

4. To serve, fill a wine glass three-fourths of the way with the sangria, using a long wooden spoon to help guide a mixture of fruit into the glass. Top off with a splash of sparkling water.

5. To garnish, submerge a thyme sprig into each glass. Thread a honeydew ball and a cantaloupe ball onto each toothpick. The toothpick will also make it easy for your guests to enjoy eating the other fruit in the sangria.

### MAKE-AHEAD GAME PLAN

- One day ahead, prepare the melon balls for the sangria and garnishes. Cover and refrigerate until ready to serve.

- Two hours before, make the sangria. Refrigerate until ready to serve.

### PAIRS WELL WITH

Easy Grilled Salmon with Mango Salsa (page 127)

Grilled Dijon Chicken with Charred Lemons (page 123)

# HOMEMADE HOT CHOCOLATE

A few things in life will always be better homemade—I call them my "non-negotiables." Homemade whipped cream is the first, and homemade hot chocolate is next. It's creamier, richer, and so much more chocolaty than anything you'll ever get from a pouch. I've been making this recipe every December with my girls to kick off our annual Hallmark movie marathon. It's a tradition that has survived well into their teenage years and has the power to lure them off their phones and onto the sofa for an evening of predictable plots and feel-good endings! Cozy socks and fluffy blankets are optional.

**_SERVES 4_** *(Makes 5 cups/1.18 L)*

## HOT CHOCOLATE

3 cups (720 ml) whole milk

1 cup (240 ml) half-and-half

8 ounces (227 g) Ghirardelli 60% cacao bittersweet chocolate, broken into pieces

1 tablespoon (15 ml) vanilla extract

## WHIPPED CREAM

1 cup (240 ml) heavy cream

1 tablespoon (15 g) powdered sugar

½ teaspoon (2.5 ml) vanilla extract

## GARNISH

1 ounce (28 g) Ghirardelli 60% cacao bittersweet chocolate (about 2 squares)

1. In the bowl of an electric mixer, add the heavy cream, powdered sugar, and vanilla extract. Whip on high until stiff peaks form. Set aside.

2. Heat the milk and half-and-half in a large saucepan over medium-high heat.

3. Add the chocolate and whisk to combine, stirring until the chocolate is completely melted, 3 to 4 minutes. Stir in the vanilla extract.

4. Transfer the whipped cream into a pastry bag fitted with a star tip.

5. Ladle the hot chocolate into mugs, filling them three-fourths of the way. Pipe the whipped cream on top. Grate the chocolate over the top with a cheese grater or microplane.

### MAKE-AHEAD GAME PLAN

- Up to one day ahead, make the whipped cream. Cover and refrigerate.

- For a larger group of eight guests, double the recipe. Make the hot chocolate 1 hour ahead and serve it in an air pot thermos. Place the whipped cream in a bowl on the side with the extra chocolate squares and a grater. It's a fun, interactive way to serve hot chocolate to a crowd.

### PAIRS WELL WITH

All-Occasion Cut Sugar Cookies (page 221)

Soft and Chewy Gingerbread Men (page 247)

# WATERMELON AGUA FRESCA

A specialty drink is a great way to make any party feel festive! And one of the easiest drinks to master is the simple yet lovely agua fresca. It's basically just three ingredients: fruit, water, and sugar. In Los Angeles, you can find a variety of flavors and fruit combinations, but I always go back to my favorite: watermelon and lime. It's a fantastic drink that I offer my guests when the temperature rises and they've been stuck in LA traffic for over an hour! Set out this drink in a pitcher, with the garnishes on the side, and let guests serve themselves. It also makes a beautiful centerpiece on a buffet table thanks to its bright pink color!

*SERVES 4* (Makes 6 cups/1.4 L)

## SIMPLE SYRUP
¼ cup (50 g) sugar

¼ cup (60 ml) water

## AGUA FRESCA
8 cups (1.2 kg) cubed seedless watermelon (from a 10-pound/4.5 kg watermelon)

Juice of 2 limes

1 to 2 cups (240 to 480 ml) cold water, divided

## GARNISH
2 tablespoons (25 g) sugar

1 tablespoon (15 ml) lime zest

Cold water (see Note)

4 fresh mint sprigs

1 lime, sliced into wedges

## NOTE
Instead of water, dip the rims in lime juice for even more zing!

1. **Make the simple syrup:** Heat the sugar and water in a small pot over medium-high heat until the sugar is completely dissolved and a syrup has formed, 5 to 8 minutes. Let cool.

2. **Make the agua fresca:** Place the watermelon chunks in a blender. (You may need to do this in two batches.) Add the lime juice and 1 cup (240 ml) water. Blend on high until the mixture is liquefied and smooth. Pour the mixture through a fine-mesh sieve into a pitcher. This will remove the foam and excess fiber, giving you a prettier drink.

3. Taste for sweetness, and add the simple syrup in 1-tablespoon (15 ml) increments until it reaches your desired level. Taste for watermelon flavor; for a lighter drink, add the remaining 1 cup (240 ml) water. Refrigerate until ready to serve.

4. **Make the garnish:** Moments before serving, mix the sugar and lime zest on a small plate or in a very shallow bowl. Fill another shallow bowl with cold water.

5. Dip the rim of each glass into the water and then into the sugar-zest mixture. Fill each glass with ice and then pour in the agua fresca. Garnish with a mint sprig in the glass and a lime wedge on the rim.

## MAKE-AHEAD GAME PLAN
Up to one day ahead, make the agua fresca. Keep refrigerated until ready to serve. Slice the lime wedges, then cover and refrigerate until ready to serve.

## PAIRS WELL WITH
Leave-It-Chunky Guacamole (page 73)

24-Hour Flank Steak with Chimichurri (page 124)

# BELLINI COCKTAILS

On my first trip to Venice, Italy, with my father, he insisted that we book a table at the iconic Harry's Bar. I've come to learn that when Dad insists on a place, I go, because it's always worth the trip. Harry's Bar is the purported birthplace of the Bellini: a two-ingredient cocktail that combines luscious white peach puree topped off with chilled prosecco. Needless to say, it's up there as one of the greatest cocktails of all time. It's a festive way to kick off a summer party, when white peaches and nectarines are at their best! If peach season is a little early or late, a dash of peach schnapps in each glass brings the flavor back up to par. Just don't overdo it! Schnapps can be strong; add too much, and your guests may not make it to dessert.

*SERVES 8 TO 12* *(Makes 14 cups/3.3L)*

5 pounds (2.2 kg) white nectarines or peaches (see Note 1)

2 tablespoons (30 ml) fresh lemon juice (from about 1 lemon; see Note 2)

1 tablespoon (13 g) sugar

Two 750 ml bottles prosecco, chilled

### GARNISH

Peach schnapps (optional; see Note 3)

8 to 12 fresh mint sprigs

### NOTES

1. I prefer to use white nectarines because the skins are smoother and a bit nicer when pureed.

2. Don't skip the lemon juice; it prevents the puree from turning brown.

3. Add 1 tablespoon (15 ml) schnapps to each glass to boost the peach flavor if needed.

4. If you don't have a large punch bowl, you can pour the puree halfway up each glass and top with the prosecco.

1. Halve the nectarines and remove the pits. Place all but one of them in a blender. Slice the remaining nectarine and set it aside for garnishing.

2. Add the lemon juice and sugar and blend to form a smooth puree. Transfer the puree to a large punch bowl or carafe (see Note 4).

3. Pour the prosecco on top of the puree and gently stir. Stir in the reserved sliced nectarines.

4. Ladle the Bellinis into champagne flutes, being sure to catch a sliced peach or two, and top with a mint sprig.

**PAIRS WELL WITH**

Easy Grilled Salmon with Mango Salsa (page 127)

Puffy Egg Bake (page 169)

# SPARKLING CHRISTMAS PUNCH

A champagne punch is an easy way to serve a specialty drink at a holiday party. It not only looks beautiful, but it's also a cinch to make! I like to keep the holiday punch light to allow guests the ability to have more than one glass and not feel, *ahem*, overserved. Traditional punch recipes that call for a mix of spirits *and* champagne can really sneak up on you! I just add a little splash of crème de cassis liqueur, which deepens the flavor of the cranberry juice. This would also be a great time to drag out your parents' vintage punch bowl or purchase one on Etsy. A silver punch bowl adds a little Victorian splendor to any holiday party.

*SERVES 8 TO 10* (Makes 11 cups/2.6 L)

64 ounces (1.89 L) Cranberry Juice Cocktail, chilled (see Note 1)

One 750 ml bottle champagne or prosecco, chilled

3 tablespoons (45 ml) crème de cassis liqueur

½ cup (45 g) frozen cranberries (see Note 2)

1 large navel orange

2 limes

1 tablespoon (11 g) pomegranate arils

3 to 4 fresh mint sprigs (see Note 3)

### GARNISH

8 to 10 fresh mint sprigs

½ cup (87 g) pomegranate arils

2 to 3 limes, sliced into wedges

### NOTES

1. Be sure to buy Cranberry Juice *Cocktail*, which is sweetened. Pure cranberry juice is unsweetened and bitter.

2. Frozen cranberries keep the punch chilled without watering it down. They look pretty, too. If frozen cranberries aren't available, buy an extra bottle of Cranberry Juice Cocktail to fill ice cube trays, and use the cranberry ice cubes in place of the cranberries.

3. Look for bunches of fresh mint in the produce section of your grocery store. The bunches will have prettier sprigs than packaged mint leaves.

1. Pour the cranberry juice and champagne into a large punch bowl. Add the crème de cassis and stir to combine. Add the cranberries.

2. Slice the orange and limes into 3 to 4 wheels each. Place the orange wheels in the punch bowl so they float on top, slightly overlapping if needed to fit in the bowl. Add the lime wheels and then sprinkle the pomegranate arils on top, followed by the mint sprigs.

3. To serve, ladle the punch into small cups. Garnish each with a mint sprig, a few pomegranate arils, and a squeeze of lime.

### MAKE-AHEAD GAME PLAN

Two hours ahead, slice the fruit and prep the garnishes. Cover and refrigerate until ready to serve.

### PAIRS WELL WITH

Baked Brie with Fig Jam, Rosemary, and Walnuts (page 66)

Gougères (aka French Cheesy Puffs; page 57)

# SNACKS AND NIBBLES

# STUFFED MUSHROOM CAPS

There comes a time during holiday entertaining, usually around New Year's Eve, when you've had just about all the gooey cheese and flaky puff pastry you can handle. That's when you turn to these delicious stuffed mushroom caps. They are hearty and flavorful without being overly decadent and filling, and you'll love the contrast between the juicy mushrooms and the savory, crunchy topping. The best part is that they can be prepped and stuffed in advance—all you have to do is pop them in the oven moments before guests arrive. Serve them alongside my Roasted Shrimp Cocktail (page 54) for an elegant New Year's Eve combo that won't take all day in the kitchen!

*MAKES 12* (serves 4 to 6)

12 cremini mushrooms (about 8 ounces/227 g; see Note 1)

1 tablespoon (14 g) salted American butter

⅓ cup (45 g) minced shallots

2 tablespoons (30 ml) minced fresh thyme

2½ teaspoons (12.5 ml) Worcestershire sauce

1 garlic clove, minced

Kosher salt and freshly cracked black pepper, to taste

3 tablespoons (15 g) panko breadcrumbs

3 tablespoons (15 g) freshly grated Parmesan

2 tablespoons (30 ml) minced Italian parsley

## NOTES

1. It's better to buy the mushrooms individually, as opposed to in a carton, to ensure they are roughly the same size.
2. The chopped stems should equal about ½ cup (40 g).

1. Preheat the oven to 350°F (175°C). Place the oven rack in the lower third of the oven.

2. Gently twist off the stem from each mushroom cap. Slice off a thin sliver of the stem's root end and discard. Mince the stems (see Note 2).

3. Melt the butter in a sauté pan over medium-high heat. Sauté the shallots in the butter until soft, 1 to 2 minutes, and then add the mushroom stems. Sauté until the mushrooms begin to release their juices, 1 to 2 minutes. Add the thyme, Worcestershire sauce, garlic, salt, and pepper, and continue to cook until the liquid has evaporated, about 10 seconds. Set aside to cool.

4. Mix the breadcrumbs, Parmesan, and parsley in a medium bowl. Add the mushroom stem mixture and stir to combine.

5. Place the mushroom caps on their backs, and spoon 1 to 2 teaspoons (5 to 10 ml) filling into each one, piling it high so it domes a little bit. Place them on a baking sheet.

6. Bake for 12 to 15 minutes, until the mushrooms begin to wrinkle and the cheese starts to brown. Serve immediately.

## MAKE-AHEAD GAME PLAN

One day ahead, fill the mushrooms. Cover and refrigerate until ready to bake.

## PAIRS WELL WITH

Roasted Shrimp Cocktail with Kick-in-the-Pants Cocktail Sauce (page 54)

Warm Spinach and Artichoke Dip (page 53)

# CRUDITÉ PLATTER
## WITH GREEN GODDESS DIP

Veggies and dip don't have to be a boring display of carrot and celery sticks with a tub of ranch dressing on the side. You can create something *so much better* with just a little effort. You'll love the fantastic blend of summery flavors this dip provides from the herbs, garlic, and lemon juice. Not to mention the bright green color, a conversation starter in itself! Set out this platter with appetizer plates and small spoons to allow guests to serve themselves and prevent double-dipping. By pairing it with a rainbow of fresh vegetables (or "crudité," as the French would say), you can really level up your veggie platter. Look for prepackaged baby vegetables, which not only look charming but also can cut down on prep (since you can serve them whole or sliced in half). Chill the rosé and get ready to welcome summer!

*SERVES 8* (Makes 2 cups/480 ml)

### DIP

1 cup (220 g) mayonnaise

1 cup (245 g) sour cream

2 garlic cloves, minced

⅓ cup (80 ml) roughly chopped fresh dill

⅓ cup (80 ml) roughly chopped fresh parsley

⅓ cup (80 ml) roughly chopped fresh tarragon

¼ cup (60 ml) roughly chopped fresh chives

2 tablespoons (30 ml) fresh lemon juice (from about 1 lemon)

Kosher salt and freshly cracked black pepper, to taste

### CRUDITÉ (see Note 1)

1 pint (340 g) cherry tomatoes

1 bunch red radishes or French breakfast radishes, halved lengthwise

1 pound (454 g) baby carrots

1 pound (454 g) mini bell peppers in assorted colors

8 ounces (227 g) baby zucchini

8 ounces (227 g) sugar snap peas

1 small head purple cauliflower, cut into florets

1 watermelon radish, sliced into ⅛-inch (3 mm) rounds (see Note 2)

1. **Make the dip:** Place the mayonnaise, sour cream, garlic, dill, parsley, tarragon, chives, lemon juice, salt, and pepper in a blender and blend on high until smooth. Cover and refrigerate until ready to serve.

2. **Make the crudité platter:** Transfer the dip to a small serving bowl. Place the bowl on a larger serving platter.

3. Nestle the vegetables around the platter, grouping by color. You can follow the pattern of the rainbow if desired or switch it up, but keep each type of vegetable together for a more cohesive design.

### MAKE-AHEAD GAME PLAN

One day ahead, make the dip. Prep the crudité platter, cover with a clean, damp kitchen towel, and refrigerate.

### PAIRS WELL WITH

Sheet-Pan Lamb with Caramelized Shallots and Provençal Tomatoes (page 110)

Easy Grilled Salmon with Mango Salsa (page 127)

### NOTES

1. The prettiest crudité platters have a variety of colors represented. Think of the rainbow and use that as your guide, picking vegetables that represent each color. A platter with a lip on it works best to ensure the vegetables don't slide off.

2. The best way to slice a watermelon radish is with a mandoline, since they are hard to cut with a knife. If you don't have one, you could replace the watermelon radish with roasted purple potatoes.

# WARM SPINACH AND ARTICHOKE DIP

Any type of gooey, cheesy appetizer is a wonderful way to greet your guests, and spinach-artichoke dip is a classic worthy of mastering. I use fresh spinach and sautéed shallots to elevate the flavor, and you'll love how the fresh lemon juice and zest complement the artichoke hearts. This is a great appetizer to serve in the early spring months (March and April), when the weather is still cool, but your taste buds are craving spring flavors. Or serve it for a crowd for game day or awards season, when guests are huddled around the TV looking for something filling and decadent. It's practically a meal in itself!

***SERVES 6 TO 8*** *(Makes 4 1/2 cups/715 g)*

1 tablespoon (14 g) salted American butter

¼ cup (28 g) minced shallots

Kosher salt and freshly cracked black pepper, to taste

5 ounces (142 g) baby spinach (see Note)

1 baguette, for serving

2 tablespoons (30 ml) olive oil

8 ounces (227 g) cream cheese, softened

½ cup (110 g) mayonnaise

1 garlic clove, minced

¼ teaspoon (1.25 ml) lemon zest

1 teaspoon (5 ml) lemon juice

¼ teaspoon (1 g) kosher salt

Freshly cracked black pepper to taste

1½ cups (113 g) finely shredded Italian blend cheese, divided

½ cup (70 g) roughly chopped artichoke hearts (from a can packed in water, drained)

1 tablespoon (15 ml) finely chopped fresh Italian parsley (optional)

## NOTE

I prefer the texture and flavor of fresh spinach, but you can also use frozen spinach. Just make sure the spinach has thawed and then pat it dry to release its moisture.

1. Melt the butter in a large skillet over medium-high heat. Add the shallots and season with salt and pepper. Cook until translucent and fragrant, 3 to 4 minutes.

2. Add the spinach and cook until wilted, 2 to 3 minutes. Transfer to a small bowl and let cool.

3. Meanwhile, cut the baguette into ½-inch (1 cm) slices and place them on a baking sheet. Brush the top side only with the olive oil. Place under the broiler to toast for 30 to 60 seconds, until golden brown. Set aside to cool.

4. Preheat the oven to 350°F (175°C). Place the oven rack in the lower third of the oven.

5. Use a wooden spoon to mix the cream cheese, mayonnaise, garlic, lemon zest, lemon juice, salt, pepper, and ¾ cup (57 g) cheese in a large bowl.

6. Fold in the shallot-spinach mixture and the artichoke hearts. Transfer to a 7×9-inch (18×23 cm) oven-safe casserole dish. Sprinkle the remaining cheese evenly on top, covering it completely.

7. Place the dish on a baking sheet. Bake for 25 minutes, or until the dip is warmed through, and then place under the broiler for 30 to 60 seconds, until the cheese is bubbling and golden.

8. Top with the parsley if desired. Serve immediately with the toasted baguette.

## MAKE-AHEAD GAME PLAN

One day ahead, assemble the dip. Cover and refrigerate. To serve, place in a preheated 350°F (175°C) oven for 30 minutes, or until the dip is warmed through. Then, place under the broiler for 30 to 60 seconds, until the cheese is golden brown and bubbly!

## PAIRS WELL WITH

Roasted Shrimp Cocktail with Kick-in-the-Pants Cocktail Sauce (page 54)

Stuffed Mushroom Caps (page 49)

# ROASTED SHRIMP COCKTAIL
## WITH KICK-IN-THE-PANTS COCKTAIL SAUCE

There's nothing that says "party" more than a shrimp cocktail! But I can't tell you how many times I've tasted a sad shrimp cocktail that feels like the air has been let out of the party balloon. The lifeless poached shrimp, just lying there with nothing to say. The flavorless cocktail sauce. You and your guests deserve better. Heck, the shrimp deserve better! This recipe isn't any more difficult than traditional shrimp cocktail, but the effort is put in where it matters. Butterflying and roasting the shrimp will make them look and taste a whole lot better! And the cocktail sauce is worthy of its name, bursting with lemony, horseradish flavor with just enough heat to loosen up those guests and get the party started!

*SERVES 4 TO 6* *(Makes 1 cup/240 ml of cocktail sauce)*

2 pounds (907 g) peeled, tail-on frozen shrimp, thawed (see Note 1)

⅓ cup (80 ml) olive oil

2 garlic cloves, minced

¼ teaspoon (1.25 ml) dried basil

¼ teaspoon (1.25 ml) red pepper flakes

Kosher salt and freshly cracked black pepper, to taste

### COCKTAIL SAUCE

1 cup (240 ml) ketchup

1 tablespoon (15 ml) prepared horseradish

1 tablespoon (15 ml) lemon juice

1 teaspoon (5 ml) lemon zest

5 to 6 dashes hot sauce

Kosher salt and freshly cracked black pepper, to taste

### GARNISH

2 tablespoons (30 ml) minced fresh Italian parsley

1 lemon, sliced into wedges

### NOTES

1. Frozen shrimp is more cost effective, but you can also use fresh shrimp if you prefer.

2. This sauce is so flavorful that it will be hard to resist the urge to "double-dip." So, it's a good idea to place a little spoon in the cocktail sauce and offer a few small appetizer plates. Guests can take a few shrimp on their plate along with a few dollops of sauce and double-dip all they want!

1. Preheat the oven to 400°F (200°C).

2. **Make the shrimp:** Butterfly each shrimp by slicing a slit up the back at least ½-inch (1 cm) deep, being careful not to cut through completely. Remove the black vein with a small paring knife and rinse the shrimp under cold water. Pat dry with a paper towel.

3. Whisk together the olive oil, garlic, basil, red pepper flakes, salt, and black pepper in a large bowl. Toss the shrimp in the mixture to coat on all sides. Transfer the shrimp to a rimmed baking sheet, forming a single layer.

4. Roast for 5 to 6 minutes, until the shrimp are pink and opaque, turning halfway through. Remove from the oven and let cool. Cover and refrigerate until ready to serve.

5. **Make the sauce:** Whisk together all the ingredients in a small bowl. Cover and refrigerate until ready to serve.

6. Transfer the cocktail sauce to a small serving bowl and place it on a platter (see Note 2). Put shrimp around the bowl, and garnish with parsley and lemon wedges.

### MAKE-AHEAD GAME PLAN

- Two days ahead, make the cocktail sauce. Keep covered and refrigerate until ready to serve.

- One day ahead, roast the shrimp and allow it to cool. Keep covered and refrigerate until ready to serve.

### PAIRS WELL WITH

Rosemary Beef Tenderloin with Horseradish Cream (page 143)

Sheet-Pan Lamb with Caramelized Shallots and Provençal Tomatoes (page 110)

# GOUGÈRES
## (AKA FRENCH CHEESY PUFFS)

Over twenty years ago, my husband and I were married in the Loire Valley of France. Part of the appeal of bringing the party to France was the opportunity to introduce French culture to our friends and family. More than sixty Americans made the trip, and to celebrate their arrival, my parents threw a big welcome luncheon. The party kicked off with the traditional French aperitif, complete with champagne and trays and trays of delicate gougères: scrumptious French cheese puffs. They are crispy on the outside and warm and chewy on the inside, a highly addictive combination. The American guests scarfed them up, two to three at a time—they were so good! There is a lot to remember about that week of festivities, but the one thing that everyone always brings up, even twenty-five years later, is "those French cheesy puffs!"

***SERVES 6 TO 8*** *(Makes 24)*

½ cup (120 ml) water

4 tablespoons (56 g) salted American butter

¼ teaspoon (1 g) kosher salt

½ cup (70 g) all-purpose flour

2 large eggs, beaten (about 120 ml/½ cup)

¾ cup (45 g) grated Gruyère cheese, plus ¼ cup (15 g) for garnish (see Note)

Fleur de sel salt, to taste

Freshly cracked black pepper, to taste

### NOTE

Grate the Gruyère on the smallest hole of a box grater.

1. Preheat the oven to 375°F (190°C). Place the oven rack in the lower third of the oven. Line two baking sheets with parchment paper.

2. Bring the water, butter, and kosher salt to a boil in a medium saucepan over medium-high heat. Whisk to combine.

3. Reduce the heat to medium and then add the flour. Stir well until a dough forms and becomes glossy, about 1 minute.

4. Remove from the heat and pat the dough down with a wooden spoon into a rough circle. The eggs will scramble if they touch the hot pan, and this gives them a safe place to land.

5. Slowly pour in the eggs, one-third at a time, stirring with a wooden spoon after each addition, until the mixture is nice and glossy. It will take some work to stir in the eggs (they may even look curdled), but just keep stirring and the dough will come together in a sticky mass. If you are having trouble with a wooden spoon, use a whisk instead. Then, stir in ¾ cup (45 g) grated Gruyère.

6. Transfer the mixture to a pastry bag fitted with a ½-inch (1 cm) round tip. Pipe twelve 1-inch (2.5 cm) rounds (about the size of a quarter), leaving about 2 inches (5 cm) of space in between, on each baking sheet.

7. Top each round with a small mound of the remaining cheese, a sprinkle of fleur de sel, and a crack of pepper. Bake one tray at a time, leaving the other on the countertop at room temperature.

8. Bake for 20 to 22 minutes, until risen and golden brown. Repeat with the second baking sheet. Serve immediately.

### MAKE-AHEAD GAME PLAN

- These are best made right before guests arrive for the lightest, fluffiest texture. But they will still be tasty if prepped ahead.

- Up to two weeks ahead, pipe the gougères onto a parchment-lined tray (omitting the fleur de sel, pepper, and cheese for garnish) and place in the freezer for 2 hours. Transfer the frozen rounds to a ziplock bag and keep in the freezer until ready to bake. No need to defrost before baking. Just add the fleur de sel, pepper, and cheese, and bake in a preheated 375°F (190°C) oven for 22 to 23 minutes, until golden brown.

### PAIRS WELL WITH

Sweet and Spicy Candied Pecans (page 69)

Rosemary Beef Tenderloin with Horseradish Cream (page 143)

# SOUR CREAM AND ONION DIP

Skip those seasoning packets in the chip aisle and make your own sour cream and onion dip. It not only will taste better but will allow you to adjust the seasoning and texture, too. Use this recipe as a jumping-off point and then add more garlic, Worcestershire sauce, or chives as desired. This makes a great game day or awards night snack. Serve with your favorite potato chips or even waffle fries! But don't put out too many fries because the combination is so good that your guests will be too full for dinner.

*SERVES 8 TO 10* *(Makes 3 cups/720 ml)*

1 tablespoon (15 ml) olive oil

1 large yellow onion, diced (about 2 cups/300 g)

1 teaspoon (6 g) kosher salt

Freshly cracked black pepper, to taste

16 ounces (454 g) sour cream

4 ounces (113 g) cream cheese, softened

1 garlic clove, minced

1 teaspoon (5 ml) onion powder

1 teaspoon (5 ml) Worcestershire sauce

3 tablespoons (45 ml) minced chives, divided

Your favorite potato chips or waffle fries, for serving (see Note)

1. Heat the olive oil in a large nonstick skillet over medium-high heat.

2. Add the onions. Season with salt and pepper and cook until soft, caramelized, and fragrant, 4 to 6 minutes. Set aside to cool.

3. Meanwhile, use a rubber spatula to mix the sour cream and cream cheese in a large bowl.

4. Whisk in the garlic, onion powder, Worcestershire sauce, and 2 tablespoons (30 ml) chives. Fold in the cooled onions.

5. Transfer to a serving bowl and garnish with the remaining chives.

6. Serve with potato chips or waffle fries.

**NOTE**

This dip is hearty, so it's best to serve it with strong chips, such as Ruffles or kettle cooked chips, which can handle the weight. Waffle fries heat up really well in the air fryer! Just pop them in frozen, and air fry at 375°F (190°C) for 10 to 15 minutes, until crispy and warmed through.

**MAKE-AHEAD GAME PLAN**

One day ahead, make the dip. Cover and refrigerate until ready to serve.

**PAIRS WELL WITH**

DIY Bloody Mary Bar (page 31)

Blazin' Hot Buffalo Wings (page 70)

# DECONSTRUCTED CHERRY TOMATO BRUSCHETTA

Bruschetta is a classic summer appetizer, but even the toastiest of bread can turn soggy under the weight of juicy, ripe tomatoes. I say let bruschetta live up to its highest potential by deconstructing it! All you have to do is grill the bread, toss the tomatoes, and pile it high on a board for an easy presentation that is both welcoming and interactive. Anything like this will get your guests mingling (and generally loosen them up), because it gives them something to do with their hands. Serve with some balsamic glaze on the side for a finishing drizzle of sweetness. Or slather on the burrata for a heartier appetizer that will keep the troops at bay while you're grilling dinner. Either way, this goes well with a chilled glass of rosé.

*SERVES 8*

## TOASTS

One 16-ounce (454 g) Italian or French loaf

½ cup (120 ml) olive oil

3 garlic cloves, minced

Pinch of Italian seasoning

Kosher salt and freshly cracked black pepper, to taste

## TOMATOES

16.5 ounces (467 g) cherry tomatoes, quartered (see Note)

1 garlic clove, minced

¼ cup (60 ml) chiffonade of fresh basil

2 tablespoons (30 ml) olive oil

Kosher salt and freshly cracked black pepper, to taste

## FOR SERVING

½ cup (120 ml) balsamic glaze

Two 8-ounce (227 g) containers burrata (optional)

### NOTE

Cherry tomatoes are a great option for bruschetta, since they don't emit as much juice as larger tomatoes and they are full of flavor! For a pretty presentation, use both yellow and red cherry tomatoes.

1. **Make the toasts:** Slice the bread into 1-inch (2.5 cm) slices. Mix the olive oil, garlic, Italian seasoning, salt, and pepper in a small bowl.

2. Brush the olive oil mixture onto both sides of the bread slices and then transfer them to a plate.

3. Grill the bread, turning the slices to form a crosshatch design, 2 to 3 minutes per side on a grill pan or 1 to 2 minutes per side on a BBQ grill.

4. **Make the tomatoes:** Mix the tomatoes, garlic, basil, olive oil, salt, and pepper. Gently toss to combine and then transfer the mixture to a small serving bowl.

5. Place the bowl of tomatoes on a serving board and arrange the toasts around the bowl.

6. Transfer the balsamic glaze to a small serving jar with a honey dipper. (The honey dipper creates a fantastic "just-enough" drizzle.)

7. Encourage guests to spoon the tomatoes over the grilled bread and then add a drizzle of balsamic glaze.

8. If serving with the burrata, place the cheese on the bread first, top with tomatoes, and finish with glaze.

### MAKE-AHEAD GAME PLAN

· One hour before serving, whisk up the olive oil mixture for the bread. Cover and leave at room temperature.

· One hour before serving, slice the tomatoes and prepare the dressing. Cover both and leave at room temperature. Keep them separated until ready to serve.

### PAIRS WELL WITH

Easy Gourmet Burgers (page 137)

Grilled Dijon Chicken with Charred Lemons (page 123)

# SOUTHERN CHEESE STRAWS
## (THE YANKEE VERSION)

You might be thinking, *What does a New Englander know about making Southern cheese straws?* Well, while I was taking a tour through the South with my father for his HGTV series, we ended up in some of the loveliest Southern living rooms, where inevitably, someone would offer us one of these delectable little nibbles, followed by a glass of something bubbly. Years later, I tried to recreate this recipe but could never find an easy-to-use cookie press that didn't make me want to pull my hair out! I was determined to develop a recipe that only required a pastry bag and tip. But it does take some muscle, so if you want an even easier route, you can skip the pastry bag and just fill the pastry tip and then push the dough through it with your fingertips. With a quick flash freeze before baking, these addictive little Southern snacks can be yours! They pair beautifully with a glass of champagne, red wine, or port.

*SERVES 10 TO 12* (Makes 80 to 120)

8 ounces (227 g) sharp cheddar, grated (see Note 1)

1 cup (226 g) salted American butter, softened

2½ cups (350 g) all-purpose flour

¾ teaspoon (3.75 ml) smoked paprika

¾ teaspoon (5 g) kosher salt

½ teaspoon (2.5 ml) cayenne, plus more to taste

### NOTES

1. I recommend using a block of Tillamook sharp cheddar cheese and grating it by hand for the best flavor and texture (pre-shredded cheese often contains anti-caking agents, which can affect the taste and texture).

2. It's better to pipe the cheese straws while the dough is soft and then freeze them before baking instead of chilling the dough first, which will make it *really* hard to pipe out!

3. Piping is a two-handed operation: Hold the top of the bag with your right hand to stabilize it, and use your left hand to squeeze and pipe out the dough. If the piping becomes too difficult, pop the dough back into your mixer with the paddle attachment, add 1 tablespoon (15 ml) of vegetable oil to the dough, and beat together; this will make it more supple and easier to pipe.

1. Line a baking sheet with parchment paper.

2. Combine the cheese and butter in the bowl of an electric mixer. Whisk together the flour, paprika, salt, and cayenne in a medium bowl.

3. Slowly add the dry ingredients, in thirds, to the cheese-butter mixture, beating in between each addition and scraping down the bowl as needed to form a cohesive dough.

4. Transfer the dough to a pastry bag fitted with a large star tip (1½ inches/4 cm at the base and ½ inch/1 cm at the tip) and pipe 2-inch (5 cm) cheese straws (see Notes 2 and 3) onto the baking sheet. Place the baking sheet in the freezer for 20 minutes.

5. Preheat the oven to 400°F (200°C). Place the oven rack in the lower third of the oven. Bake for 10 to 11 minutes, until golden brown.

6. Let cool slightly and then serve. Or let cool completely and then store in an airtight container at room temperature until ready to serve.

### MAKE-AHEAD GAME PLAN

One week ahead, bake the cheese straws and allow them to cool completely. Place them in a resealable plastic bag and freeze. To reheat, place them on a parchment-lined baking sheet and bake in a preheated 300°F (150°C) oven for 5 to 7 minutes.

### PAIRS WELL WITH

Sour Cream and Onion Dip (page 58)

A Little Bit Lighter Gazpacho (page 96)

# CREAMY HUMMUS
## WITH GRILLED PITA

The secret to this smooth and creamy hummus is baking soda. That's right: baking soda! Ten years ago, this was the tip heard around the internet, and I'm still grateful to have come upon it. Normally, this technique involves dried chickpeas, but I think using canned is way easier. Though canned chickpeas are already softened, they can also result in lumpy, grainy hummus. The baking soda will melt all that graininess away! Simmering canned chickpeas with baking soda allows them to get even softer, loosening their skins in the process. The result is the creamiest, smoothest hummus, much better than anything you'll buy from the store. Making your own hummus is also the easiest way to adjust the flavor, adding more zing with the lemon juice, more kick with the garlic, or more salt to your liking. Skip the chips in favor of freshly grilled pita for a winning combo that will disappear in minutes.

***SERVES 4 TO 6*** *(Makes 3½ cups /770 g)*

### HUMMUS
Two 15-ounce (425 g) cans
    chickpeas

1 teaspoon (4 g) baking soda

⅔ cup (160 ml) tahini

2 garlic cloves

¼ cup (60 ml) fresh lemon juice
    (from about 2 lemons)

2 teaspoons (10 ml) ground
    cumin, plus more for garnish

1 teaspoon (6 g) kosher salt

½ cup (120 ml) olive oil, plus
    more for drizzling

1 tablespoon (15 ml) chopped
    fresh Italian parsley

### PITA
One 12-ounce (340 g) package of
    your favorite pita bread

1 tablespoon (15 ml) olive oil

Sprinkle of fleur de sel salt

### NOTE
I like my hummus on the thinner side. If that sounds like you, too, add up to 2 tablespoons (30 ml) lemon juice or water to thin. First, taste it: If you like the flavor, add water; if you'd like a bit more zing, add lemon juice.

1. **Make the hummus:** Drain and rinse the chickpeas, setting aside 1 tablespoon (15 ml) chickpeas for the garnish. Fill the cans with water.

2. Place the chickpeas in a medium pot, and pour the water from the cans over them. Stir in the baking soda. Simmer until the chickpea skins start to loosen, about 10 minutes.

3. Drain the chickpeas and rinse with cold water to remove any baking soda taste. If a few skins remain, that's okay; they will just get processed up.

4. Place the chickpeas in a food processor with the tahini and process until smooth. Add the garlic, lemon juice, cumin, and salt, and process again until smooth.

5. With the food processor running, slowly add the olive oil. Taste for seasoning, and add more salt or cumin as desired (see Note).

6. Transfer the hummus to a serving bowl, drizzle with a little more olive oil to taste, and garnish with the reserved chickpeas, a sprinkle of cumin, and parsley.

7. **Make the pita:** Brush the pita with the olive oil on both sides. Grill on a grill pan or BBQ until grill marks form and the pita is soft and warm, about 1 minute on each side.

8. Stack the pita and cut the stack into quarters. Sprinkle with fleur de sel. Serve the pita with the hummus.

### MAKE-AHEAD GAME PLAN
One day ahead, make the hummus. Place it in an airtight container and refrigerate until ready to serve.

### PAIRS WELL WITH
Fresh and Fruity White Wine Sangria (page 36)

Crudité Platter with Green Goddess Dip (page 50)

# BAKED BRIE
## WITH FIG JAM, ROSEMARY, AND WALNUTS

Brie, fig jam, and rosemary is one of my favorite flavor combinations, and I've been making a version of this appetizer for years. It results in a molten, bubbly skillet of goodness that is just divine slathered over gourmet raisin crackers or slices of crusty baguette. At our house, and I suspect at yours soon, this is the holiday-defining appetizer that kicks off Thanksgiving, sails into Christmas, and gets one last hoorah on New Year's Eve. You can switch up the jams and nuts to suit your tastes or the occasion; sour cherry jam and raw almonds or apricot jam and raw pistachios work nicely with the rosemary, too!

*SERVES 4*

One 13.2-ounce (374 g) wheel Brie or Camembert (see Note 1)

3 tablespoons (45 ml) fig jam

1 tablespoon (15 ml) chopped fresh rosemary

2 tablespoons (30 ml) finely chopped raw walnuts

### FOR SERVING

Two 5.3-ounce (150 g) packages raisin crackers or 1 baguette (see Note 2)

1 pound (454 g) seedless red grapes

### NOTES

1. In the US, it can be hard to find small wheels of Brie, but Alouette Cheese makes one, and their 13.2-ounce (374 g) size fits perfectly in a 6-inch (15 cm) cast-iron skillet.

2. If using this as an appetizer before dinner, serve it with crackers, which are less filling. The baguette toasts are better for a cocktail party.

1. Preheat the oven to the broiler setting. Slice the baguette into 1-inch slices (2.5 cm) and place on a baking sheet. Toast both sides under the broiler for 1 to 3 minutes, until golden brown. Set aside, keeping them at room temperature, until ready to serve.

2. Lower the oven to 375°F (190°C). Place the oven rack in the lower third of the oven.

3. Score the Brie by slicing four slits horizontally, about 1 inch (2.5 cm) apart, and four slits vertically, creating a checkerboard pattern.

4. Place the Brie in a 6-inch (15 cm) mini cast-iron skillet, oval gratin dish, or other oven-safe dish. Spread the jam over the Brie, add the rosemary, and sprinkle the walnuts on top.

5. Place the skillet on a baking sheet and bake for 12 to 15 minutes, until the cheese starts to ooze out of the slits and the nuts are golden brown.

6. Transfer the skillet to a heat-safe surface, and add the crackers and grapes around the skillet before serving.

### MAKE-AHEAD GAME PLAN

- Up to four hours ahead, assemble the Brie, loosely cover, and refrigerate until ready to bake.

- Up to 30 minutes ahead, toast the baguette slices. Allow to cool completely. Keep at room temperature loosely covered with a sheet of foil.

### PAIRS WELL WITH

Sparkling Christmas Punch (page 44)

Stuffed Mushroom Caps (page 49)

## SWEET AND SPICY
# CANDIED PECANS

As far as snacks go, is there anything more addictive than a warm candied nut? They are the perfect little cocktail nibble around the holidays, and they look extra fancy when placed in a silver dish or a footed serving bowl. Serve them on their own or toss them into my Thankful Thanksgiving Salad (page 103). They are also a fantastic food gift idea; you can place them in a cellophane bag tied up with raffia, faux evergreen, and berries. I love to use pecans in this recipe because of their buttery texture. It is a perfect match for the sweet and salty flavor and the kick of cayenne!

***SERVES 6*** *(Makes 1 pound/454 g)*

1 teaspoon (5 ml) vegetable oil

2 tablespoons (28 g) salted American butter

2 tablespoons (30 ml) honey

2 tablespoons (20 g) light brown sugar

½ teaspoon (2.5 ml) pumpkin pie spice or ground cinnamon

½ teaspoon (3 g) kosher salt

¼ teaspoon (1.25 ml) cayenne

1 pound (454 g) raw pecan halves (see Note)

### NOTE
If desired, you can substitute raw walnuts or cashews for the pecans.

1. Preheat the oven to 350°F (175°C). Grease a large, rimmed baking sheet with the vegetable oil.

2. Melt the butter and honey in a large nonstick skillet over medium heat. Add the brown sugar, pumpkin pie spice, salt, and cayenne. Whisk to combine.

3. Add the pecans and toss with a spatula to coat. Spread the pecan mixture out in a single layer on the baking sheet.

4. Bake for 10 minutes and then toss the pecans with a spatula and bake for 3 minutes more, or until they look darker, smell fragrant, and start to dry out.

5. Remove the pecans from the oven and let them cool, dry, and harden for 10 minutes.

6. Serve immediately or store in an airtight container at room temperature for up to 5 days.

### MAKE-AHEAD GAME PLAN
One day ahead, bake the pecans and then allow them to dry and harden. Transfer them to an airtight container at room temperature until ready to serve.

### PAIRS WELL WITH
Baked Brie with Fig Jam, Rosemary, and Walnuts (page 66)

The Thankful Thanksgiving Salad (page 103)

# BLAZIN' HOT BUFFALO WINGS

Even if you couldn't care less about game day, at some point, you will probably live with someone who does. To make these afternoons more enjoyable, I say bring on the food! Food (along with the cute horse commercials) will get you through the day if you don't even know who's playing. Fair warning: These wings are not for the faint of heart. They are blazing hot, which also makes them curiously delicious. Pair them with ranch dressing or my Crisp and Creamy Coleslaw (page 155) to further extinguish the heat. These wings are extra crispy because they're tossed in baking powder along with the spices before baking. Better yet, if you have an air fryer, use it; they'll be even crisper that way!

*SERVES 4*

### HOT SAUCE

5 tablespoons (70 g) salted American butter (see Note 1)

¼ cup (60 ml) sriracha (see Note 2)

2 teaspoons (10 ml) white vinegar

1 teaspoon (5 ml) Worcestershire sauce

¼ teaspoon (1.25 ml) garlic powder

### RANCH DRESSING

1 cup (240 g) sour cream

½ cup (120 ml) buttermilk

½ cup (110 g) mayonnaise

2 teaspoons (10 ml) garlic powder

1 teaspoon (5 ml) lemon zest

½ teaspoon (2.5 ml) celery seed

2 tablespoons (30 ml) fresh chives

2 tablespoons (30 ml) fresh dill

Freshly cracked black pepper

### WINGS

3 pounds (1.4 kg) bone-in chicken wings (1 party pack drums and flats)

3 teaspoons (12 g) baking powder

1 teaspoon (6 g) kosher salt

Freshly cracked black pepper, to taste

1 teaspoon (5 ml) garlic powder

1. Preheat the oven to 450°F (230°C). Line a baking sheet with foil and place a rack on top. (To make these in an air fryer, see Note 3.)

2. **Make the sauce:** Melt the butter in a small saucepan over medium heat. Add the sriracha, vinegar, Worcestershire sauce, and garlic powder.

3. **Make the dressing:** Place the sour cream, buttermilk, mayonnaise, garlic powder, lemon zest, and celery seed in a blender. Blend until smooth.

4. Add the chives, dill, and pepper, and pulse until just combined. Don't over-pulse, or you'll have a green dressing that will resemble green goddess dip! Pour into a container and refrigerate until ready to serve.

5. **Make the wings:** Pat the wings dry with a paper towel. Whisk the baking powder, salt, pepper, and garlic powder in a large bowl. Add the wings in batches and toss to coat. Lay the wings in a single layer on the rack.

6. Bake for 15 minutes and then flip the wings over and bake for 10 more minutes, or until golden brown and crispy.

7. Place the wings in a large, clean bowl and pour in the hot sauce. Toss to coat.

8. Transfer the wings to a serving platter and serve with the ranch dressing.

#### MAKE-AHEAD GAME PLAN

- One day ahead, prepare the hot sauce. Allow it to cool, then cover and refrigerate. Reheat the sauce in a small saucepan over medium-high heat until warmed through, about 5 minutes. Proceed as directed.

- One day ahead, make the ranch dressing. Cover and refrigerate until ready to serve.

#### PAIRS WELL WITH

Crisp and Creamy Coleslaw (page 155)

Crudité Platter with Green Goddess Dip (page 50)

### NOTES

1. If the sauce is too spicy for your taste, add another 1 tablespoon (14 g) butter.

2. The thick consistency of the sriracha allows the sauce to coat the wings better than traditional vinegar-based hot sauces.

3. To cook in an air fryer, follow your manufacturer's instructions for air frying chicken. Usually, this is between 375°F to 400°F (190°C to 200°C) and takes about 20 minutes. Shake the basket to flip the wings halfway through.

# LEAVE-IT-CHUNKY GUACAMOLE

I'll admit that the first time I saw guacamole sold in France, my Californian pride was a bit bruised. The "Avocado Dip," as it was labeled, had been whipped beyond recognition, making it look more like baby food than guacamole. To be fair, the French aren't the only ones at fault; I've seen Americans do this, too. Years later, when my French nephews visited us in Los Angeles, I made them my version of this party favorite, and they were hooked.

I explained that there should be no pureeing, no whipping or blending of any kind. The avocados should remain recognizable—just cubed and gently tossed with a fork, which creates its own gentle mashing. Load the guacamole with other chunky vegetables like tomatoes and onions, and keep the flavors clean and fresh. I skip cumin and garlic, which I find are too overpowering for the delicate avocado. But I do like a little heat in the form of a few dashes of hot sauce. Serve this chunky guacamole with artisan-style tortilla chips that can withstand the weight!

*SERVES 4* *(Makes 2 cups /480 g)*

2 ripe avocados, cubed (see Note 1)

1 cup (140 g) vine-ripened tomatoes, chopped

¼ cup (37 g) diced red onion

2 tablespoons (30 ml) chopped fresh cilantro (plus a few leaves for garnish)

2 tablespoons (30 ml) fresh lime juice (from 1 or 2 limes; see Note 2)

½ teaspoon (2.5 ml) hot sauce

¼ teaspoon (1 g) kosher salt

Freshly cracked black pepper, to taste

Your favorite tortilla chips, for serving

1. Place the avocado, tomatoes, onions, cilantro, lime juice, hot sauce, salt, and pepper in a medium bowl. Gently toss with a fork to combine.

2. Transfer to a serving bowl and top with a few cilantro leaves. Serve immediately.

### MAKE-AHEAD GAME PLAN

- One hour before guests arrive, place all the ingredients, except the avocados, in a bowl. Cover and leave at room temperature on your countertop.

- Moments before guests arrive, cut the avocados, toss with the rest of the ingredients, and serve immediately.

### PAIRS WELL WITH

24-Hour Flank Steak with Chimichurri Sauce (page 124)

Better BBQ Chicken (page 133)

### NOTES

1. Don't buy ripe avocados. They are typically too bruised inside from all the squeezing they have endured from other customers. Instead, buy the unripe ones, which no one ever touches, and let them ripen at home for 3 to 4 days, free from any manhandling. You'll end up with an avocado that is beautifully soft and buttery inside.

2. If your limes are hard, they won't release much juice. Roll them on your counter firmly with the palm of your hand to loosen the membranes. If that doesn't help, pop them in the microwave on high for 5 seconds, and they'll be nice and juicy!

# WARM CRAB PLATTER
## WITH HOMEMADE AIOLI

One of the easiest starters for wowing a crowd is a generous pile of crab legs and claws. It's also a very festive first course for Christmas or New Year's Eve. The legs and claws are sold cooked, so all you have to do is heat them up, which takes less than 10 minutes. Then, whip up the aioli: a garlicky homemade mayonnaise. The French take their mayonnaise very seriously. On one of our first trips to France, we spent a lovely weekend at a friend's home. Langoustines were in season, and it's customary to serve them with homemade mayonnaise. I had never seen how mayonnaise was made, so our friend's mother, a very elegant woman in her mid-eighties, whisked me off into the kitchen to show me just how it was done. She even let me hold the whisk. I swung into action, mixing in the oil with great gusto, until I felt her perfectly manicured hands firmly grip my wrist and pry the whisk out of my eager little fingers. She uttered something in French, and a chorus of laughter erupted. It wasn't until hours later that I learned exactly what she'd said: "That's enough! We cannot let an American be in charge of the mayonnaise!" Apparently, I was whisking too fast to create the proper emulsion. Years later, with the help of my French sisters-in-law, I mastered the technique!

*SERVES 4* *(Makes ¾ cup/180 ml aioli)*

1½ pounds (680 g) golden king crab legs, thawed if frozen

2½ pounds (1.1 kg) Dungeness crab claws, thawed if frozen

1 large egg yolk (see Note 1)

1½ teaspoon (7.5 ml) Dijon mustard

⅔ cup (160 ml) neutral oil (such as vegetable, grapeseed, or canola)

2 garlic cloves, minced

1 tablespoon (15 ml) snipped fresh chives

Kosher salt and freshly cracked black pepper, to taste

2 lemons, sliced into wedges

### NOTES

1. It may be tempting to use store-bought mayonnaise and doctor it up. But the texture, flavor, and consistency of homemade mayonnaise is totally different. To avoid the raw egg yolk, you can use 1 tablespoon (15 ml) of a pasteurized egg product instead.

2. An emulsion is a mixture of two liquids that don't naturally combine, like the oil and the egg yolk. Adding them together slowly will create an even better texture.

1. Preheat the oven to 350°F (175°C).

2. Fill a large roasting pan with ¼ inch (6 mm) of water. Place the crab legs and claws inside, cover with foil, and "steam bake" for 8 to 10 minutes.

3. Meanwhile, make the aioli: Whisk the egg yolk and mustard in a small bowl and then slowly add the oil in a steady drizzle, whisking all the while and pausing the drizzle to make sure the oil is combining and creating an emulsion (see Note 2). The mixture should become creamier and thicker. Do not add the oil too quickly, or the emulsion will separate or "break" and you'll have to start over.

4. Whisk in the garlic, chives, salt, and pepper. Serve with the crab, and garnish with lemon wedges.

### MAKE-AHEAD GAME PLAN

Two hours ahead, make the mayonnaise. Cover and refrigerate until ready to serve.

### PAIRS WELL WITH

Make-Ahead Beef Stew (page 130)

Rosemary Beef Tenderloin with Horseradish Cream (page 143)

# SOUPS AND SALADS

# BUTTERNUT SQUASH SOUP
## WITH RAISIN BREAD CROUTONS

Butternut squash is like a pretty girl who doesn't need much makeup. You don't want to mask her natural beauty, just enhance what Mother Nature gave her. The squash becomes extra flavorful and sweet when roasted in the oven. Once the soup is pureed, I spruce it up a bit by adding a splash of maple syrup and a little dash of curry powder. The curry powder creates this fantastic sensation that reaches down into your soul and warms you from within. The raisin bread croutons are unexpected but feel right at home with all the other fall flavors. I love to serve this soup as a starter in the cooler months, when the thought of welcoming guests with a chilled salad just doesn't seem civilized. They will thank you for this warming soup instead!

*SERVES 4 TO 6* (*Makes 6 cups/1.4 L*)

3 pounds (1.4 kg) butternut squash

2 tablespoons (30 ml) olive oil, divided

Kosher salt and freshly cracked black pepper, to taste

½ large yellow onion, diced (about 1 cup/150 g)

2 medium carrots, diced (about ½ cup/60 g)

1 small celery stalk, diced (about ⅓ cup/45 g)

1 garlic clove, minced

4 cups (960 ml) vegetable broth

1 tablespoon (15 ml) maple syrup

1 teaspoon (5 ml) curry powder

### CROUTONS

2 cups (140 g) cubed pecan raisin bread (see Note)

Olive oil spray

### GARNISH

2 tablespoons (30 g) sour cream or crème fraîche

1 teaspoon (5 ml) warm water

1 teaspoon (5 ml) fresh thyme leaves

### NOTE

Look for an "artisan-style" raisin loaf in the bakery department of your grocery store. It should have a nice weight to it so it can form a crunchy crouton. Avoid breakfast-style cinnamon swirl raisin bread: It will be too sweet and won't have the same effect.

1. Preheat the oven to 425°F (215°C).

2. Halve the squash lengthwise. Scoop out the seeds. Place on a baking sheet and then drizzle 1 tablespoon (15 ml) olive oil over the halves. Season with salt and pepper.

3. Roast for 1 hour, until the flesh is very tender when pierced with a knife. Let cool.

4. Reduce the oven temperature to 375°F (190°C).

5. Heat the remaining olive oil in a Dutch oven over medium-high heat.

6. Add the onions, carrots, and celery, and sauté until fragrant and tender, 8 to 10 minutes. Add the garlic and cook for 1 more minute. Add the broth and then remove from the heat and set aside.

7. **Make the croutons:** Put the bread cubes in a medium bowl and coat lightly with olive oil spray, tossing the cubes to distribute the oil. Place the cubes on a baking sheet and bake for 10 to 12 minutes, until golden brown and crunchy.

8. Scoop out the flesh of the squash with a melon baller, loosening it away from the peel. (A melon baller is sharp and will help release the squash more easily than a spoon.) Transfer the flesh to a blender. Add the vegetable mixture and then puree the soup on high until smooth. Wipe out the Dutch oven.

9. Transfer the soup to the Dutch oven and heat over medium-high until hot, about 3 to 4 minutes. If the soup feels too thick for your liking, thin with vegetable broth or water in ¼-cup (60 ml) increments until you achieve your desired consistency.

10. Taste for seasoning and add more salt and pepper if desired. Whisk in the maple syrup and the curry powder, and taste and add more syrup or curry powder if desired.

11. **Make the garnish:** Thin the sour cream with the warm water.

12. Ladle the soup into bowls, and add a drizzle of the thinned sour cream, the fresh thyme leaves, and the croutons.

### MAKE-AHEAD GAME PLAN

- One day ahead, make the soup. Let cool and then refrigerate until ready to reheat and serve.
- Two hours ahead, mix up the sour cream garnish. Cover and refrigerate.
- One hour ahead, make the croutons. Let cool and then store in an airtight container at room temperature.

### PAIRS WELL WITH

Cast-Iron Roast Chicken (page 107)

Fennel-Crusted Pork Loin with Spiced Parsnips and Apples (page 134)

# LITTLE GEM CAESAR SALAD
## WITH CROUTON TOASTS

A composed salad is a lovely way to kick off a dinner party, and using baby lettuce makes it even prettier. This way, you don't have to cut and toss romaine lettuce and serve out portions, which never ends up looking very pretty. If you're prepping the house for a party—and putting out fresh flowers—you can spiff up this classic salad to match the surroundings. I serve it with crouton toasts instead of traditional croutons because small croutons can sometimes be hard to stab with a fork and eat gracefully. Guests can nibble on the toasts with their fingertips while enjoying the traditional flavors of a classic Caesar salad!

*SERVES 4*

### DRESSING

½ cup (110 g) mayonnaise

1 teaspoon (5 ml) lemon zest

3 tablespoons (45 ml) fresh lemon juice (from about 1½ lemons)

2 tablespoons (30 ml) olive oil

1 teaspoon (5 ml) anchovy paste

½ teaspoon (2.5 ml) Worcestershire sauce

½ cup (40 g) freshly grated Parmesan (see Note 1)

### CROUTON TOASTS

1 high-quality baguette (not too squishy!)

2 tablespoons (30 ml) olive oil

Kosher salt and freshly cracked black pepper, to taste

½ cup (40 g) freshly grated Parmesan

1 teaspoon (5 ml) dried basil

### SALAD

5 ounces (142 g) Baby Gem or Little Gem lettuce (see Note 2)

¼ cup (35 g) pine nuts

### NOTES

1. Don't be tempted to save time and buy pre-shredded Parmesan; freshly grated will taste much better.
2. If you can't find this type of lettuce, look for baby romaine.

1. **Make the dressing:** Whisk together the mayonnaise, lemon zest and juice, olive oil, anchovy paste, and Worcestershire sauce. Then, whisk in the cheese.

2. Gently toast the pine nuts in a nonstick pan over medium-high heat until golden brown, 3 to 4 minutes. Set aside to cool.

3. **Make the crouton toasts:** Slice the bread into ¼-inch (6 mm) slices. Transfer the slices to a baking sheet. Brush both sides of the bread with olive oil and season with salt and pepper.

4. Place under the broiler until golden brown and toasted, 1 to 2 minutes. Remove from the oven and flip the bread over. Sprinkle with the Parmesan and basil on the untoasted side only. Place back under the broiler to melt the cheese and toast the bread, about 1 minute.

5. To assemble the salads, place 7 to 8 lettuce leaves on each plate. Add the dressing with a fork (instead of a spoon) so it drizzles onto the salad. Place the toasted pine nuts on top and add some freshly cracked pepper.

6. Place 1 to 2 crouton toasts on each plate and serve immediately.

### MAKE-AHEAD GAME PLAN

- One day ahead, make the dressing. Cover and refrigerate until ready to serve.

- Four hours ahead, toast the pine nuts. Let cool and then cover and leave at room temperature.

- One hour ahead, make the croutons. Allow to cool then loosely cover and leave at room temperature.

### PAIRS WELL WITH

Old-School Lasagna (page 120)

Rosemary Beef Tenderloin with Horseradish Cream (page 143)

# ROASTED BEET SALAD
## WITH ORANGES AND HERBS

Growing up in the States, I had no problem passing by the cooked beets while cruising the salad bar. On the few occasions that I did try them, they always tasted like, well, dirt. But my husband's family changed my ways. My mother-in-law and sisters-in-law each have a version of a roasted beet salad that they serve as a starter: It's typically tossed in a mustardy vinaigrette and topped with lots of fresh parsley. I came to love this simple salad and looked forward to it any time we were in France. Back in the US, I started to experiment with different flavors. When I made it for my family one Easter, the expressions on their faces were priceless. It was clear that they hadn't ever enjoyed a roasted beet, either, so I like to think I changed their ways, too!

**SERVES 4 TO 6**

4 pounds (1.8 kg) red beets, greens removed

2 large navel oranges

2 tablespoons (30 ml) fresh mint leaves, sliced into thin ribbons

2 tablespoons (30 ml) fresh parsley, sliced into thin ribbons

1 tablespoon (7 g) minced shallots

### DRESSING

2 tablespoons (30 ml) champagne vinegar

1 tablespoon (15 ml) Dijon mustard

6 tablespoons (90 ml) grapeseed oil

2 teaspoons (10 ml) orange zest, from the navel oranges

1 tablespoon (15 ml) snipped chives

Kosher salt and freshly cracked black pepper, to taste

### NOTES

1. Don't let the beets cool too long, or they will be harder to peel. When they're warm, the skins will easily slip off.
2. You may want to use latex gloves for this part, since the beets can stain your hands and turn your fingernails pink.
3. Add crumbled goat cheese and chopped pistachios for a heartier starter.

1. Preheat the oven to 425°F (215°C).

2. Remove the greens from the beets and a sliver off each top. Leave the pointy root end intact. Wrap each beet individually in foil.

3. Place the foil packets on a baking sheet and roast until a knife easily pierces the beet. This can take 25 minutes for beets the size of a lemon and over 45 minutes for beets the size of an orange.

4. Let the beets sit for 10 to 15 minutes, until they are cool enough to handle (see Note 1).

5. Run each beet under cool water, removing the skin at the same time, and then transfer it to a medium bowl to cool further (see Note 2).

6. **Meanwhile, make the dressing:** Whisk the vinegar and mustard in a small bowl. Slowly add the grapeseed oil, whisking until emulsified and creamy. Then, add the orange zest, the chives, and salt and pepper to taste.

7. To segment each orange, slice a thin sliver off the bottom to stabilize and then a sliver off the top to reveal the fruit below. Place your knife at the top of the orange and slice around the curve at an angle to remove the peel in sections. Then, take another turn of the orange with your knife to remove any of the white pith that remains. Insert the knife between the orange segment and the dividing membranes to release the orange segment. Continue all the way around the orange until all the segments are removed and then transfer them to a small bowl.

8. Assemble the salad on individual plates so the beets don't turn the whole salad pink. Slice the beets into vertical wedges and place 3 to 4 wedges on a plate. Nestle in 3 to 4 orange segments, and sprinkle on the herbs and shallots. Drizzle the dressing on top (see Note 3).

### MAKE-AHEAD GAME PLAN

- Two days ahead, roast the beets and peel them. Cover and refrigerate until ready to serve, and slice them just before serving.
- Two days ahead, make the dressing. Hold off on adding the zest, chives, salt, and pepper until right before serving.

### PAIRS WELL WITH

Grilled Dijon Chicken with Charred Lemons (page 123)

Pan-Seared Salmon with Lemon Butter Caper Sauce (page 113)

# HORSERADISH POTATO SALAD
## WITH CARAMELIZED SHALLOTS

I didn't realize how polarizing potato salad can be until I moved to the West Coast. Upon further digging, I learned that it's the mayonnaise that gets people all worked up. See, there's no "gray area" with mayo: You either love it or hate it. And if a perfectly delicious potato salad is drenched in it, well then, game over. I love this recipe because it relies on sour cream for its dressing, with just an obligatory two-tablespoon nod to the mayonnaise for silkiness. The horseradish is a "flavor diversion" that keeps the Mayo Haters concentrating on the great kicky taste. The caramelized shallots are also not to be missed! They add a wonderful sweetness and look pretty placed on top. I prefer to leave the hard-boiled eggs out because—let's face it—that's what egg salad is for. I'm a purist when it comes to potato salad. Serve this salad with chicken or steak for a classic meat-and-potatoes summer dinner menu.

*SERVES 4*

1½ pounds (680 g) baby new potatoes (see Note 1)

⅓ cup (80 g) sour cream

2 tablespoons (30 ml) prepared horseradish

2 tablespoons (30 g) mayonnaise

1 tablespoon (15 ml) minced fresh chives, with blossoms if desired

1 tablespoon (15 ml) minced fresh dill

1 teaspoon (5 ml) Dijon mustard

1 teaspoon (5 ml) apple cider vinegar

### CARAMELIZED SHALLOTS

1 tablespoon (15 ml) olive oil

4 medium-sized shallots, sliced into half-moons (about 1½ cups/170 g)

Kosher salt and freshly cracked black pepper, to taste

1 teaspoon (5 ml) balsamic vinegar

1 teaspoon (5 ml) minced fresh rosemary

### NOTES

1. You can use any color potatoes you like. Red or multicolored new potatoes will add a nice color to this dish.

2. If you make this salad ahead of time, reserve about ¼ cup (60 ml) of the dressing. The potatoes will drink up the dressing if you add it too far in advance, leaving your salad a bit dry. It's nice to have a little extra dressing to toss in before serving to freshen it up. Extra dressing also makes a great sandwich spread for a roast beef sandwich or BLT!

1. Place the potatoes in a large pot of cold water. Bring to a boil and cook until fork-tender, 15 to 20 minutes. Drain and let cool. Refrigerate, uncovered, until ready to serve.

2. **Meanwhile, whisk up the dressing:** Mix the sour cream, horseradish, mayonnaise, chives, dill, mustard, and vinegar in a small bowl. Cover and refrigerate until ready to serve.

3. **Make the shallots:** Heat the olive oil in a large nonstick pan over medium-high heat. Sauté the shallots until they turn brown and slightly crispy, 4 to 6 minutes. Season with salt and pepper to taste.

4. Add the vinegar and cook until the shallots are coated and most of the liquid has evaporated, about 30 seconds. Stir in the rosemary and then set aside to cool. Cover and refrigerate until ready to serve.

5. Before serving, slice the potatoes in half (or quarters if they are large) and then toss with the dressing, the herbs, and half of the shallot mixture. Don't use all the dressing in one go; add a little bit at a time until it reaches the level of coverage you desire (see Note 2).

6. Transfer the salad to a serving bowl and sprinkle the top with the remaining shallots. If you grow your own chives and have some flowering blossoms, they are edible, and you can sprinkle a few of them on top for a pretty garnish.

### MAKE-AHEAD GAME PLAN

- Two days ahead, cook the potatoes. Cover and refrigerate.

- One day ahead, mix the dressing. Cover and refrigerate.

- One to two hours before serving, toss the salad with the dressing.

### PAIRS WELL WITH

24-Hour Flank Steak with Chimichurri (page 124)

Grilled Dijon Chicken with Charred Lemons (page 123)

# PHILIPPE'S PESTO ORZO SALAD

If this salad could talk! We've whipped it up on both sides of the Atlantic and shuttled it around to potlucks and school picnics, and it still remains my husband Philippe's favorite summer side dish. It's just so easy and delicious! It's also a very filling side dish, so if you're grilling and short on time, you can get away with this as your only side dish. It's starchy from the orzo and fresh from the veggies, so it feels like you've covered all of your bases. Philippe and I have debated about which cheese is better in this salad: pearl mozzarella balls or crumbled goat cheese. For years, I swore the mozzarella was better, but now I think he's right! I've crossed over to Team Goat Cheese; it really does add so much more flavor. Try for yourself and decide, or add both—that's an option, too!

*SERVES 6 TO 8*

6 quarts (5.7 L) water

Kosher salt, for the pasta water

1 pound (454 g) orzo pasta

8 ounces (227 g) sugar snap peas

4 ounces (113 g) crumbled goat cheese or pearl mozzarella balls (or both)

¾ cup (110 g) sun-dried tomatoes in oil, sliced

½ cup (120 ml) julienned basil

½ cup (70 g) pine nuts

**PESTO** (SEE NOTE 1)

2 cups (480 ml) basil leaves

3 tablespoons (45 ml) pine nuts

1 garlic clove, minced

½ teaspoon (3 g) kosher salt

½ cup (120 ml) olive oil

¼ cup (20 g) freshly grated Parmesan (see Note 2)

### NOTES

1. To save time, you can use a good-quality store-bought pesto sauce from the refrigerated section of your supermarket. The flavor will be better than anything in a shelf-stable jar.
2. Resist the temptation to buy pre-shredded Parmesan. That's fine for cooked things like lasagna, but the freshly grated cheese will give your pesto a better flavor and texture!

1. Salt the water and bring it to a boil in a large pot. Add the orzo and cook, slightly covered, until the pasta is tender, stirring occasionally to prevent it from sticking to the bottom, 10 to 11 minutes. Drain the pasta and run it under cold water to stop the cooking process, and transfer to a large bowl.

2. **Make the pesto:** Add the basil leaves, pine nuts, garlic, and salt to a food processor. Process until the basil is minced, scraping down the bowl as needed. With the food processor running, slowly add the oil to form a thick sauce. Remove the blade and gently stir in the Parmesan.

3. Transfer the pesto to the bowl and toss with the pasta. Add the snap peas, goat cheese, and tomatoes, and toss to coat. Stir in the julienned basil and pine nuts.

4. Serve immediately to allow the goat cheese to soften slightly from the warmth of the pasta (this makes it really yummy!). Otherwise, cover and refrigerate until ready to serve.

**MAKE-AHEAD GAME PLAN**

One day ahead, make the salad. Cover and refrigerate until ready to serve.

**PAIRS WELL WITH**

24-Hour Flank Steak with Chimichurri (page 124)

Grilled Dijon Chicken with Charred Lemons (page 123)

# CREAMY ASPARAGUS SOUP
## WITH CRÈME FRAÎCHE

I love to serve soup as a starter in the spring when there is still a little bit of chill in the air. This soup is filled with vibrant springtime flavors. It's smooth and creamy from the potato, and the addition of the crème fraîche and lemon zest takes it to a whole new level. It works well for Easter, Mother's Day, and baby or bridal showers, and the whole thing can be made the day before. All you have to do is reheat, garnish, and serve! My kind of starter.

*SERVES 4 AS A STARTER* (Makes 5½ cups/1.3 L)

2 tablespoons (28 g) salted American butter

½ large yellow onion, diced (about 1 cup/150 g)

2 celery stalks, diced (about ½ cup/65 g)

1 shallot, diced (about ¼ cup/28 g)

Kosher salt and freshly cracked black pepper, to taste

4 cups (960 ml) chicken broth

1 large russet potato, peeled and diced (about 1 cup/160 g)

1 garlic clove, sliced

1 pound (454 g) fresh asparagus, tough ends removed, chopped into 1-inch (2.5 cm) pieces

### GARNISH

¼ cup (60 g) crème fraîche or sour cream (see Note 1)

Grated lemon zest, to taste

3 tablespoons (45 ml) snipped fresh chives (see Note 2)

Freshly cracked black pepper, to taste

### NOTES

1. It's worth seeking out crème fraîche over sour cream. The flavor is subtler, and the texture is more luxurious. My favorite brand is Bellwether Farms, which you can find at most American supermarkets.
2. If you grow your own herbs, plant some onion chives or flowering thyme. They both blossom in the spring with gorgeous purple edible flowers that you can use for garnishing this soup. The purple against the green is a beautiful spring color combination!

1. Melt the butter in a large Dutch oven over medium-high heat. Add the onions, celery, and shallot, and cook until tender and fragrant, 2 to 3 minutes. Season with salt and pepper.

2. Add the broth, potatoes, and garlic. Cover and simmer until the potatoes are fork-tender, about 5 minutes. Add the asparagus and simmer for 5 minutes (and no longer, or the flavor and color will fade).

3. Transfer the soup to a blender and blend on high until ultrasmooth.

4. Clean out the Dutch oven and then pour in the soup. Taste and season with more salt and pepper if needed.

5. Ladle the soup into shallow bowls. Top with a dollop of crème fraîche and swirl with a fork. Add lemon zest to taste, a sprinkle of chives (and chive blossoms if you have them), and a crack of black pepper.

**MAKE-AHEAD GAME PLAN**

Two days ahead, make the soup. Cover and refrigerate until ready to serve.

**PAIRS WELL WITH**

Easy Grilled Salmon with Mango Salsa (page 127)

Sheet-Pan Lamb with Caramelized Shallots and Provençal Tomatoes (page 110)

# SOUTHAMPTON CHICKEN SALAD

This salad is inspired by a lunch I had years ago when visiting Southampton, New York. It's the kind of salad that is made using ingredients found at the local farm stands and is great for packing up into sandwiches to take to the beach. It's practically a full meal in itself, with meat, potatoes, and a side of fruit all tossed up into one yummy salad! If you can't find shelled pistachios, you can swap them out with raw pecans or use my Sweet and Spicy Candied Pecans (page 69) for a sweet and salty crunch. I love to spoon the salad in between thick slices of pumpernickel bread with Bibb lettuce and slices of ripe heirloom tomatoes. Don't forget to pack the Dangerously Delicious Chocolate Chip Cookies (page 203) or Better than Box-Mix Brownies (page 204)!

*SERVES 6 TO 8*

## CHICKEN SALAD

1½ pounds (680 g) bone-in, skin-on chicken breasts (about 2 breasts; see Note 1)

Kosher salt and freshly cracked black pepper

1 pound (454 g) red baby new potatoes (see Note 2)

¾ cup (180 g) sour cream

¼ cup (55 g) mayonnaise

2 teaspoons (10 ml) Dijon mustard

¼ cup (60 ml) chopped fresh dill

¼ cup (60 ml) chopped fresh tarragon

Kosher salt and freshly cracked black pepper, to taste

1½ cups (235 g) red grapes, halved lengthwise

1 cup (122 g) raw pistachios, shelled (see Note 3)

## SANDWICHES

8 leaves Bibb lettuce

2 medium ripe heirloom tomatoes, cut into 8 slices

Sliced rustic bread (such as pumpernickel, hearty whole wheat, or sourdough)

## NOTES

1. To make this recipe even quicker, you can use 2 cups (705 g) shredded store-bought rotisserie chicken.
2. I leave the skin on the potatoes for a more colorful salad and a bit more texture.
3. Look for raw, shelled pistachios at Trader Joe's or your local Mediterranean market.

1. Preheat the oven to 375°F (190°C). Place the oven rack in the lower third of the oven. Line a baking sheet with foil.

2. **Make the salad:** Season the chicken, under the skin, with salt and pepper.

3. Roast the chicken on the baking sheet for 45 minutes, until cooked through. Set aside to cool.

4. Meanwhile, boil the potatoes in a large pot of water until fork-tender, 10 to 15 minutes. Drain and let cool. Cut the potatoes into quarters and set aside.

5. Whisk the sour cream, mayonnaise, and mustard in a large bowl. Add the dill, tarragon, salt, and pepper. Set aside.

6. Remove the chicken skin. Use two forks to shred the chicken meat into long bite-size pieces, removing the meat from the bones.

7. Add the chicken, potatoes, grapes, and pistachios to the bowl, and toss to coat in the dressing. Check for seasoning, adding more salt or pepper as desired.

8. Cover and refrigerate until ready to serve. Place a big scoop on a Bibb lettuce leaf for a dainty lunch, or prepare sandwiches by placing lettuce, tomato slices, and chicken salad on sliced bread and take them to the beach.

### MAKE-AHEAD GAME PLAN

This salad is best made a few hours before serving. However, if you would like to make it a day ahead, it's better to prepare all the components, place them in a bowl minus the dressing, and refrigerate. Toss in the dressing a few hours before serving. That way, the salad won't dry out.

### PAIRS WELL WITH

Sweet and Spicy Candied Pecans (page 69)

A Little Bit Lighter Gazpacho (page 96)

# GRILLED PANZANELLA SALAD

The first year we planted our vegetable garden in Los Angeles, I "grew" a panzanella salad. I had eight planters devoted to growing tomatoes, and each planter contained a different heirloom variety. You see, I had a plan—once July rolled around, each one of those tomatoes would play a starring role in this salad. I can't tell you how rewarding it was to serve my "homegrown" panzanella salad with all those beautiful multicolored tomatoes! But there's no need to plant a vegetable garden to make this salad. Today's grocery stores and farmers markets offer a wide selection of heirloom tomatoes, which are not only beautiful but also have incredible flavor. Since panzanella is *all about the tomatoes*, choose them wisely! It also helps to let them sit on your windowsill for 3 to 4 days to fully ripen. Grilling the bread adds another layer of summery flavor to this recipe, even if you need to use a grill pan to get a nice charring. Go for it—it's worth the effort!

---

### SERVES 4

---

### VINAIGRETTE

3 tablespoons (45 ml) red wine vinegar

1 garlic clove, minced

¼ teaspoon (1.25 ml) Italian seasoning

Kosher salt and freshly cracked black pepper, to taste

¼ cup (60 ml) extra virgin olive oil

### BREAD

1 tablespoon (15 ml) olive oil

1 garlic clove, minced

¼ teaspoon (1.25 ml) Italian seasoning

Kosher salt and freshly cracked black pepper, to taste

Nine 1-inch-thick (2.5 cm) slices (about 10.5 ounces/300 g) ciabatta or other rustic Italian bread

### SALAD

2½ pounds (1.1 kg) ripe heirloom tomatoes, cut into wedges (see Note)

10 ounces (283 g) multicolored cherry tomatoes, halved

½ cup (120 ml) chiffonade of fresh basil, plus more for garnish

### NOTE

Purchasing a variety of tomatoes in different colors and shapes will add greater interest to this salad. Look for red, yellow, and orange tomatoes for the base of the salad, and throw in a Green Zebra or Cherokee Purple tomato for some nice accent colors.

1. **Make the vinaigrette:** Combine the vinegar, garlic, Italian seasoning, salt, and pepper in a small bowl. Slowly add the olive oil in a steady stream, whisking all the while, to form a dressing. Taste for acidity. If it's too acidic for your liking, add more oil; if it's not acidic enough, add more vinegar.

2. **Make the bread:** Place the olive oil in a small bowl and add the garlic, the Italian seasoning, and salt and pepper to taste. Combine with a fork. Brush the garlic oil on both sides of each slice of bread. Grill until nicely toasted and charred, 2 or 3 minutes per side. Remove from the grill and set aside to cool.

3. **Make the salad:** Place the heirloom and cherry tomatoes in a large bowl. Add the vinaigrette and basil, and gently mix to combine.

4. Slice the grilled bread into 1-inch (2.5 cm) chunks and toss with the tomato mixture to lightly coat the bread with the vinaigrette. It's better to add the bread last so it doesn't get too soaked and soggy.

5. Transfer the salad to a shallow serving platter to show off the colors of the tomatoes and to prevent the bread from getting too squished under their weight. Garnish with fresh basil.

### MAKE-AHEAD GAME PLAN

One hour before serving, grill the bread and leave it at room temperature. Cover loosely with a sheet of foil only when the bread is completely cooled; otherwise, condensation will form and make your bread soggy. Make the dressing and let sit at room temperature. Slice the tomatoes, cover, and leave at room temperature.

### PAIRS WELL WITH

Better BBQ Chicken (page 133)

Grilled Dijon Chicken with Charred Lemons (page 123)

# SUMMER CORN CONFETTI SALAD

This salad is inspired by the roadside farm stands of Long Island and the family friends who would invite us to their homes every summer when I was growing up. Their casually chic dinner parties were a highlight of my childhood, and they would serve up big summer salads like this in large antique bowls, which made them seem even more special. This salad doesn't need a heavy dressing because Mother Nature has already done most of the work for you. Make it in July or August when these ingredients are at their peak, and you'll see what I mean: You'll be rewarded with vegetables so sweet they taste like candy. Tossed with a good fistful of fresh herbs and a tangy vinaigrette, this salad promises big summer flavor in every little bite.

*SERVES 8*

Vegetable oil, for greasing

6 large ears fresh corn, husked, rinsed, and patted dry

10 ounces (283 g) cherry tomatoes, quartered

2 medium English cucumbers, peeled and diced (about 2 cups/280 g)

2 medium orange bell peppers, diced (about 1½ cups/205 g; see Note)

6 to 8 large radishes, diced (about ½ cup/ 75 g)

⅓ cup (45 g) diced shallots

½ cup (120 ml) chiffonade of fresh basil

¼ cup (60 ml) chopped fresh parsley

## DRESSING

½ cup (120 ml) olive oil

2 garlic cloves, minced

2 tablespoons (30 ml) white wine vinegar

2 teaspoons (10 ml) minced fresh dill

Kosher salt and freshly cracked black pepper, to taste

## NOTE

Try to keep all the diced vegetables roughly the same size; this will add to the colorful confetti-like nature of this salad.

1. Grease an outdoor grill or grill pan with vegetable oil and heat to medium-high.

2. Grill the corn until slightly charred on all sides, turning occasionally, 10 to 15 minutes. Remove the corn and allow it to cool.

3. Transfer the corn to a cutting board and stand it upright. Use a chef's knife to slice the corn off the cob, trying to keep large chunks of the corn rows intact; this will make for a prettier presentation.

4. Transfer the corn kernels to a large bowl. Then, add the tomatoes, cucumber, bell peppers, radishes, and shallots. Set aside.

5. **Make the dressing:** Whisk together the olive oil, garlic, vinegar, dill, salt, and pepper in a small bowl.

6. Drizzle the dressing over the vegetables and toss to coat. Then, add the basil and parsley and toss to combine. Serve immediately.

## MAKE-AHEAD GAME PLAN

- One day ahead, dice the peppers and cucumbers and then cover and refrigerate.

- A few hours ahead, grill the corn, cut it off the cob, cover, and refrigerate.

- One hour ahead, dice the other vegetables, assemble the salad, and make the dressing. Keep the salad and dressing separated and refrigerated and then toss them together right before serving.

## PAIRS WELL WITH

Easy Gourmet Burgers (page 137)

Easy Grilled Salmon with Mango Salsa (page 127)

# A LITTLE BIT LIGHTER GAZPACHO

Traditional gazpacho soup usually calls for adding bread to the recipe to thicken it, but I make this soup in the heat of the summer, and the bread always makes it feel too heavy. I started leaving it out, and now I think it's even better this way! This is such an easy summer starter, especially for a beginner, because it's basically a veggie smoothie: Just add all the ingredients to a blender and whirl it up. You can even leave it in the blender, pop it in your fridge, and then pour it into something glass and footed when it comes time to serve. Martini glasses or footed ice cream bowls work well. This soup also has a pretty garnish on top, so between the fantastic flavors and the pretty presentation, you're sure to get lots of *oohs* and *ahs* when you bring this to the table.

***SERVES 4 AS A STARTER*** *(5 cups/1.6 L)*

8 medium ripe Roma tomatoes, chopped (about 4 cups/680 g; see Note 1)

1 large English cucumber, chopped and peeled (about 1 cup/150 g)

1 large yellow bell pepper, chopped (about 1 cup/116 g)

1 large red bell pepper, chopped (about 1 cup/116 g)

1 large white onion, chopped (about 1 cup/140 g)

2 garlic cloves, minced

¼ cup (60 ml) olive oil

¼ cup (40 g) chopped fresh Italian parsley

3 tablespoons (45 ml) red wine vinegar (see Note 2)

1½ teaspoons (7.5 ml) hot sauce (see Note 3)

1 teaspoon (6 g) kosher salt

Freshly cracked black pepper, to taste

**GARNISH**

Drizzle of extra virgin olive oil

3 radishes, diced

¼ cup (38 g) peeled and diced English cucumber

¼ cup (60 ml) roughly chopped fresh dill

Freshly cracked black pepper, to taste

**NOTES**

1. For the best tomato flavor, place the tomatoes on your windowsill for 3 to 4 days to ripen before making this recipe.

2. Gazpacho should have a nice bite from the vinegar to be refreshing. Before deciding to add any more vinegar, let the soup sit for 4 hours in the refrigerator so the flavor becomes more pronounced.

3. Feel free to increase the amount of hot sauce to your liking. Or serve some hot sauce on the side for guests to turn up the heat if desired.

1. Place the tomatoes, cucumber, peppers, onions, and garlic in a blender and blend until smooth.

2. Add the olive oil, parsley, vinegar, hot sauce, salt, and pepper. Pulse to combine.

3. Keep refrigerated for at least 4 hours before serving. The flavors will become more pronounced the longer it sits in the refrigerator, and it will be nicely chilled, too.

4. Ladle the soup into bowls or glasses and garnish with a drizzle of olive oil and some diced radishes, diced cucumbers, dill, and pepper.

**MAKE-AHEAD GAME PLAN**

• Two days ahead, make the soup. Keep it in the blender in the refrigerator. Right before serving, whirl it in the blender again to freshen it up and then serve immediately.

• A few hours before serving, prepare and refrigerate the garnishes.

**PAIRS WELL WITH**

Better than Store-Bought Cheddar Scones (page 187)
Southampton Chicken Salad sandwiches (page 91)

# COOL AS A CUCUMBER SALAD
## WITH CRÈME FRAÎCHE, DILL, AND MINT

Cucumber salad is a classic summer side dish that doesn't have to be complicated. In fact, my motto is the simpler, the better! This salad is a mainstay in France with my husband's family, who typically serve it as a summer starter. It's simply tossed with crème fraîche, fleur de sel, and lots of freshly cracked pepper. I like the addition of radishes for a cooling bite, and the dill and mint just give it a little something extra. I like to peel the cucumbers in stripes to make it a bit more decorative. The best part about this salad is that you can dress it up or down!

*SERVES 6 TO 8*

4 large English cucumbers (about 30 ounces/850 g)

1 bunch of radishes (about 12 ounces/340 g)

5 ounces (142 g) crème fraîche (see Note)

One 0.5-ounce (14 g) package fresh dill, minced

2/3 cup (160 ml) fresh mint leaves, julienned

Kosher salt and freshly cracked black pepper, to taste

### NOTE

*Crème fraîche and sour cream are often used in similar preparations, but in this instance, I encourage you to seek out the crème fraîche. It comes in a 5-ounce (142 g) container, so all you have to do is open the tub and toss it in!*

1. Peel the cucumber skin in stripes ¾ inch (2 cm) apart. Slice into ¼-inch (6 mm) wheels. Transfer to a large bowl.

2. Remove the tops from the radishes and slice lengthwise into quarters. Add to the bowl.

3. Add the crème fraîche and toss the vegetables to coat.

4. Add the dill, mint, salt, and pepper, and toss.

5. Serve immediately or keep chilled for up to 2 hours before serving.

### MAKE-AHEAD GAME PLAN

- One day ahead, prep the vegetables. Cover and refrigerate until ready to serve.

- Two hours ahead, make the salad, but wait on the dill and mint. Cover and refrigerate. Toss in the herbs just before serving so the flavor will be more pronounced.

### PAIRS WELL WITH

Easy Gourmet Burgers (page 137)

Easy Grilled Salmon with Mango Salsa (page 127)

# SILKY SMOOTH
# POTATO AND LEEK SOUP

This potato soup is so silky smooth and creamy, you would swear it had a ton of heavy cream in it! But it doesn't have a drop. It gets its texture from my favorite secret ingredient: cauliflower, the wonder vegetable! It may not seem like much to celebrate when raw, but cooked cauliflower develops a creamy, silky texture that is ideal for thickening blended soups. This is my husband's favorite soup recipe, and we often turn to it for an easy weeknight meal by adding chunks of rotisserie chicken and frozen peas to it. It also freezes beautifully!

**SERVES 8 AS A STARTER AND 4 AS A MAIN COURSE** *(Makes 8 cups/1.9 L)*

2 tablespoons (30 ml) olive oil

1 large yellow onion, diced (about 2 cups/250 g)

3 large leeks, white parts only, sliced into rings (about 1¾ cups/125 g)

2 celery stalks, diced (about ½ cup/60 g)

2 garlic cloves, chopped

Kosher salt and freshly cracked black pepper, to taste

4 cups (960 ml) chicken broth, plus ½ cup (120 ml) for thinning if desired (see Note)

2 large russet potatoes, peeled and cut into ½-inch (1 cm) cubes (about 4 cups/620 g)

¾ cup (95 g) small cauliflower florets

2 tablespoons (30 ml) minced chives

## CROUTONS

1 small baguette

2 tablespoons (30 ml) olive oil

1 garlic clove, minced

Kosher salt and freshly cracked black pepper, to taste

## NOTE

Unless it's for dietary restrictions, I would not recommend low-sodium chicken broth for this recipe. The flavor is not as pronounced.

1. Heat the olive oil in a large stock pot or Dutch oven over medium heat. Sauté the onions, leeks, celery, and garlic until soft and fragrant, 2 to 3 minutes. Season with salt and pepper to taste.

2. Add the broth, potatoes, and cauliflower. Simmer until fork-tender, 10 to 12 minutes.

3. Transfer the soup to a blender, and puree in batches until smooth. Then, transfer the soup to a clean stock pot. Taste for seasoning and add salt and pepper if desired. Thin with additional broth if a thinner consistency is desired.

4. Preheat the oven to 375°F (190°C).

5. **Make the croutons:** Cut the baguette into 1-inch (2.5 cm) slices and then into bite-size chunks. Toss with the olive oil, garlic, salt, and pepper and then place the slices on a baking sheet.

6. Bake for 8 to 10 minutes, until golden brown, shaking the pan halfway through to toss the croutons.

7. Ladle the soup into bowls, and top with a sprinkle of chives and a few croutons.

## MAKE-AHEAD GAME PLAN

- Two days ahead, make the soup. Let cool and then transfer to an airtight container and refrigerate until ready to serve. Reheat over medium-high heat, whisking to warm through and thinning with more chicken broth if desired.

- One day ahead, make the croutons. Store in an airtight container at room temperature.

## PAIRS WELL WITH

Cast-Iron Roast Chicken (page 107)

Fennel-Crusted Pork Loin with Spiced Parsnips and Apples (page 134)

# THE THANKFUL THANKSGIVING SALAD

Most guests don't make a beeline to the Thanksgiving buffet looking for salad, but when they spoon this onto their plates, they'll be thankful they did! It has everything going for it: toasty pecans and chewy cranberries as well as refreshing grapes and pomegranate seeds, tossed in a nutty balsamic vinaigrette. It's a welcome palate cleanser on a plate that's typically loaded with heavy carbs and gravy. Consider it a culinary halftime, allowing you and your guests to go the extra mile to finish your plates!

*SERVES 6*

2 cups (480 ml) water

1 cup (180 g) tricolor quinoa (see Note 1)

1 cup (114 g) raw pecan halves

1 large bunch lacinato kale (about 10 large leaves)

1 small head radicchio, quartered and sliced into ½-inch (1 cm) ribbons

1 large ripe Bartlett pear, sliced

1 cup (144 g) red grapes, halved lengthwise

One 4-ounce container pomegranate arils (about ¾ cup/113g)

⅔ cup (90 g) dried cranberries (see Note 2)

### DRESSING

2 tablespoons (30 ml) balsamic vinegar

1 tablespoon plus 1 teaspoon (20 ml) Dijon mustard

½ cup (120 ml) walnut oil (see Note 3)

Kosher salt and freshly cracked black pepper, to taste

1. Preheat the oven to 350°F (175°C).

2. Place the water and quinoa in a large saucepan. Bring to a boil and then reduce to a low simmer and cover. Cook until all the liquid has evaporated, about 15 minutes. Fluff with a fork and set aside to cool.

3. Place the pecans on a baking sheet and bake for 5 to 8 minutes, until fragrant. Let cool and then set aside.

4. **Make the dressing:** Whisk together the balsamic vinegar and mustard in a small bowl. Slowly whisk in the walnut oil, a little bit at a time, pausing between each addition to allow the mixture to emulsify and thicken before adding more oil. Season with salt and pepper.

5. Remove the kale stems by slicing off the leaves on either side. Then, stack the leaves and slice them into wide 2-inch (5 cm) ribbons.

6. Place the quinoa, kale, and radicchio in a large salad bowl. Add the pear, grapes, pecans, pomegranate arils, and cranberries.

7. Drizzle in the dressing according to taste or serve it on the side. (If you don't use all of it, you can refrigerate it for up to a week.) Toss the salad and serve immediately.

### NOTES

1. You can find tricolor quinoa at Trader Joe's. I like the color it provides for fall, but any quinoa will taste the same.

2. Look for Ocean Spray dried cranberries; they have the best flavor.

3. The walnut oil is the unsung hero of this salad. It's worth seeking out for the great nutty flavor it provides. Alternatively, you can use grapeseed oil.

### MAKE-AHEAD GAME PLAN

- Two days ahead, cook the quinoa. Cover and refrigerate.

- One day ahead, make the dressing and slice the grapes. Cover and refrigerate.

- Two hours ahead, prepare the kale and the radicchio. Cover and refrigerate.

### PAIRS WELL WITH

Cheesy Italian Potato Bake (page 148)

Butternut Squash Soup with Raisin Bread Croutons (page 79)

# THE
# MAIN EVENT

# CAST-IRON ROAST CHICKEN

Years ago, before I could afford a fancy roasting pan, I plopped a chicken in the largest pan I had—a 12-inch (30 cm) cast-iron skillet—and put it in the oven to roast. The fantastic conductive quality of the cast iron produced the most amazing roast chicken: It was crispy on the outside and tender and juicy on the inside. From then on, there was no turning back! It's now my go-to way to roast a chicken. This chicken is extra flavorful thanks to the rosemary-garlic butter I place under the skin, a little French trick I learned from my husband.

*SERVES 4*

One 4-pound (1.8 kg) kosher whole chicken (see Note 1)

3 tablespoons (42 g) salted American butter, plus 1 tablespoon (14 g) for greasing

1 garlic clove, minced

1 tablespoon (15 ml) minced fresh rosemary

Kosher salt and freshly cracked black pepper, to taste

1 tablespoon (15 ml) olive oil

## NOTES

1. For extra juiciness, buy a kosher chicken. They are processed with salt, which acts like a brine, tenderizing the chicken.

2. Before roasting the chicken, check the cavity for giblets. I once roasted a chicken with a plastic bag of giblets inside the cavity. You can bet I now check every single time!

3. Ask any cast-iron aficionado how to care for cast iron, and they will tell you not to wash the pan with soap! It will strip the patina you've worked so hard to get. Here's what you should do instead: Scrape off any drippings with a plastic spatula or plastic dough scraper. Then, rinse the pan with warm water to remove any stubborn pieces. Yes, your pan will be greasy but take a paper towel and wipe it dry. Place it back in your oven, which has been turned off but will still be warm. Leave it there overnight, and the heat from the cooling oven will set the grease and add to your pan's patina.

1. Preheat the oven to 350°F (175°C). Place the oven rack in the lower third of the oven. Let the chicken come to room temperature, about 15 minutes.

2. Melt 3 tablespoons (42 g) butter in a small saucepan over medium heat. Add the garlic, rosemary, salt, and pepper. Remove from the heat and set aside to cool.

3. Insert a spoon between the breast meat and the skin to loosen the pocket (see Note 2). Spoon half of the butter mixture into the pocket of each breast. Massage the skin to distribute the butter over the breast meat.

4. Grease a 12-inch (30 cm) cast-iron pan (see Note 3) with the remaining butter. Place the chicken in the pan. Tie the legs together with butcher's twine.

5. Brush the skin of the chicken all over with olive oil. Sprinkle the skin with salt and pepper to taste.

6. Place the skillet in the oven for 1 hour and 30 minutes, or until the internal temperature has reached 165°F (74°C) in the thickest part of the thigh. Every 20 minutes or so, spoon the pan juices over the chicken.

7. Remove the skillet from the oven, transfer the chicken to a cutting board, and let rest for 10 minutes.

8. Carve the chicken by removing the legs and wings first and then removing the entire breasts and carving them on your board. Place the sliced chicken on a platter.

9. Transfer the pan drippings into a fat separator or remove the fat from the pan with a large spoon by skimming it off the top. Spoon the remaining sauce over the chicken.

## MAKE-AHEAD GAME PLAN

One day ahead, prep the chicken by adding the butter under the skin and trussing it. Place the chicken in a Pyrex dish in the refrigerator (don't refrigerate it in the cast iron). Transfer the chicken to the cast-iron skillet when it is time to roast.

## PAIRS WELL WITH

Silky Smooth Potato and Leek Soup (page 100)

Roasted Ratatouille (page 151)

# SHEET-PAN LAMB
## WITH CARAMELIZED SHALLOTS AND PROVENÇAL TOMATOES

Typically, the fallback for Easter is ham, but I think nothing is more festive than roasted lamb. And when you see how this recipe comes together, nothing will seem easier! This is a complete holiday meal on one sheet pan. It's a quick sear to lock in the flavor of the meat and then a slow roasting to tenderize it, which creates a wonderful caramelized exterior and a very tender interior. While the lamb roasts in the oven, the shallots and tomatoes cook right along with it. The flavor combination of the sweet shallots and the savory lamb, combined with the zing of the mustard sauce, makes this very simple dish appear extra fancy and festive!

# SHEET-PAN LAMB
## WITH CARAMELIZED SHALLOTS AND PROVENÇAL TOMATOES

*SERVES 8*

**LAMB**

Two 1¾-pound (794 g) racks of lamb (see Note 1)

2 tablespoons (30 ml) minced fresh rosemary

1 teaspoon (6 g) kosher salt

Freshly cracked black pepper, to taste

1 tablespoon (15 ml) olive oil

**TOMATOES**

8 medium tomatoes

6 tablespoons (40 g) breadcrumbs

2 tablespoons (10 g) panko breadcrumbs

2 teaspoons (10 ml) olive oil

1 teaspoon (5 ml) herbes de Provence

Kosher salt and freshly cracked black pepper, to taste

**SHALLOTS**

6 medium shallots, quartered and peeled (see Note 2)

Kosher salt and freshly cracked black pepper, to taste

1 teaspoon (5 ml) balsamic vinegar

**MUSTARD SAUCE**

2 cups (480 ml) heavy cream

2 tablespoons (30 ml) Dijon mustard

2 tablespoons (30 ml) whole grain mustard

2 to 3 dashes Worcestershire sauce

1 tablespoon (15 ml) chopped fresh tarragon

Eight 1-inch (2.5 cm) tarragon sprigs

1. **Make the lamb:** Season all sides of the lamb with the rosemary, salt, and pepper, pressing the seasonings in so they stick. Place the racks in large resealable plastic bags and refrigerate overnight (see Note 3).

2. Preheat the oven to 325°F (165°C). Place the oven rack in the lower third of the oven.

3. **Make the tomatoes:** Slice the tops off the tomatoes and just a sliver off the bottoms to stabilize them. If desired, you can roast the tops to serve on top of the finished tomatoes for a cute presentation. Mix the breadcrumbs, panko, olive oil, herbes de Provence, salt, and pepper in a small bowl. Sprinkle the mixture on each tomato and then place it on a baking sheet.

4. **Cook the lamb:** Brush the rosemary off the lamb (this will prevent burnt rosemary in your pan). Heat the olive oil in a large skillet over medium-high heat until shimmering. Sear the lamb on all sides until golden brown, 3 to 4 minutes. Transfer the lamb to a plate to rest.

5. **Make the shallots:** Place the shallots in the pan drippings, cut side down. Don't move them until they start to caramelize and turn golden brown, about 2 minutes. Flip the shallots and sauté until golden brown and fork-tender, 2 to 4 minutes more. Season with salt and pepper to taste. Then, add the balsamic vinegar, deglazing the pan and tossing the shallots to coat.

6. Transfer the lamb and shallots to the baking sheet with the tomatoes. Roast for 25 minutes, or until a meat thermometer registers 135°F to 144°F (57°C to 62°C) for medium doneness.

7. **Meanwhile, make the sauce:** Add the heavy cream, Dijon mustard, whole-grain mustard, and Worcestershire sauce to a large saucepan. Bring to a simmer and allow the sauce to thicken, 5 to 8 minutes. Keep warm on a low simmer, and right before serving, whisk in the chopped tarragon.

8. Transfer the lamb to a carving board. Cover with foil to keep warm and let rest for 15 minutes. Keep the tomatoes and shallots on the pan. The residual heat from the pan will keep them warm, and they are okay to serve at room temperature.

9. Place the lamb on a cutting board with the meaty side down and the bones up in the air. Carve out single chops in between the bones.

10. Serve two chops per person, crisscrossing the bones at the top of the plate, with a few shallots tucked in at the bottom of the plate.

11. Drizzle the chops with the mustard sauce and garnish with a tarragon sprig. Place the tomatoes on the side of each plate and serve.

## NOTES

1. Ask your butcher to trim the lamb. A proper trimming should take the fat off all the way to the meat line, exposing the bones entirely. This will provide you with more elegant chops.

2. Quarter the shallots first and *then* peel them. They'll be much easier to peel that way.

3. The bags will take up less room in your fridge than a casserole dish. You can even use the crisper drawers to store it.

## MAKE-AHEAD GAME PLAN

One day ahead, season the lamb, place it in the bags, and refrigerate. Make the mustard sauce, excluding the fresh tarragon. Keep refrigerated until ready to serve. Then, reheat and add the tarragon right before serving.

## PAIRS WELL WITH

Creamy Asparagus Soup with Crème Fraîche (page 88)

Perfect Lemon Bars (page 236)

# PAN-SEARED SALMON
## WITH LEMON BUTTER CAPER SAUCE

Salmon may seem like a main course better suited for warmer weather, but it can also be wonderful for fancy winter occasions, especially when paired with a rich and decadent sauce. France's Loire Valley is famous for their beurre blanc sauce, a classic French butter and wine sauce that's as decadent as it gets. But beurre blanc can be a bit fussy to prepare—one false move, and the sauce can separate or "break." This lemon butter caper sauce is way easier and just as delicious. It's inspired by a sauce I discovered at my local grocery store in France. Only in France can you get excellent lemon butter caper sauce in a jar. This would be an easy recipe for Christmas or New Year's Eve. Most of it can be prepped ahead of time, and all you have to do is cook the fish and reheat the sauce. Serve it with my Crispy Hasselback Potatoes (page 160) or Easy Roasted Potatoes (page 152)—but make sure to give the potatoes an ample head start. They can stay warm in a 350°F (175°C) oven while you bake the fish.

*SERVES 4*

### LEMON BUTTER CAPER SAUCE

1 tablespoon (15 ml) olive oil

2 tablespoons (14 g) minced shallots

Kosher salt and freshly cracked black pepper, to taste

⅓ cup (80 ml) dry white wine (chardonnay or sauvignon blanc)

3 tablespoons (42 g) salted American butter

2 teaspoons (10 ml) lemon zest

1 garlic clove, minced

½ cup (120 ml) heavy cream

1 tablespoon (15 ml) capers, drained

1 tablespoon (15 ml) minced fresh dill, plus 4 small sprigs

### SALMON

Four 8-ounce (227 g) skin-on salmon filets

Kosher salt and freshly cracked black pepper, to taste

1 tablespoon (15 ml) coconut oil

### NOTES

1. It is much better to take the fish out if it is ready than to overcook it by keeping it warm in the oven. Pouring the hot sauce over the fish will reheat it without overcooking it.

2. If you would like to serve more sauce on the side, double the sauce recipe.

1. Preheat the oven to 350°F (175°C). Place the oven rack in the lower third of the oven.

2. **Make the sauce:** Heat the olive oil in a medium saucepan over medium-high heat. Add the shallots, season with salt and pepper, and cook until translucent and fragrant, 1 to 2 minutes.

3. Add the wine and simmer until reduced by half, 1 to 2 minutes. Add the butter, lemon zest, and garlic and simmer for 1 minute to infuse the butter with the other flavors.

4. Add the heavy cream and simmer until bubbling and thickened slightly, 2 to 3 minutes. Turn off the heat.

5. **Make the fish:** Pat each filet dry with a paper towel. Season with salt and pepper.

6. Place a 12-inch (30 cm) nonstick skillet with an oven-safe handle over medium-high heat. Add the coconut oil, swirling around the pan to coat until shimmering and hot.

7. Place the filets in the pan, skin side up. Sear the filets without touching them, until the bottom layer is opaque and the edges are golden brown, 2 to 3 minutes.

8. Flip each filet and then transfer the skillet to the oven for 7 to 8 minutes. Check the fish at 6 minutes by inserting a knife into the thickest part of the center to see if the fish is still translucent. Take it out once it is fully opaque (see Note 1).

9. Reheat the sauce and then stir in the capers and minced dill.

10. Place the filets on a plate and top with the sauce (see Note 2). Garnish with the dill sprigs and pepper.

**MAKE-AHEAD GAME PLAN**

- One day ahead, prepare the sauce, minus the capers and dill. Cover and refrigerate until ready to reheat. Then, add the capers and dill as directed.

- One hour before, season the fish. Cover and refrigerate until ready to cook.

**PAIRS WELL WITH**

Crispy Hasselback Potatoes (page 160)

Easy Roasted Potatoes (page 152)

# FRENZY-FREE CHICKEN POT PIE

I love the idea of serving chicken pot pies for a winter dinner party. But getting them on the table with the filling piping hot and the pastry puffed up takes some doing! Putting cold puff pastry over hot filling is just asking for disaster—it results in soggy pastry that puffs up in some places and not others. And worse yet, it creates an awkward kitchen frenzy in front of your guests, who feel compelled to get up and help when you really wish they wouldn't, because wrestling with puff pastry is a one-person job. Thankfully, I've discovered a better way: Make the filling the day before, and all you have to do is reheat it on the stovetop. Meanwhile, the puff pastry gets baked in the oven, separately, in large, generous rectangles. This allows it to reach its full puffed-up potential and golden-brown perfection! These "pies" have enough flaky puff pastry for every little bite of filling, with no awkward kitchen theatrics!

---

*SERVES 4*

**CHICKEN**

3 pounds (1.4 kg) bone-in, skin-on chicken breasts (about 4 breasts)

1 teaspoon (6 g) kosher salt

**FILLING**

4 tablespoons (56 g) salted American butter

3 medium carrots, diced (about 1 cup/120 g)

1 large yellow onion, diced (about 1 cup/150 g)

Kosher salt and freshly cracked black pepper, to taste

8 ounces (227 g) cremini mushrooms, sliced

2 teaspoons (10 ml) Worcestershire sauce

1 teaspoon (5 ml) dried thyme

⅓ cup (80 ml) dry white wine (chardonnay or sauvignon blanc)

½ cup (70 g) all-purpose flour

4 cups (960 ml) chicken broth

1 cup (135 g) frozen peas

¼ cup (60 ml) heavy cream

1 garlic clove, minced

2 tablespoons (30 ml) chopped fresh Italian parsley

2 tablespoons (30 ml) chopped fresh thyme

**TOPPING**

All-purpose flour, for dusting

One 14-ounce (397 g) package Dufour puff pastry, thawed (see Note)

1 large egg, beaten

Fleur de sel salt and freshly cracked black pepper, to taste

Four 1-inch (2.5 cm) fresh thyme sprigs

1. Preheat the oven to 375°F (190°C). Place the oven rack in the lower third of the oven. Put a roasting rack on a baking sheet.

2. **Make the chicken:** Loosen the pockets of skin covering the chicken breasts. Rub the kosher salt under the skin and over each breast, massaging it into the meat. Transfer the chicken to the baking sheet.

3. Roast the chicken for 45 to 50 minutes, until cooked through. Set aside to cool.

4. Increase the oven temperature to 400°F (200°C). Line a baking sheet with parchment paper.

5. **Make the filling:** Melt the butter in a large Dutch oven over medium heat until foamy. Add the carrots and onions. Season with kosher salt and pepper to taste and cook until tender, 3 to 4 minutes.

6. Add the mushrooms and cook until they release their juices, 1 to 2 minutes. Add the Worcestershire sauce, the dried thyme, and more kosher salt and pepper to taste.

7. Add the wine and cook until the wine is reduced by half, about 1 minute. Add the flour and stir to coat the vegetables. Cook for 1 minute and then add the broth and whisk to combine. Simmer over medium-high heat until thickened, 2 to 3 minutes.

8. Reduce the heat to low and then add the peas, heavy cream, and garlic. Stir until the peas are warmed through. Then, add the parsley and fresh thyme and simmer on low to keep warm.

9. Shred the chicken off the bone into bite-size pieces. Add the chicken to the pot of filling and add kosher salt and pepper to taste. Turn off the heat and keep covered.

10. **Make the topping:** Roll out the puff pastry on a floured surface. Trim the dough into 6×5-inch (15×13 cm) rectangles.

11. Place the pastry on the baking sheet. Brush each rectangle with the beaten egg and then top with a sprinkle of fleur de sel and pepper. Place a thyme sprig in the center of each rectangle.

12. Bake for 25 to 30 minutes, until the pastry has puffed up and is a rich golden brown.

13. Reheat the filling if needed. Ladle out the filling into four shallow bowls and top each with a puff pastry rectangle. Serve immediately.

## NOTES

I love Dufour puff pastry for this recipe because it's creased into four rectangles, so all you have to do is trim it slightly to size. Be sure to thaw it in the refrigerator the night before using.

## MAKE-AHEAD GAME PLAN

• Two days ahead, prepare the filling, but wait to add the fresh thyme and parsley until after you reheat it so the flavor is more pronounced.

• One day ahead, prepare the puff pastry rectangles, trim them, and add the egg wash, seasoning, and thyme sprigs. Cover tightly with plastic wrap and refrigerate. Remove the plastic wrap and bake the pastry for 20 minutes before heating the filling. That way, both will be ready to plate at the same time.

## PAIRS WELL WITH

Stuffed Mushroom Caps (page 49)

Go-To Chocolate Bundt Cake (page 225)

# FALL-OFF-THE-BONE STICKY RIBS

The title alone describes what I think makes the perfect rib: It should be sticky and sweet, and the meat should be so tender that it falls off the bone. These ribs are the perfect dinner to kick off the summer grilling season, whether that be for Memorial Day or Father's Day. But a word of caution—this is the kind of dinner best enjoyed with good friends or family because eating it is no dainty affair. It's messy and a bit "caveman-like," but that's the part that loosens everybody up and ensures a good time. Don't forget the Handi Wipes!

*SERVES 4 TO 6*

**BBQ SAUCE**

1 cup (240 ml) ketchup

⅓ cup (55 g) brown sugar

⅓ cup (80 ml) molasses

¼ cup (60 ml) white wine vinegar

1 teaspoon (5 ml) hot sauce

1 teaspoon (5 ml) Dijon mustard

½ teaspoon (2.5 ml) Worcestershire sauce

2 garlic cloves, minced

**RIBS**

2 tablespoons (20 g) brown sugar

1 tablespoon plus 1 teaspoon (20 ml) ground cumin

1 tablespoon plus 1 teaspoon (20 ml) smoked paprika

2 teaspoons (10 ml) ground coriander

2 teaspoons (10 ml) garlic powder

2 teaspoons (12 g) kosher salt

2 racks pork spareribs (about 5 pounds total/2.2 kg)

1. **Make the sauce:** Place the ketchup, brown sugar, molasses, vinegar, hot sauce, mustard, Worcestershire sauce, and garlic in a small saucepan and simmer until fragrant, about 5 minutes. Let cool and then transfer to a small heat-safe Pyrex pitcher (this will make it easier to reheat), cover, and refrigerate until ready to grill.

2. Preheat the oven to 350°F (175°C).

3. **Make the ribs:** Whisk together the brown sugar, cumin, paprika, coriander, garlic powder, and salt in a small bowl.

4. Lay out two large pieces of foil and then fasten them together by folding the seams. Place the foil diagonally across a baking sheet (this is the only way the ribs will fit). You'll do this for each rack, so you will need four pieces of foil and two baking sheets.

5. Place the racks on the foiled baking sheets and then rub the dry rub mixture onto both sides of the ribs.

6. Seal up the ribs in the foil. Then, place the baking sheets in the oven for 2 hours, rotating each rack (from the top to the bottom of your oven) halfway through.

7. Reheat the BBQ sauce in the microwave on high in 30-second increments until hot.

8. Preheat an outdoor grill to medium-high. Grill the ribs for 3 to 5 minutes on each side for desired charring. Brush with BBQ sauce on both sides and flip to set the sauce quickly without burning.

9. Cut the racks into single ribs and place them on a platter. Brush with more sauce as needed.

**MAKE-AHEAD GAME PLAN**
- Three days ahead, make the BBQ sauce.
- One day ahead, season the ribs, place in foil, and refrigerate until ready to grill.

**PAIRS WELL WITH**
Crisp and Creamy Coleslaw (page 155)

Eleventh-Hour Corn Pudding (page 156)

# OLD-SCHOOL LASAGNA

My mom is a nice Irish girl who married into a large Italian family. One New Year's Eve, Mom, who was nine months pregnant with me, spent all day making a homemade lasagna to impress the matriarch of my dad's family, Big Nonna. When Big Nonna arrived for dinner, Mom eagerly blurted out, "I made a homemade lasagna!" Big Nonna looked a bit puzzled and said, "What's so hard about that?" This was a woman who could make a lasagna with her eyes closed. But I won't sugarcoat it: Lasagna is work. It's practically devotional. Still, everyone should know how to make a great one, and for me, that means going old school by skipping the ricotta cheese and using the traditional béchamel sauce instead. It's the kind of dish you'll turn to for big family gatherings or a lazy Sunday lunch with friends and their kids (what kid won't eat lasagna?).

# OLD-SCHOOL LASAGNA

*SERVES 6*

## MEAT SAUCE

2 tablespoons (30 ml) olive oil

1 large yellow onion, diced (about 1 cup/ 150 g)

2 small carrots, diced (½ cup/60 g)

1 small celery stalk, diced (about ⅓ cup/ 45 g)

Kosher salt and freshly cracked black pepper, to taste (see Note 1)

1 pound (454 g) 90% lean ground beef

½ pound (227 g) sweet Italian pork sausage, casings removed (about 2 links)

1 tablespoon (15 ml) Italian seasoning

1 teaspoon (5 ml) fennel seed

1 cup (240 ml) white wine

One 15-ounce (425 g) can tomato sauce

One 14.5-ounce (411 g) can diced tomatoes

¼ cup (60 ml) tomato paste

2 garlic cloves, minced

2 tablespoons (30 ml) chopped fresh Italian parsley

## BÉCHAMEL SAUCE

4 tablespoons (56 g) unsalted butter

¼ cup (35 g) all-purpose flour

4 cups (960 ml) whole milk

2 garlic cloves, minced

2 teaspoons (10 ml) minced fresh thyme

1 teaspoon (6 g) kosher salt

Pinch of ground nutmeg

## ASSEMBLY

Unsalted butter, for greasing

16 no-boil (oven-ready) lasagna noodles (see Note 2)

16 ounces (454 g) shredded Italian blend cheese

Freshly cracked black pepper, to taste

Italian seasoning, to taste

1 tablespoon (15 ml) chopped fresh Italian parsley, for garnish

1. **Make the meat sauce:** Heat the olive oil in a large Dutch oven over medium-high heat. Sauté the onions, carrots, and celery until fragrant and translucent, 3 to 5 minutes. Season with salt and pepper to taste.

2. Add the beef, sausage, Italian seasoning, and fennel seed. Brown the meat until cooked through completely, 5 to 8 minutes. Add the wine and simmer until the liquid is reduced by one-third, 3 to 4 minutes. Add more salt and pepper to taste, if needed.

3. Add the tomato sauce, diced tomatoes, and tomato paste, and stir to combine. Then, add the garlic. Simmer for 15 minutes, until the sauce sweetens up as the tomato acid mellows in flavor. Remove from the heat, stir in the parsley, and set aside.

4. **Make the béchamel sauce:** Melt the butter in a large sauté pan over medium-high heat until foamy. Add the flour and whisk to form a paste. Slowly add the milk, whisking until combined.

5. Simmer over medium-high heat until the sauce thickens and coats the back of a spoon, 8 to 10 minutes. Remove from the heat. Whisk in the garlic, thyme, salt, and nutmeg.

6. Preheat the oven to 325°F (165°C). Place the oven rack in the lower third of the oven. Grease a 9×12-inch (23×30 cm) oven-safe casserole dish with butter.

7. Spread a thin layer of meat sauce onto the bottom of the dish. Turn your lasagna pan vertically. Place four lasagna noodles in the dish vertically in a single layer, overlapping slightly at the ends. You will have gaps in between the noodles, but the noodles will expand as they cook.

8. Add 1½ cups (360 ml) béchamel sauce on top of the noodles and then 1½ cups (360 ml) meat sauce on top, spreading it out with the back of a spoon to cover. Top with 1 cup (110 g) cheese. Repeat this process two more times to create three layers of noodles, sauce, and cheese.

9. For the final layer, place four more noodles on top, cover with the remaining béchamel sauce, and top with the remaining cheese. Top with pepper and a sprinkle of Italian seasoning.

10. Cover with foil and bake for 45 minutes. Then, uncover and bake for 5 to 10 minutes, until the cheese is golden brown. For extra browning, place under the broiler for 1 to 2 minutes.

11. For ease of slicing, let cool for 10 minutes. Garnish with fresh parsley. Then, slice into squares and serve.

## NOTES

1. Italian sausage can be notoriously salty or unsalty! It really depends on where you buy it. In fact, it can be so salty at times that you may not need to add any salt to your sauce. Or it could be lacking salt and you'll need to add a good couple of pinches. Best to keep tasting your sauce, once the meat is cooked through, and adjust the salt as needed.

2. Depending on the brand, you may need two boxes of lasagna noodles.

## MAKE-AHEAD GAME PLAN

In the morning, assemble the lasagna. Cover and refrigerate and then bake right before serving. If you bake it ahead and try to reheat it, it will dry out.

## PAIRS WELL WITH

Tossed salad with 1, 2, 3 French Vinaigrette (page 181)

Just a Scoop of Tiramisu (page 231)

# GRILLED DIJON CHICKEN
## WITH CHARRED LEMONS

In the heat of summer, when it's just too hot to cook and burgers on the grill have lost their appeal, turn to this recipe! It's a fantastic, quick, and easy grilled chicken that fits into an elegant summer menu when paired with my Cool as a Cucumber Salad with Crème Fraîche, Dill, and Mint (page 99) or Phillipe's Pesto Orzo Salad on (page 87). The white wine in the marinade tenderizes the chicken, making it succulent and juicy, but be sure you give it the full 4 hours of marinating to work its magic. You'll also love the charred lemons. Not only do they look pretty on the platter, but the warm lemon juice squeezed on top of the chicken at the end is a lovely bright finish. Leftover chicken is delicious served cold, cut into cubes, and tossed with the leftover orzo salad. It's a tasty summer lunch to pack up and take to the beach!

### SERVES 6 TO 8

1 cup (240 ml) dry white wine (chardonnay, sauvignon blanc, or pinot grigio)

¼ cup (60 ml) olive oil

2 garlic cloves, minced

2 tablespoons (30 ml) Dijon mustard

1 teaspoon (5 ml) Worcestershire sauce

2 tablespoons (30 ml) minced fresh thyme, plus 4 to 5 sprigs

½ teaspoon (3 g) kosher salt

Freshly cracked black pepper, to taste

2½ pounds (1.1 kg) pounded chicken cutlets (see Note)

4 lemons, halved horizontally

Vegetable oil, for greasing

### NOTE

Look for pounded chicken cutlets at the store. They are pounded evenly, which helps them cook at the same rate. If you can't find them, halve chicken breasts vertically, place them between two sheets of wax paper, and pound them thinly with a meat mallet.

1. Whisk together the wine, olive oil, garlic, mustard, and Worcestershire sauce in a 9×14-inch (23×36 cm) casserole dish. Whisk in the thyme, salt, and pepper.

2. Place the chicken cutlets in the marinade, spooning it over the chicken to coat well. Cover and refrigerate for at least 4 hours or overnight.

3. Grease an outdoor grill or indoor grill pan with vegetable oil and heat to medium-high.

4. Use a pastry brush to lightly brush the lemons with vegetable oil. Use tongs to pick up the chicken, shaking it gently to let any excess marinade drip off.

5. For nice grill marks, grill each chicken breast vertically on the horizontal grates for 2 minutes on each side and then flip and position the chicken horizontally and grill on each side to create a cross-hatch pattern, 1 to 2 minutes more. The chicken is done when it is firm and no longer soft to the touch. Transfer to a plate.

6. Grill the lemons, cut side down, until softened and nicely charred on the bottom with grill marks, 3 to 4 minutes.

7. Transfer the chicken to a platter, and garnish with the charred lemons and thyme sprigs. Encourage guests to squeeze the warm lemon juice over the chicken for a bright, lemony finish.

### MAKE-AHEAD GAME PLAN

One day ahead, marinate the chicken. Cover and refrigerate until ready to grill.

### PAIRS WELL WITH

Cool as a Cucumber Salad with Crème Fraîche, Dill, and Mint (page 99)

Philippe's Pesto Orzo Salad (page 87)

# 24-HOUR FLANK STEAK
## WITH CHIMICHURRI

I love to make grilled flank steak in the summer because it's an easy and affordable way to serve steak for a crowd. A successful flank steak boils down to three key components: the marinade, the grilling, and the way that it's sliced. Flank steak is a tougher cut of meat, but not to worry: My 24-hour marinade will have it slicing like butta! The chimichurri sauce provides a delicious herby kick, and a squeeze of lime is the perfect finish.

*SERVES 8*

½ cup (120 ml) balsamic vinegar

⅓ cup (80 ml) honey

¼ cup (60 ml) olive oil

¼ cup (60 ml) soy sauce

4 garlic cloves, minced

1 tablespoon (15 ml) fresh lime juice (from about ½ lime)

2 teaspoons (10 ml) Dijon mustard

2 tablespoons (30 ml) minced fresh rosemary

1 teaspoon (6 g) kosher salt

Freshly cracked black pepper

2 pounds (907 g) flank steak

Vegetable oil, for greasing

**CHIMICHURRI SAUCE**

2 garlic cloves, minced

1 tablespoon (7 g) minced shallots

1 tablespoon (15 ml) red wine vinegar

1 cup (240 ml) chopped Italian parsley, stems and all (see Note 1)

½ cup (120 ml) olive oil

1 tablespoon (15 ml) fresh lemon juice (from about ½ lemon)

½ teaspoon (2.5 ml) dried oregano

Kosher salt and freshly cracked black pepper, to taste

1 to 2 pinches red pepper flakes (optional)

**GARNISH**

Sprinkle of fleur de sel salt

3 to 4 rosemary sprigs

4 to 6 lime wedges

1. Whisk the vinegar, honey, olive oil, soy sauce, garlic, lime juice, and mustard in a 9×14-inch (23×36 cm) casserole dish. Then, whisk in the rosemary, kosher salt, and black pepper.

2. Submerge the steak in the marinade and then flip it over and spoon the marinade on top to cover it. Cover the dish and refrigerate for 24 hours (see Note 2).

3. **Just before grilling, make the sauce:** Combine the garlic, shallots, and vinegar in a medium bowl. Add the parsley, olive oil, lemon juice, and oregano, and stir to combine.

4. Season with kosher salt and black pepper to taste and add the red pepper flakes if desired. Transfer to a small, shallow serving bowl, and keep covered at room temperature until ready to serve, for up to 1 hour (otherwise, keep refrigerated).

5. Grease an outdoor grill or indoor grill pan with vegetable oil and heat to medium-high.

6. Remove the steak from the marinade, and place on a baking sheet. Pat the steak dry with paper towels, and brush off as many rosemary leaves you can (see Note 3).

7. Flank steak is best served at medium temperature, between 135°F and 140°F (57°C and 60°C). To achieve this doneness and create nice crosshatch grill marks, place the steak on the grill vertically (to create horizontal grill marks) for 6 minutes with the grill lid closed. Flip vertically and grill for another 3 minutes, until the steak is caramelized and a bit soft to the touch in the center.

8. Flip and reposition horizontally for another 90 seconds. Then, flip horizontally and cook the other side for 90 seconds, until the steak is a bit firmer to the touch. Transfer the steak to a clean baking sheet and let rest for 15 to 20 minutes.

9. Transfer the steak to a carving board and slice against the grain, with your knife blade at an angle (not straight down), into ¼-inch (6 mm) slices. This will create ribbony beef that will be more tender than thick, straight cuts.

10. Place the beef on a platter, sprinkle with a pinch or two of fleur de sel, and garnish with fresh rosemary and lime wedges. Serve with some chimichurri sauce drizzled lightly on top and the rest on the side.

### NOTES

1. Be sure to use the stems, not just the leaves. The stems have even more flavor!

2. Don't rush this part: Some recipes will say 5 or 12 hours is enough time for marinating flank steak, and I've fallen for this, too, only to experience mediocre results. Go the full 24 hours, and you'll be glad you did.

3. To achieve a nice sear, the steak needs to be dry when it hits the hot grill; otherwise, it will steam up. Removing the rosemary leaves prevents them from burning on the grill.

**MAKE-AHEAD GAME PLAN**

• One day ahead, marinate the beef. If you're planning to grill at 7 pm, start making the marinade at 6 pm the night before.

• One hour before serving, make the chimichurri sauce. It's best made right before serving to keep the flavors fresh; they dull a bit if refrigerated.

**PAIRS WELL WITH**

Roasted Ratatouille (page 151)

Horseradish Potato Salad with Caramelized Shallots (page 84)

# EASY GRILLED SALMON
## WITH MANGO SALSA

There comes a time in our entertaining journey when a summer dinner invitation expands beyond "come for burgers on the grill." When you are ready to go further and make something kinda fancy (but still really easy!), turn to this grilled salmon recipe. It makes an instant impression because it's so elegant and summery. It's also hard to imagine that something this delicious could be this simple! A party of four is the perfectly sized group for serving this meal because it will allow you to spend a little more time on the "wow factor" for this dish: the plating. Don't skip the grated radish garnish at the end, which resembles tiny flower petals under the twinkle of candlelight. This would be a beautiful dish for Mom on Mother's Day, too!

*SERVES 4*

### MANGO SALSA
2 cups (375 g) diced ripe mango

½ cup (75 g) diced red onion

2 tablespoons (22 g) pomegranate arils

1 tablespoon (15 ml) chopped fresh cilantro

½ jalapeño, diced (about 1 tablespoon/10 g)

¼ teaspoon (1.25 ml) lime zest

Juice of ½ lime

Kosher salt and freshly cracked black pepper, to taste

### SALMON
Vegetable oil, for greasing

Four 6-ounce (170 g) skin-on salmon filets

Kosher salt and freshly cracked black pepper, to taste

### GARNISH
8 small cilantro sprigs

1 lime, sliced into 4 wedges

1 radish (See Note 1)

### NOTES

1. If you don't typically have radishes in the crisper drawer (and since you only need one radish for the garnish), serve this meal with the Crudité Platter with Green Goddess Dip (page 50) or A Little Bit Lighter Gazpacho (page 96) as a starter, since both recipes call for radishes.

2. You can also make a tiny incision in the top to check for doneness. You will be spooning the salsa over the fish, so don't worry—it will hide the cut.

1. **Make the salsa:** Combine the mango, onion, pomegranate arils, cilantro, jalapeño, lime zest and juice, salt, and pepper in a medium bowl.

2. **Make the salmon:** Grease an outdoor grill or indoor grill pan with vegetable oil and heat to medium-high.

3. Season the top of the fish with salt and pepper. Grill the fish, skin side up, until ¼ inch (6 mm) at the bottom is opaque, 4 to 6 minutes. Then, flip and cook until the fish starts to crack a little bit on top, 4 to 6 minutes more (see Note 2).

4. Divide the fish among four plates and then spoon the salsa over the fish. Garnish each plate with 1 to 2 cilantro sprigs and a lime wedge.

5. Use a coarse hand grater to grate the radish over the fish and plates, working the radish around so you are continually getting the red part. (It will be prettier that way.)

### MAKE-AHEAD GAME PLAN
- Two hours ahead, season the fish, cover, and refrigerate until ready to serve.
- One hour ahead, combine the ingredients for the salsa, leaving out the cilantro and the lime zest and juice. Cover and refrigerate. Add the remaining ingredients just before serving for the best flavor.

### PAIRS WELL WITH
A Little Bit Lighter Gazpacho (page 96)

Lemon-Scented Strawberry Shortcakes (page 211)

# MAKE-AHEAD
# BEEF STEW

When the holidays roll around and the menu planning begins, we all dream of that festive make-ahead recipe: the kind we can effortlessly reheat in the oven, with a glass of champagne in one hand and an egg timer in the other. When our girls were young and Christmas meant twenty-four hours of mayhem, beef stew was the go-to recipe for Christmas dinner. My parents would take the kids out for the day, which left me all alone in the kitchen, whistling along to Christmas carols while I made two big batches of this stew to serve to a crowd. The best part is that it has all the food groups represented in one bowl, eliminating the need for a side dish, *and* it can all be made the day before. Yes, it takes 2½ hours in the oven, but you will be rewarded with tender bites of beef that will melt in your mouth, so don't rush the process! If you have children at home and visiting relatives are looking for ways to help, have them entertain the kids while you prepare this stew. Because the prep is even better when you're left all alone in the kitchen whistling to Christmas carols.

# MAKE-AHEAD BEEF STEW

*SERVES 6*

3 tablespoons (45 ml) olive oil, divided

2 large carrots, cut into 2-inch (5 cm) pieces (about 2 cups/280 g; see Note 1)

2 cups (130 g) frozen pearl onions

2 medium celery stalks, chopped (about ½ cup/70 g)

2 teaspoons (10 ml) dried thyme

Kosher salt and freshly cracked black pepper, to taste

½ cup (70 g) all-purpose flour

1½ pounds (680 g) beef stew meat (such as top or bottom round or chuck steak; see Note 2)

1 cup (240 ml) red wine (côtes du Rhône, pinot noir, or merlot)

7 cups (1.7 L) beef stock

¼ cup (60 ml) tomato paste

2 teaspoons (10 ml) Worcestershire Sauce

2 bay leaves, fresh or dried

2 garlic cloves, minced

1½ pounds (680 g) peeled Baby Dutch potatoes

1 tablespoon (14 g) salted American butter

8 ounces (227 g) cremini mushrooms, quartered

2 tablespoons (20 g) cornstarch

2 tablespoons (30 ml) very cold water

## NOTES

1. Cut the carrots on the diagonal for a pretty presentation.
2. My favorite meat for stews is Trader Joe's All Natural Lean Beef Stew Meat.
3. Be sure your Dutch oven doesn't have a plastic knob, or it will melt.

1. Heat 1 tablespoon (15 ml) olive oil in a large Dutch oven over medium-high heat. Add the carrots, onions, and celery. Cook the vegetables until fragrant, 2 to 3 minutes, and then add the thyme, salt, and pepper. Transfer to a bowl.

2. Preheat the oven to 350°F (175°C).

3. Place the flour in a shallow bowl. Season half the beef pieces with salt and pepper on all sides. Then, dredge through the flour, coating on all sides and shaking off any excess.

4. Heat 1 tablespoon (15 ml) olive oil in the Dutch oven over medium-high heat. Add the first batch of floured beef to the pot, giving each piece room to sear. Brown the beef on all sides, 2 to 4 minutes. (It doesn't need to be cooked through at this stage.) Transfer to a plate to rest.

5. Repeat steps 3 and 4 with the second batch of beef. Add more olive oil if needed, but don't clean out the pot!

6. Deglaze the pot with the red wine, scraping up the brown bits with a wooden spoon and allowing the liquid to reduce slightly. Add the beef stock, tomato paste, Worcestershire sauce, bay leaves, and garlic. Whisk to combine.

7. Add the beef, vegetables, and any juices. Stir to combine before stirring in the potatoes. Cover the pot and place in the oven for 90 minutes (see Note 3).

8. Meanwhile, melt the butter in a small skillet over medium-high heat. Sauté the mushrooms until golden brown, 2 to 3 minutes. Season with salt and pepper to taste.

9. Mix the cornstarch and water in a small bowl to form a slurry.

10. After the 90 minutes is up, remove the pot from the oven, add the mushrooms and the slurry, and whisk to combine.

11. Return the pot to the oven for 1 more hour, until the meat is tender and easily pulls apart with a fork. If the meat is still tough, bake for another 15 to 20 minutes, until tender. Remove the bay leaves and serve.

## MAKE-AHEAD GAME PLAN

· One month ahead, freeze the stew. Complete the full recipe, and allow it to cool completely before freezing. Thaw in the refrigerator the night before and then reheat it on the cooktop until warmed through. Thin with beef stock if needed.

· Two days ahead, make the stew. It's even better made a day or two ahead! Refrigerate until ready to serve. It will thicken as it sits, so have some extra beef stock on hand to thin it out if needed. Place in a preheated 350°F (175°C) oven for 30 to 40 minutes, stirring occasionally.

## PAIRS WELL WITH

Tossed salad with 1, 2, 3 French Vinaigrette (page 181)

Go-To Chocolate Bundt Cake (page 225)

# BETTER BBQ CHICKEN

As soon as Memorial Day arrives, I start to crave a BBQ chicken dinner with all the trimmings! But over the years, I've realized that there are a few pitfalls to achieving really good BBQ chicken at home. Either the sauce slides off the chicken and never really sets, or it burns on the grill, thereby burning the chicken, or it looks great on the outside but remains raw on the inside! Then, I discovered the secret: The best BBQ chicken is a two-step process. Start the chicken on the grill and finish it in the oven. This ensures that the BBQ sauce sets in layers, which creates more flavor. The grill chars it, and the oven beautifully caramelizes and sets it. The final layer is one last slather of BBQ sauce just before serving.

*SERVES 4 TO 6*

## BBQ SAUCE

1 cup (240 ml) ketchup

⅓ cup (55 g) brown sugar

⅓ cup (80 ml) molasses

¼ cup (60 ml) white wine vinegar

2 garlic cloves, minced

1 teaspoon (5 ml) hot sauce

1 teaspoon (5 ml) Dijon mustard

½ teaspoon (2.5 ml) Worcestershire sauce

## CHICKEN

3½ pounds (1.6 kg) cut-up chicken (breasts, legs, wings, etc.)

2 tablespoons (30 ml) vegetable oil

Kosher salt and freshly cracked black pepper, to taste

### NOTE

Don't rush this part: This is when the sauce caramelizes onto the chicken and sets it. It also allows you time to get your side dishes ready.

1. **Make the BBQ sauce:** Place the ketchup, brown sugar, molasses, vinegar, garlic, hot sauce, mustard, and Worcestershire sauce in a small saucepan. Simmer until fragrant, about 5 minutes. Let cool and then transfer to a 2-cup (480 ml) glass measuring cup. (This will make it easier to reheat in the microwave and hold the basting brush upright while grilling the chicken and basting.) Cover and refrigerate until ready to grill.

2. **Make the chicken:** Place the chicken on a baking sheet and pat dry with a paper towel. Brush the chicken with vegetable oil and season with salt and pepper on both sides.

3. If you made the sauce in advance (see Make-Ahead Game Plan), reheat it in the microwave in 30-second intervals until hot (or simmer on the stovetop). Set ⅓ cup (80 ml) aside for the final basting.

4. Heat an outdoor grill or large grill pan to medium-high heat. Preheat the oven to 350°F (175°C).

5. **Prepare to grill:** Take the pan of chicken, BBQ tongs, a clean baking sheet, clean tongs, the BBQ sauce, and a silicone basting brush out to the grill.

6. Place the chicken on the grill, skin side down, and cover. Grill the chicken until nicely browned, 5 to 8 minutes, and then flip and cook for 5 to 8 minutes on the other side.

7. Baste the chicken skin with the sauce and cover. Then, continue to grill for 3 minutes until the sauce has set. Flip, baste the other side with sauce, and cover for 3 minutes more, until both sides are nicely charred. Use the clean tongs to transfer the chicken to the clean baking sheet.

8. Baste the chicken with the sauce on the skin side one more time. Then, transfer the baking sheet to the oven and bake for 10 to 15 minutes (see Note), until the sauce on the chicken has caramelized and set and the chicken reaches an internal temperature of 165°F (74°C).

9. Use a clean basting brush to baste the chicken with the reserved sauce one final time, and serve.

### MAKE-AHEAD GAME PLAN

Two days ahead, make the BBQ sauce. Cover and refrigerate until ready to use.

### PAIRS WELL WITH

Horseradish Potato Salad with Caramelized Shallots (page 84)

Summer Corn Confetti Salad (page 95)

# FENNEL-CRUSTED PORK LOIN
## WITH SPICED PARSNIPS AND APPLES

A roast pork loin is a typical Sunday lunch for my husband's French family. It's an economical cut of meat that will feed a crowd, and it's an easy dish for entertaining too, since you can throw in a few veggies to cook at the same time! I love to serve this in the fall, when the thought of a one-pan dinner is too tempting to pass up. You'll love the combination of the caramelized spiced parsnips and apples with the fennel-crusted pork—a flavor match made in heaven. Spoon over the easy pan sauce, and you'll have an elegant Sunday meal.

*SERVES 8*

### PORK LOIN

2 tablespoons (30 ml) fennel seed

2 teaspoons (10 ml) dried basil

2 teaspoons (10 ml) dried oregano

2 teaspoons (10 ml) dried thyme

1 teaspoon (6 g) kosher salt

Freshly cracked black pepper, to taste

3 pounds (1.4 kg) boneless center-cut pork loin roast, patted dry (see Note 1)

2 tablespoons (30 ml) olive oil

### PARSNIPS AND APPLES

2 pounds (907 g) parsnips, peeled and sliced lengthwise into quarters

2 pounds (907 g) Honeycrisp apples, sliced into wedges (see Note 2)

2 tablespoons (30 ml) olive oil

½ teaspoon (2.5 ml) grated fresh ginger

¼ teaspoon (1.25 ml) ground cinnamon

¼ teaspoon (1.25 ml) ground nutmeg

Kosher salt and freshly cracked black pepper, to taste

### PAN SAUCE

⅓ cup (80 ml) dry white wine (chardonnay or sauvignon blanc)

2 cups (480 ml) chicken broth

½ teaspoon (2.5 ml) Dijon mustard

3 to 4 dashes Worcestershire sauce

1 tablespoon (10 g) cornstarch (optional)

1 tablespoon (15 ml) very cold water (optional)

### NOTES

1. Be sure to buy a pork tenderloin roast, which is a larger cut of meat than a pork tenderloin. Pork roast takes longer to cook, which fits perfectly with the amount of time it will take to roast the parsnips and apples.

2. If you can't find Honeycrisps, use any other sweet, crisp apples. Leave the skins on to allow the pectin to create a jammy consistency as the apples cook down.

3. Alternatively, you can sear the pork in a large skillet and transfer it to a baking sheet to roast. Don't wash out the skillet; save it and the collected drippings to make the pan gravy.

1. Preheat the oven to 400°F (200°C). Place the oven rack in the lower third of the oven.

2. **Make the pork:** Mix the fennel seed, basil, oregano, thyme, salt, and pepper in a small bowl. Press the spices into the pork on all sides.

3. **Make the parsnips and apples:** Toss the parsnips and apples in a large bowl with the olive oil, ginger, cinnamon, nutmeg, salt, and pepper until well coated.

4. **Cook the pork:** Heat the olive oil over medium-high heat in a large heavy-bottomed roasting pan suitable for use on a cooktop. Sear the pork until golden brown, 2 to 3 minutes per side (see Note 3).

5. Transfer the parsnips and apples to the roasting pan, and spread them onto a single layer around the pork. Roast for 1 hour, or until the internal temperature of the pork reaches 165°F (74°C), tossing the parsnips and apples occasionally in the pork juices.

6. Transfer the pork to a carving board to rest for 10 to 15 minutes. Move the parsnips and apples to a baking sheet for even cooking and return them to the oven. Increase the oven temperature to 425°F (215°C) to allow them to caramelize for 5 to 10 minutes.

7. **Make the pan sauce:** Place the roasting pan on the stovetop over medium-high heat. Deglaze the pan with the wine, scraping up the brown bits on the bottom with a wooden spoon, until the liquid is reduced by one-third. Add the broth and simmer until reduced slightly, 3 to 4 minutes. Whisk in the mustard and Worcestershire sauce and simmer until hot, 3 to 4 minutes.

8. **If desired, thicken the sauce with a cornstarch slurry:** Whisk the cornstarch and water in a small bowl. Bring the sauce to boil and slowly add the slurry, whisking all the while until the sauce thickens.

9. Carve the pork into ¼-inch (6 mm) slices and transfer to a long platter, keeping the slices together and splayed out (for a pretty presentation). Nestle the parsnips and apples on either side. Transfer the pan sauce to a gravy boat and serve on the side.

**MAKE-AHEAD GAME PLAN**

Two days ahead, season the pork. Place it in a Pyrex dish, cover, and keep refrigerated. Remove it from the refrigerator 30 minutes before searing to come up to room temperature.

**PAIRS WELL WITH**

Roasted Broccoli with Garlic and Parmesan (page 147)

Butternut Squash Soup with Raisin Bread Croutons (page 79)

# EASY GOURMET BURGERS

The easiest way to upgrade a regular backyard BBQ burger is with the fixin's. I don't like to mess around too much with the burger itself; just a little light seasoning and a hot grill will provide all the flavor you need. It's what you put *on top of the burger* that matters. For me, that means caramelized shallots, smoky ketchup, gooey Swiss cheese, and chopped cornichons. It's all held together with a buttery, toasted brioche bun. Can it get any better?!

## SERVES 4

### BURGERS

2 tablespoons (30 ml) Worcestershire sauce

1 teaspoon (5 ml) garlic powder

¾ teaspoon (5 g) kosher salt

Freshly cracked black pepper, to taste

2 pounds (907 g) 80% to 85% lean ground beef (see Note)

1 tablespoon (15 ml) vegetable oil

### CARAMELIZED SHALLOTS

1 tablespoon (15 ml) olive oil

3 large shallots, sliced into half-moons

1 teaspoon (5 ml) balsamic vinegar

1 teaspoon (5 ml) minced fresh rosemary

Kosher salt and freshly cracked black pepper, to taste

### SMOKY KETCHUP

1 cup (240 ml) ketchup

2 teaspoons (10 ml) smoked paprika

### FIXIN'S

4 brioche buns

2 tablespoons (28 g) salted American butter, melted

4 slices Swiss cheese

4 leaves Bibb lettuce

8 cornichons, chopped

### NOTE

Avoid anything over 85% lean; you'll need some fat to keep your burger moist.

1. **Make the burgers:** Whisk together the Worcestershire sauce, garlic powder, salt, and pepper in a large bowl. Add the beef and work the seasoning into the meat, gently tossing to coat. Cover and refrigerate until ready to grill.

2. **Make the shallots:** Heat the olive oil in a medium nonstick pan. Add the shallots and cook until caramelized, wilted, and fragrant, 2 to 3 minutes. Add the vinegar and cook until most of the liquid has evaporated, about 1 minute.

3. Add the rosemary, salt, and pepper. Let cool and then cover and refrigerate until ready to serve at room temperature or chilled.

4. **Make the ketchup:** Whisk the ketchup and paprika in a small bowl. Refrigerate until ready to serve.

5. Divide the burger mixture into four ½-pound (227 g) patties. Brush each one lightly with vegetable oil.

6. Heat an outdoor grill or an indoor grill pan to medium-high heat. Lightly brush the inside of each brioche bun with melted butter.

7. Take the patties, buns, and cheese out to the grill, along with a clean plate and an extra clean spatula or tongs for removing the cooked burgers (to avoid cross contamination).

8. Grill each burger until it starts to look juicy on top, or about 5 minutes. Flip, add the cheese, and grill, covered, for 2 to 3 minutes more. For medium doneness, the burger will be firm to the touch but soft in the middle.

9. Grill the buns until nicely toasted, about 1 minute.

10. Place a leaf of lettuce on the bottom of each bun and then add a burger, ketchup, shallots, and cornichons. Top with a bun and serve.

### MAKE-AHEAD GAME PLAN

- Two days ahead, make the shallots and smoky ketchup. Cover and refrigerate until ready to serve.

- One day ahead, make the burger mixture and form it into patties. Cover and refrigerate until ready to grill.

### PAIRS WELL WITH

Horseradish Potato Salad with Caramelized Shallots (page 84)

Summer Corn Confetti Salad (page 95)

# BEGINNER'S ROAST TURKEY
## (AND GRAVY)

You can avoid roasting a turkey for as long as possible, until one day, you can't. Thanksgiving will eventually find its way to your house, and you'll long for a Norman Rockwell–type bird to grace your table. I promise, this is not a pipe dream. Especially once you start thinking of a turkey as just a big chicken. In my house growing up, the holiday turkey was always a team effort: Mom on the turkey, Dad on the gravy, and our dear friend Michael on the carving. In the chaos of holiday cooking, sometimes it takes a village. Not only does this group approach lessen the burden for the host, but there's also something sweet about everyone stepping up to the plate and sharing their unique talents to guarantee success. When Thanksgiving reached my house back in 2009, I felt like a deer in headlights, staring at a twenty-pound bird and not sure where to begin. Mom walked me through it, step by step (over the phone!). So that shows you just how easy it can be!

# BEGINNER'S ROAST TURKEY
## (AND GRAVY)

***SERVES 10*** *(with leftovers)*

### TURKEY

4 tablespoons (56 g) salted American butter, melted

2 tablespoons (30 ml) minced fresh rosemary

2 tablespoons (30 ml) minced fresh sage

2 tablespoons (30 ml) minced fresh thyme

1 teaspoon (6 g) kosher salt

½ teaspoon (2.5 ml) freshly cracked black pepper

One 20-pound (9 kg) turkey (see Turkey Note 1)

1 tablespoon (15 ml) olive oil

4 cups (960 ml) chicken broth

½ cup (120 ml) dry white wine (chardonnay or sauvignon blanc)

### GRAVY

Pan juices from the turkey

½ cup (120 ml) dry red wine (merlot or cabernet sauvignon)

1 tablespoon (15 ml) cornstarch

1 tablespoon (15 ml) cold water

3 cups (720 ml) chicken broth

1 bay leaf (fresh or dried)

1 tablespoon (15 ml) Dijon mustard

¼ teaspoon (1.25 ml) curry powder

A few dashes Worcestershire sauce

Kosher salt and freshly cracked black pepper, to taste

1. **Make the turkey:** Preheat the oven to 325°F (165°C). Remove all oven racks except the lowest one; this will prevent the turkey from burning.

2. Combine the butter, rosemary, sage, thyme, salt, and pepper in a small bowl.

3. Unwrap the turkey in the sink and remove the neck and giblets from the cavity. Keep the neck and discard the giblets. Remove any plastic packaging around the cavity.

4. Rinse the turkey and then place it on a rack in a heavy-bottomed 13×18-inch (33×46 cm) roasting pan (see Turkey Note 2). Pat dry with paper towels. Clean your sink well with hot, soapy water.

5. Being careful not to tear the skin, use your hands to loosen the skin under the breast meat. (I know it's a bit slimy, but this isn't the time to be squeamish. Just soldier on. Your turkey will taste all the better for it, and this is how you earn your Thanksgiving stripes.)

6. Spoon the butter-herb mixture under the skin. Then, carefully use your hands under the skin to work the mixture over the breast meat. Tie the legs together with butcher's twine.

7. Use a silicone pastry brush to brush the skin with olive oil to allow it to crisp up. Season with more salt and pepper. Add 1 cup (240 ml) chicken broth, the white wine, and the reserved turkey neck to the bottom of the pan.

8. Tent the entire turkey loosely with foil (you may need to use two sheets folded together) and roast for 2 hours, adding more chicken broth to the bottom of the pan, in 1-cup (240 ml) increments, if it gets below about 1 inch (2.5 cm) of liquid.

9. Remove the foil, and roast for 45 minutes to 1 hour more, until the internal temperature of the thickest part of the thigh reaches 160°F (70°C). Baste the turkey with the pan juices every 20 minutes to help the turkey brown.

10. Let the turkey rest in the pan at room temperature for 20 minutes before carving (this will bring it up to 165°F/74°C and allow it to retain its juices).

11. Transfer the turkey to a carving board. Remove the rack and discard the turkey neck.

12. **Make the gravy:** Pour the pan drippings through a fat separator to separate the fat from the sauce. Place the roasting pan on the stovetop over medium-low heat, and deglaze the pan with the red wine, reducing it by one-third. Add the pan sauce from the fat separator. Discard the fat in the trash (not down the drain). Mix the cornstarch and water in a small bowl to form a slurry.

13. Add the chicken broth. Bring to a boil and then add the cornstarch slurry to thicken (see Turkey Note 3). Add the bay leaf, mustard, curry powder, and Worcestershire sauce. Simmer for 3 to 4 minutes and then remove the bay leaf.

14. Add salt and pepper to taste if needed. Transfer to a gravy boat and serve with the carved turkey.

**TURKEY NOTES**

1. Thaw a frozen turkey in the refrigerator for at least 24 hours for every 4 to 5 pounds (1.8 to 2.2 kg). Keep it in its packaging and place it in a large pan to catch any juices that may leak.

2. The roasting pan should have a heavy bottom, and you should be able to put it over a low flame on your cooktop.

3. For cornstarch to work its magic, the liquid you are trying to thicken must be boiling, and the water used to make the cornstarch slurry must be very cold. For a thicker gravy, double the quantity of the cornstarch slurry.

**PAIRS WELL WITH**

Fresh Green Bean Casserole (page 159)

Sweet Potato Casserole with Toasted Marshmallows (page 164)

# HOMEMADE CRANBERRY SAUCE

My mother, for some reason, always had an attachment to jellied cranberry sauce, the kind that comes in a can and keeps its exquisite shape even after sliding out onto the plate. But when my husband and I inherited Thanksgiving, the canned cranberry sauce was the first thing to go. And what did Mom rave about most that year? The homemade cranberry sauce! It's laughable how easy homemade cranberry sauce is. In fact, it's so simple that you can practically do it in your sleep, which is why it's always the last recipe I make the night before Thanksgiving, when I'm exhausted and running on autopilot.

***SERVES 10*** *(Makes 2½ cups/600 ml)*

1 large navel orange

One 12-ounce (340 g) bag fresh cranberries

1 cup (240 ml) water

½ cup (100 g) sugar

1 cinnamon stick (see Sauce Note)

¼ teaspoon (1 g) kosher salt

Large pinch of ground cloves

**SAUCE NOTE**

If you don't have a cinnamon stick, swap for a large pinch of ground cinnamon.

1. Using a vegetable peeler, peel off 6 to 8 orange peels, 2 inches (5 cm) in length. Juice the orange.

2. Place the cranberries, water, orange peels and juice, sugar, cinnamon stick, salt, and cloves in a large saucepan.

3. Bring to a boil and then reduce the heat and simmer for 5 to 10 minutes. If you prefer large chunks and less syrup (that's how I like it!), cook for 5 minutes; for a smoother sauce, cook for 10 minutes.

4. Remove from the heat and let cool (the sauce will thicken as it cools). Leave the cinnamon stick and orange peels in; they will add additional flavor as the sauce cools in the refrigerator.

5. Transfer to an airtight container and refrigerate until ready to serve. Before serving, remove the cinnamon stick (I like to keep the peels in).

**MAKE-AHEAD GAME PLAN**

Two days ahead, make the sauce. Cover and refrigerate until ready to serve.

**PAIRS WELL WITH**

Make-Ahead Thanksgiving Stuffing (page 163)

Beginner's Roast Turkey (and Gravy) (page 140)

# ROSEMARY BEEF TENDERLOIN
## WITH HORSERADISH CREAM

Nothing says "special occasion" more than a beef tenderloin. It's an important recipe to master because you can serve it for Christmas, New Year's Eve, Mother's Day, or Easter. Guests are always delighted by a melt-in-your-mouth, center-cut beef tenderloin, also known as the chateaubriand cut. It comes from the same tenderloin as a filet mignon, but I choose to serve it whole as one roast (because it's way easier!) and carve off slices just before serving. It's become a go-to holiday meal in recent years since it's so easy to prepare and holds up to the chaos of holiday entertaining. You'll love the combination of the tender beef with the bite of the horseradish cream. Serve it with my Crispy Hasselback Potatoes (page 160; see Note 1) for an elegant side dish that just screams holiday entertaining!

*SERVES 6 TO 8*

### BEEF

2 tablespoons (30 ml) whole black peppercorns

1 tablespoon (15 ml) freshly minced rosemary

2 teaspoons (12 g) kosher salt

4 pounds (1.8 kg) boneless beef tenderloin (center or chateaubriand cut)

2 tablespoons (30 ml) vegetable oil

### HORSERADISH CREAM

2 cups (480 g) sour cream

¼ cup (60 ml) prepared horseradish

2 tablespoons (30 ml) snipped fresh chives

Kosher salt and freshly cracked black pepper, to taste

1. **Make the beef:** Place the peppercorns in a resealable plastic bag, seal, and whack with a rolling pin or hammer to crush the peppercorns into a coarse grind. Put the crushed peppercorns, rosemary, and salt in a small bowl, and toss to combine.

2. Pat the beef dry with a paper towel, and rub the dry rub all over the beef. Place the beef in a shallow casserole dish, cover, and refrigerate overnight (see Note 2).

3. Remove the beef from the refrigerator and let stand at room temperature for 30 minutes.

4. Meanwhile, preheat the oven to 425°F (215°C). Place the oven rack in the lower third of the oven.

5. Add the vegetable oil to a heavy-bottom roasting pan suitable for a cooktop. Heat on medium-high until the oil shimmers. Add the beef and cook, turning the meat, until a nice crust forms on all sides (including the ends), 5 to 10 minutes.

6. Transfer the roasting pan to the oven and roast the beef for 15 to 20 minutes, until a meat thermometer registers 140°F (60°C) for medium rare (see Note 2) in the thickest part of the meat.

7. Remove the roasting pan and let rest on your cooktop for 10 minutes. Transfer the beef to a carving board and cover with foil for another 10 minutes.

8. **Meanwhile, make the horseradish cream:** Whisk the sour cream, horseradish, chives, salt, and pepper in a medium bowl.

9. Carve the beef into 1-inch-thick (2.5 cm) slices and serve with the horseradish cream.

### NOTES

1. If serving the Crispy Hasselback Potatoes (page 160) with the beef, give the potatoes a head start. Place them in the oven 35 minutes before the beef. At the 35-minute mark, brush the potatoes with butter. Move the potatoes to the lower rack, and place the beef on the middle rack. Reduce the oven temperature to 425°F (215°C). Roast the beef for 15 to 20 minutes, brushing the potatoes with butter at the 15-minute mark and then check the beef for doneness at the same time. Continue to roast the beef until a meat thermometer registers 140°F (60°C) for medium in the thickest part of the meat. The potatoes can roast a bit longer if needed while the beef rests before carving.

2. If you have guests who prefer different doneness levels, cut the tenderloin into two or three separate cuts before searing and then pull them out of the oven when they're cooked to rare (120 to 125°F/50 to 51°C), medium (130 to 135°F/54 to 57°C), or well done (160°F/70°C).

### MAKE-AHEAD GAME PLAN

One day ahead, make the horseradish cream. Cover and refrigerate until ready to serve. Season the beef with the dry rub, cover, and refrigerate it overnight.

### PAIRS WELL WITH

Crispy Hasselback Potatoes (page 160)

Roasted Ratatouille (page 151)

# SIDE DISHES

# ROASTED BROCCOLI
## WITH GARLIC AND PARMESAN

When you need an impressive vegetable side that's equally easy and delicious, turn to this roasted broccoli. It reminds me of an overpriced side dish you may order at a trendy restaurant when you realize your main dish doesn't "come with anything." The broccoli is flavorful and nicely charred since it roasts at a high temperature, and the garlic roasts right along with it, becoming toasted and sweet. Top it off with some freshly grated Parmesan for a hearty, creamy finish.

### SERVES 4

6 tablespoons (90 ml) olive oil, divided

24 ounces (680 g) broccoli florets

6 garlic cloves, sliced vertically in thirds

Kosher salt and freshly cracked black pepper, to taste

Freshly grated Parmesan, to taste

#### NOTE

The flat side will help with charring. Cut the florets from a full head of broccoli; you'll get prettier, fresher florets than anything pre-cut.

1. Preheat the oven to 475°F (245°C). Brush two baking sheets with 1 tablespoon (15 ml) olive oil each.

2. Halve each broccoli floret vertically to expose a flat side (see Note).

3. Place 12 ounces (340 g) broccoli in a large bowl with 2 tablespoons (30 ml) olive oil, three of the sliced garlic cloves, salt, and pepper. Toss to coat.

4. Place the florets on one of the baking sheets, cut side down; this will allow them to brown nicely. Set aside and then repeat step 3 with the remaining broccoli, oil, and garlic, adding salt and pepper to taste.

5. Place both pans in the oven (one on the middle rack and one on the lower rack) and roast for 20 minutes, rotating the pans halfway through, until the broccoli is bright green and nicely browned on the bottom.

6. Remove from the oven and transfer to a shallow platter or bowl. Top with freshly grated Parmesan.

#### MAKE-AHEAD GAME PLAN

One day ahead, slice the broccoli and garlic. Refrigerate until ready to roast.

#### PAIRS WELL WITH

Cast-Iron Roast Chicken (page 107)

Grilled Dijon Chicken with Charred Lemons (page 123)

# CHEESY ITALIAN POTATO BAKE

This cheesy potato bake has been a mainstay at our Thanksgiving table ever since I was a kid. It's the kind of side dish that I imagine every family has, the one that, if it's not made on Thanksgiving Day, will cause sulking into Christmas. The origins of this recipe can be traced back to my father's large Italian family, the Ruggieros. His family was so big that they roasted two turkeys at Thanksgiving, but that never made enough stuffing for everyone, so they added this recipe to stretch out the starchy side dishes. Little did they know that the "stretcher" would be the side dish that everyone would clamor for generations later!

*SERVES 8*

1 tablespoon (15 ml) olive oil

1 pound (454 g) sweet Italian pork sausage, casings removed (about 4 links; see Note)

1½ teaspoons (7.5 ml) Italian seasoning

1 teaspoon (5 ml) fennel seed

3½ pounds (1.6 kg) russet potatoes

Kosher salt and freshly cracked black pepper, to taste

½ cup (113 g) salted American butter

2 cups (480 ml) whole milk

8 ounces (227 g) shredded mozzarella

Paprika, to taste

1 tablespoon (15 ml) roughly chopped fresh Italian parsley

### NOTE

For a spicy kick, try hot Italian sausage.

1. Heat the olive oil in a large nonstick sauté pan over medium-high heat. Add the sausage, breaking it into bite-size chunks with a wooden spoon. Add the Italian seasoning and fennel seed and cook the sausage until browned on all sides and cooked through, 8 to 10 minutes. Remove the sausage with a slotted spoon and drain it on a paper towel–lined plate. Let cool.

2. Meanwhile, wash and peel the potatoes. Cut the potatoes into quarters, place them in a large pot of cold water, and salt the water to taste. Boil the potatoes until fork-tender, 15 to 20 minutes. Drain.

3. Preheat the oven to 350°F (175°C). Place the oven rack in the lower third of the oven.

4. Place the butter in a large bowl. Process the potatoes through a ricer or transfer them into the bowl of a stand mixer (a large bowl and a hand mixer works, too).

5. Whisk or beat the potatoes and the butter until the butter has melted. Add the milk and combine well. Season with salt and pepper to taste.

6. Stir in the sausage. Transfer the mixture to a 9×13-inch (23×33 cm) oven-safe casserole dish, and top with the cheese. Sprinkle with paprika.

7. Bake until potatoes are warmed through, about 20 minutes. Place the casserole, uncovered, under the broiler for 1 to 2 minutes, until the cheese is golden brown and bubbling. Remove and garnish with the parsley.

### MAKE-AHEAD GAME PLAN

One day ahead, assemble the casserole, adding ¼ cup (60 ml) more milk in step 5. Let cool and then cover with the cheese and refrigerate. To reheat, place the covered casserole in a preheated 350°F (175°C) oven for 45 minutes, or until the potatoes are warmed through. Remove the foil and place under the broiler for 1 to 2 minutes to melt and bubble the cheese.

### PAIRS WELL WITH

Beginner's Roast Turkey (and Gravy) (page 140)

Rosemary Beef Tenderloin with Horseradish Cream (page 143)

# ROASTED RATATOUILLE

Ratatouille is a fantastic vegetable dish that you'll want in your repertoire because it can be made ahead of time; in fact, it's even better that way, since the flavors have time to marry and become more pronounced. Most traditional ratatouille recipes are made on the stovetop, but I prefer to roast the vegetables in the oven because they become even sweeter, almost candied. It also dries them out a bit, preventing any flavor dilution coming from watery, simmered vegetables. This is also why I break with tradition and leave the zucchini out: It's just too watery! Ratatouille is also extremely versatile. You can serve it hot, at room temperature, or cold. The leftovers are also fantastic in an omelet with a sprinkle of Gruyère cheese and fresh thyme.

*SERVES 4 TO 6*

¼ cup (60 ml) plus 1 tablespoon (15 ml) olive oil, divided

2 large onions, sliced into ¼-inch-thick (6 mm) half-moons (about 3½ cups/350 g)

1 large eggplant, sliced into ¼-inch-thick (6 mm) half-moons (about 5 cups/400 g)

5 large Roma tomatoes, quartered

1 large red bell pepper, cut into strips

1 large yellow bell pepper, cut into strips

4 garlic cloves, quartered

1 tablespoon (15 ml) herbes de Provence

½ teaspoon (3 g) kosher salt

Freshly cracked black pepper, to taste

2 tablespoons (30 ml) chopped fresh thyme

1. Preheat the oven to 425°F (215°C). Place the oven rack in the lower third of the oven.

2. Brush 1 tablespoon (15 ml) olive oil onto a large baking sheet.

3. Layer the pan with the onions, eggplant, tomatoes, peppers, and garlic, in that order.

4. Drizzle the remaining olive oil over the vegetables. Sprinkle with herbes de Provence, salt, and pepper.

5. Roast, untouched, for 30 minutes, until the vegetables start to soften.

6. Increase the oven temperature to 450°F (230°C) and roast for an additional 20 to 25 minutes, tossing occasionally with a wooden spoon, until the vegetables are cooked down, caramelized, and tender.

7. Remove from the oven and season to taste with salt, pepper, and a pinch or two more of herbes de Provence.

8. Transfer the ratatouille to a shallow serving bowl and garnish with thyme.

**MAKE-AHEAD GAME PLAN**

Two days ahead, make the ratatouille. Let cool and then cover and refrigerate. Reheat, uncovered, at 425°F (215°C) for 10 minutes, tossing occasionally.

**PAIRS WELL WITH**

24-Hour Flank Steak with Chimichurri (page 124)

Cast-Iron Roast Chicken (page 107)

# EASY ROASTED POTATOES
## WITH SMOKY KETCHUP

In theory, oven-roasted potatoes seem like a no-brainer of a recipe. Cut, toss, and bake, right? Well, if you've ever had a potato stick to the pan, crumble apart, or turn into a wannabe home fry, then you understand that there's a bit more to it. This easy technique will create a highly addictive roasted potato that is crispy on the outside and fluffy on the inside. The two-ingredient smoky ketchup? That's the sweet reward for getting it right.

---

*SERVES 4*

---

### SMOKY KETCHUP

1 cup (240 ml) ketchup

2 teaspoons (10 ml) smoked paprika

### ROASTED POTATOES

3 pounds (1.4 kg) small Yukon Gold or Baby Dutch potatoes

3 tablespoons (45 ml) olive oil

1 tablespoon (15 ml) minced fresh rosemary

Kosher salt and freshly cracked black pepper, to taste

Fleur de sel salt, for finishing (optional)

### NOTE

Take out your most well-loved, "seasoned" rimmed baking sheet. Newer pans are very porous; they will grab food and it will stick. Old pans have been exposed to hours of heat and oil over the years and develop a kind of "patina," which creates a better nonstick surface. Even if your pan looks like it should be dropped off at Goodwill, don't get rid of it! It's perfect for roasting potatoes.

1. Preheat the oven to 350°F (175°C). Place the oven rack in the lower third of the oven.

2. **Make the ketchup:** Whisk together the ketchup and paprika in a small bowl. Cover and refrigerate until ready to serve.

3. **Make the potatoes:** Rinse the potatoes and pat them dry. This is an important step; wet potatoes will steam up, and dry potatoes will crisp up!

4. Cut the potatoes into quarters. For a dressier potato, quarter lengthwise; for a rustic potato, halve lengthwise and then quarter horizontally.

5. Toss the potatoes with the olive oil, rosemary, kosher salt, and pepper in a large bowl. Transfer to a large baking sheet (see Note), making sure they fit in a single layer. They will roast better if they are not crowded.

6. Roast for 20 minutes and then shake the pan (don't flip the potatoes with a spatula). By shaking them, you won't force the ones that aren't ready and risk tearing the skin or the potato itself.

7. Roast for another 20 minutes and then shake the pan again. Continue roasting for another 10 minutes (the potatoes will be great at this point, but for an extra-crispy potato, go for *another* 10 minutes).

8. Transfer the potatoes to a shallow serving bowl and season with fleur de sel if using. Potatoes drink up the salt, and finishing salt will result in the best flavor. It will add a nice little crunch, too.

### MAKE-AHEAD GAME PLAN

Two days ahead, make the ketchup. Cover and refrigerate until ready to serve.

### PAIRS WELL WITH

Cast-Iron Roast Chicken (page 107)

Puffy Egg Bake (page 169)

# CRISP AND CREAMY COLESLAW

You might think of coleslaw as one of those obligatory side dishes that comes with your deli sandwich. And let's be honest, this variety never tastes that good. It's typically soggy, watery, and lacking in flavor. But after making homemade coleslaw, I've become a bit of a "coleslaw snob." I just can't eat it unless I've made it myself. I use freshly sliced cabbage for the crispiest results, but you could also use the store-bought ready-to-use slaw. But just don't add the dressing that comes with it, because what I have waiting for you below is way better!

*SERVES 8*

## DRESSING

1 cup (220 g) mayonnaise

½ cup (120 ml) apple cider vinegar

2 tablespoons (20 g) brown sugar

2 tablespoons (30 ml) Dijon mustard

2 teaspoons (10 ml) celery seed

¼ teaspoon (1 g) kosher salt

¼ teaspoon (1.25 ml) freshly cracked black pepper

## SLAW

5 cups (250 g) thinly sliced green cabbage (see Note 1)

4 cups (290 g) thinly sliced red cabbage

⅓ cup (50 g) diced red onion

1 large carrot, peeled into ribbons with a potato peeler

4 scallions, sliced diagonally, divided

2 tablespoons (30 ml) chopped fresh parsley

## NOTES

1. Slice the cabbage ¼ inch (6 mm) thick for best results.
2. It takes a bit of tossing to allow the dressing to permeate into the cabbage. Store any extra dressing in the refrigerator for up to 2 days and use it for dinner salads or as a spread on sandwiches.

1. **Make the dressing:** Whisk together the mayonnaise, vinegar, brown sugar, and mustard in a medium bowl until smooth. Add the celery seed, salt, and pepper.

2. **Make the slaw:** Add the green cabbage, red cabbage, onions, carrot, two of the scallions, and the parsley to a large bowl.

3. Add half of the dressing and toss to coat. Then, slowly add the remaining dressing to taste (see Note 2).

4. Transfer to a serving bowl and garnish with the remaining scallions.

### MAKE-AHEAD GAME PLAN

- Two days ahead, prepare the dressing, cover, and refrigerate.
- One day ahead, prepare the vegetables, cover, and refrigerate.
- One hour before, add the dressing to the slaw and toss. Keep refrigerated until ready to serve. Don't add the dressing the day before, or the coleslaw will start to turn purple from the red cabbage.

### PAIRS WELL WITH
Better BBQ Chicken (page 133)
Fall-Off-the-Bone Sticky Ribs (page 117)

# ELEVENTH-HOUR CORN PUDDING

There comes a time during every Thanksgiving when that one person will say, "Do you think we need one more side dish?" and you'll agree, thinking you'll just whip something up real quick! If that sounds like you, then this corn pudding is the ticket. It's quick, it's easy, and the whole thing can be mixed up in a blender! This recipe was my eleventh-hour side dish one year, and everyone went nuts for "that seriously good corn pudding thing." It's light and airy and full of sweet corn flavor, almost like a cornbread soufflé. It's just as decadent as mashed potatoes or stuffing, but not as filling. So, you can eat even more of it!

### SERVES 6 TO 8

Two 12-ounce (340 g) bags
    frozen yellow corn, divided

4 large eggs

1 cup (240 ml) heavy cream

¾ cup (180 ml) whole milk

½ cup (113 g) salted American
    butter, melted and cooled,
    plus 1 tablespoon (14 g),
    melted, for greasing

⅓ cup (66 g) granulated sugar

1½ teaspoons (9 g) kosher salt

⅓ cup (46 g) all-purpose flour

1 teaspoon (4 g) baking powder

2 tablespoons (30 ml) minced
    fresh chives

Freshly cracked black pepper,
    to taste

1. Preheat the oven to 350°F (175°C). Place the oven rack in the lower third of the oven.

2. Grease a 9×12-inch (23×30 cm) oven-safe casserole dish with 1 tablespoon (14 g) butter. (If using a 9×14-inch/23×36 cm dish, lessen the baking time by 5 to 10 minutes.)

3. Add one bag of corn and the eggs, heavy cream, milk, sugar, salt, and the remaining butter to a blender. Blend on high until smooth, about 1 minute. Transfer to a large bowl.

4. Whisk together the flour and baking powder in a small bowl.

5. Add the flour mixture to the blended mixture, whisking to combine. Add the second bag of corn, the chives, and pepper to taste. Stir to combine.

6. Pour the batter into the casserole dish and bake for 45 to 50 minutes, until the top is slightly golden brown and a toothpick comes out clean. Serve immediately.

**THANKSGIVING MAKE-AHEAD GAME PLAN**

One day ahead, you can mix the batter for the corn pudding, cover the bowl, and refrigerate until ready to bake. You can make corn pudding batter in advance, but it's best not to bake it ahead of time. While your turkey rests, pour the batter into a prepared casserole dish and bake at 350°F (175°C) for 45 to 50 minutes.

**PAIRS WELL WITH**

Beginner's Roast Turkey (and Gravy) (page 140)

Fall-Off-the-Bone Sticky Ribs (page 117)

# FRESH GREEN BEAN CASSEROLE
## (FOR THOSE WHO DON'T LIKE GREEN BEAN CASSEROLE)

No other side dish at Thanksgiving stirs up more debate than the green bean casserole. Love it or hate it, its origin story began in the Campbell's test kitchen in 1955, and for better or worse, it has since stood the test of time. As a child, I too passed it over on my way to Mom's Sweet Potato Casserole with Toasted Marshmallows (page 164) and Dad's Cheesy Italian Potato Bake (page 148). But as I got older, I took another look at this American classic and wondered how I could, well, make it better. This version uses fresh green beans and slathers them in a *homemade* creamy mushroom sauce loaded with three types of mushrooms, which each provide a different texture and flavor. Because it's the holidays, after all, we might as well go big. It then gets topped with the classic crispy, fried French's onions, because that part of the tradition should *not* be messed with!

*SERVES 8*

Kosher salt and freshly cracked black pepper, to taste

2 pounds (907 g) green beans

2 tablespoons (28 g) salted American butter

2 medium shallots, sliced into half-moons (about ¾ cup/85 g)

4 ounces (113 g) cremini mushrooms, sliced

4 ounces (113 g) shiitake mushrooms, sliced

1 large (85 g) portobello mushroom, sliced and halved lengthwise

2 tablespoons (30 ml) chopped fresh thyme

1 tablespoon (15 ml) Worcestershire sauce

One 6-ounce (170 g) container French's Fried Onions

**BÉCHAMEL SAUCE**

4 tablespoons (56 g) salted American butter

¼ cup (35 g) all-purpose flour

4 cups (960 ml) whole milk

3 garlic cloves, minced

¾ teaspoon (5 g) kosher salt

Freshly cracked black pepper, to taste

1 to 2 pinches of ground nutmeg

¼ cup (20 g) freshly grated Parmesan

1. Bring a large pot of water to a boil. Salt the water to taste. Then cook the green beans until tender but still a bit crisp, 5 to 6 minutes. Fill a large bowl with ice water.

2. Transfer the green beans to the bowl of ice water to stop the cooking. Stir the beans in the ice bath to cool and then drain them through a colander. Transfer the beans to a 9×12-inch (23×30 cm) oven-safe casserole dish, pat them dry with a clean kitchen towel, and set aside.

3. Meanwhile, melt the butter in a large skillet over medium-high heat until foamy. Add the shallots and cook until fragrant and wilted, 1 to 2 minutes, and then add the mushrooms. Cook, stirring occasionally, until the mushrooms release their juices, 3 to 5 minutes. Season with salt and pepper and then add the thyme and Worcestershire sauce. Spoon the mushroom mixture on top of the beans in the casserole dish to cover them.

4. **Make the béchamel sauce:** Melt the butter in a large, deep skillet over medium-high heat until foamy. Add the flour, whisk to form a loose paste, and then slowly whisk in the milk. Bring to a low boil, 3 to 5 minutes, and then reduce the heat to a simmer until the sauce thickens, 5 to 8 minutes.

5. Add the garlic, salt, pepper, and nutmeg. Then, add the Parmesan and stir until melted and smooth. Pour the sauce over the beans and the mushroom mixture, making sure to cover both.

6. Preheat the oven to 350°F (175°C). Top the casserole with the crispy onions, cover, and bake for 25 minutes. Uncover and bake for 5 more minutes, until the fried onions start to glisten. Serve immediately.

**MAKE-AHEAD GAME PLAN**

One day ahead, make the casserole; just don't add the onions yet. Cover and refrigerate and then proceed to step 6 when ready to bake.

**PAIRS WELL WITH**

Cheesy Italian Potato Bake (page 148)

Beginner's Roast Turkey (and Gravy) (page 140)

# CRISPY HASSELBACK POTATOES

Hasselback potatoes are *the* potato side dish for Christmas dinner or New Year's Eve. They are crispy and buttery and look so elegant on the plate. They are also a cinch to make! There are a lot of recipes out there for Hasselback potatoes. Most recipes call for leaving the skin on. Some use russet potatoes, others Yukon Gold. But I've found to get the *crispiest* Hasselback potato with a beautiful fluffy interior, you must use a russet potato *and peel it*. Peeling the potato allows the exterior to get extra crispy! And using a starchy potato like a russet delivers on the gorgeous fluffiness.

*MAKES 4*

4 large russet potatoes, peeled

3 tablespoons (45 ml) olive oil

Kosher salt and freshly cracked black pepper, to taste

6 tablespoons (84 g) salted American butter

3 garlic cloves, minced

3 tablespoons (45 ml) minced fresh thyme

Fleur de sel salt and freshly cracked black pepper, to taste

1. Preheat the oven to 450°F (230°C). Place the oven rack in the lower third of the oven.

2. Slice a small sliver off a potato's underside to stabilize it. Position the potato horizontally in front of you.

3. Place the handles of two wooden spoons or two chopsticks on either side of the potato to prevent yourself from slicing all the way through it.

4. Slice vertical 1/16-inch (1.5 mm) slits horizontally across the potato. Repeat steps 2 through 4 with the remaining potatoes.

5. Rub each potato with olive oil, massaging it into the slits where you can. They will open up as they roast, allowing you to baste more inside.

6. Place the potatoes on a baking sheet, and season with salt and pepper. Bake for 35 minutes, until the tops begin to turn slightly golden brown.

7. Meanwhile, melt the butter in a small saucepan and then add the garlic and thyme. Stir to combine.

8. At the 35-minute mark, using a pastry brush, baste each potato with the garlic butter. Bake for another 15 minutes. Baste with the garlic butter again, trying to work the butter into the slits, and then bake for 10 minutes more.

9. Remove the potatoes from the oven and baste a final time with whatever butter is left. Garnish with fleur de sel and pepper.

**MAKE-AHEAD GAME PLAN**

One day ahead, measure out the butter, garlic, and thyme in a small heat-safe Pyrex pitcher. Cover and refrigerate and then microwave to melt the butter just before using.

**PAIRS WELL WITH**

Pan-Seared Salmon with Lemon Butter Caper Sauce (page 113)

Rosemary Beef Tenderloin with Horseradish Cream (page 143)

# MAKE-AHEAD
# THANKSGIVING STUFFING

Stuffing is one of my favorite Thanksgiving side dishes. There's something so delicious about a savory bread dish that is soft and fluffy on the inside and browned and crispy on the outside. This recipe is an updated version of the classic stuffing my mom made when I was growing up in the 1970s. But instead of including the store-bought dried bread cubes she used back then, I'm giving this stuffing a bit of a makeover. I swap the dried cubes for a day-old sourdough loaf and add fresh herbs and a good helping of a dry white wine. The results feel like an homage to Mom, but brought up to date. This stuffing is even better when made a day ahead. It also reheats beautifully at 350°F (175°C), which allows it to play nicely with the other side dishes you need to reheat at the same temperature. Just pop it under the broiler for a few minutes to get that wonderful crispy top!

*SERVES 6 TO 8*

6 tablespoons (84 g) salted American butter, melted, plus 1 tablespoon (14 g) for greasing

2 tablespoons (30 ml) olive oil

1 large yellow onion, chopped (about 1 cup/140 g)

2 medium celery stalks, chopped (about ½ cup/70 g)

2 medium carrots, chopped (about ½ cup/60 g)

1 medium leek, white parts only, chopped (about ½ cup/35 g)

8 ounces (227 g) cremini or baby bella mushrooms, chopped

Kosher salt and freshly cracked black pepper, to taste

1 teaspoon (5 ml) herbes de Provence

½ cup (120 ml) dry white wine (chardonnay or sauvignon blanc)

1 tablespoon (15 ml) chopped fresh parsley

1 tablespoon (15 ml) plus 1 teaspoon (5 ml) chopped fresh thyme, divided

1 tablespoon (15 ml) minced fresh sage

One 14-ounce (397 g) loaf day-old sourdough bread (see Note 1)

2 cups (480 ml) chicken stock

2 large eggs, beaten

5 to 6 pumps olive oil spray

1. Preheat oven to 350°F (175°C). Place the oven rack in the lower third of the oven.

2. Grease a 11×15-inch (28×38 cm) gratin dish with butter (see Note 2).

3. Heat the olive oil in a large sauté pan over medium-high heat. Sauté the onions, celery, carrots, and leeks until translucent and tender, about 3 minutes. Add the mushrooms and cook until they soften and release their juices, another 3 minutes.

4. Season with salt and pepper and then stir in the herbes de Provence. Add the wine and simmer until the liquid is reduced by one-third, 1 to 2 minutes. Stir in the parsley, 1 tablespoon (15 ml) thyme, and the sage. Remove from the heat and let cool.

5. Meanwhile, cut the bread into 1-inch (2.5 cm) cubes and place them in a large bowl. Add the melted butter and toss to combine. Then, add the stock and eggs and toss again to combine. Stir in the cooked vegetables.

6. Transfer the stuffing to the gratin dish and gently coat with the olive oil spray for an extra-crispy top. Sprinkle with the remaining thyme.

7. Bake for 35 to 40 minutes, until the egg is cooked, the stuffing is hot inside, and the top is beginning to brown and crisp. If desired, place under the broiler for 1 to 3 minutes to crisp further. Serve immediately or let cool if making a day ahead (see Make-Ahead Game Plan).

## NOTES

1. Buy a whole loaf and cut it yourself (do not buy sliced sandwich bread). If the bread is not day-old, bake the cubes at 250°F (120°C) for 10 to 15 minutes, until they begin to dry out. Or cut it the day before and let it dry out.

2. The shallower the pan is, the better; that way, everyone gets a bit of the crispy topping.

## MAKE-AHEAD GAME PLAN

One day ahead, make the stuffing, bake, and let cool completely. Cover and refrigerate. To reheat, keep covered and bake at 350°F (175°C) for 20 minutes. Uncover, bake for 5 minutes more, and then place under the broiler for 1 to 3 minutes to crisp up. Set a timer for this part; since Thanksgiving is a multitasking affair, it's easy to forget about the stuffing and burn it!

## PAIRS WELL WITH

Fresh Green Bean Casserole (For Those Who Don't Like Green Bean Casserole) (page 159)

Beginner's Roast Turkey (and Gravy) (page 140)

# SWEET POTATO CASSEROLE
## WITH TOASTED MARSHMALLOWS

Sweet potato casserole with marshmallows is a legendary Thanksgiving side, and now, thanks to my husband, Philippe, it's also a bit legendary in a tiny corner of France. Philippe makes no bones about being perplexed by the flavors of Thanksgiving. He just can't get on board with the combination of sweet and salty. When he explains Thanksgiving to our French friends and relatives, he always makes sure to emphasize that we "put *confiture* on the turkey" and "serve up a crazy sweet potato dish with a marshmallow *gratin*!" Our French friends can't believe it, and I wince as he undermines decades of progress by confirming that Americans have no culinary sophistication. But this has never deterred me. I stand proud of our sweet potato casserole, and anyone who holds a US passport should know how to make a great one. And by the way, this dish is the first thing that ends up on the plate of any French national who happens to be at our house on the fourth Thursday in November.

---

### SERVES 8 TO 10

---

Four 40-ounce (1.13 kg) cans Princella sweet potatoes in syrup (see Note 1)

4 tablespoons (56 g) salted American butter

½ cup (120 ml) heavy cream

1 teaspoon (5 ml) ground nutmeg

½ teaspoon (3 g) kosher salt

One 10-ounce (283 g) bag mini marshmallows (see Note 2)

#### NOTES

1.  I have tried to make this dish with fresh sweet potatoes, only to have the most disappointing results! But my own mother warned me: It only works with canned sweet potatoes. (The Princella brand sold at nearly every American supermarket does the trick!)

2.  We always buy some extra marshmallows just in case we burn the first batch! If you don't need them, you can always use them up at Christmas on top of my Homemade Hot Chocolate (page 39).

1.  Preheat the oven to 350°F (175°C). Place the oven rack in the lower third of the oven.

2.  Transfer 2 tablespoons (30 ml) of syrup from each can of sweet potatoes (8 tablespoons/120 ml total) into a large Dutch oven. Drain the sweet potatoes and then add them to the pot.

3.  Set over medium-low heat. Add the butter and mix with a hand mixer until smooth and creamy, 10 to 15 minutes. The longer the sweet potatoes heat in the Dutch oven, the more the lumps will soften. Add the heavy cream, nutmeg, and salt. Continue to beat until most of the lumps disappear. (They will also soften and dissolve while baking, so don't feel you need to get rid of all of them at this stage.)

4.  Transfer the mixture to a 9×13-inch (23×33 cm) oven-safe casserole dish. Place in the oven for 15 to 20 minutes, until the casserole is hot throughout.

5.  Top with an even layer of marshmallows and place under the broiler for 1 to 2 minutes, until golden brown. Don't walk away; the marshmallows will burn quickly! If they do burn, simply scrape them off and add a fresh layer.

**MAKE-AHEAD GAME PLAN**

One day ahead, make the casserole without the marshmallows. Cover and refrigerate. To reheat, keep covered and place the casserole in a 350°F (175°C) oven for 35 to 40 minutes, until hot. Then, proceed to step 5.

**PAIRS WELL WITH**

Fresh Green Bean Casserole (For Those Who Don't Like Green Bean Casserole) (page 159)

Beginner's Roast Turkey (and Gravy) (page 140)

BRUNCH

# PUFFY EGG BAKE

This breakfast casserole is your MVP of brunch dishes. It sees you through Easter, Mother's Day, bridal and baby showers, Christmas morning, and beyond! It's almost unfathomable that something so simple and so easy can be so incredibly delicious. It's light and fluffy like a soufflé, but without any pesky, time-consuming—do-I-really-have-to—egg separating. All thanks to a little cottage cheese. *Whaaaat?!* I know you're thinking, *but I don't like cottage cheese!* I know, no one does, but trust me on this one: No one will ever know it's in there. In fact, if I didn't tell you, you wouldn't know it. But now that the cat is out of the bag, just trust the process!

## SERVES 8

½ cup (113 g) salted American butter, melted, plus 1 tablespoon (14 g) for greasing

12 large eggs

16 ounces (454 g) small curd cottage cheese

½ cup (70 g) all-purpose flour

1 teaspoon (4 g) baking soda

16 ounces (454 g) finely shredded Mexican blend cheese (see Note 1)

Hot sauce or salsa, for serving

### NOTES

1. Look for finely shredded Mexican cheese because it melts into the casserole more evenly than the larger shreds.

2. Add a small can of fire-roasted chiles or jalapeños to the batter for additional heat. But stop there—this casserole doesn't like too many mix-ins. It will lose its fluffiness.

3. If the casserole gets too browned on top while baking, cover it with foil until fully baked inside.

1. Preheat the oven to 350°F (175°C). Place the oven rack in the lower third of the oven.

2. Grease a 9×13-inch (23×33 cm) oven-safe casserole dish with 1 tablespoon (15 ml) melted butter.

3. Whisk the eggs in a large bowl. Stir in the cottage cheese and add ½ cup (120 ml) melted butter. Whisk until combined.

4. Whisk together the flour and baking soda in a small bowl. Whisk the dry ingredients into the egg mixture.

5. Stir in the cheese with a wooden spoon or spatula (see Note 2). Pour the batter into the casserole dish.

6. Bake on the lowest rack of the oven for 30 to 35 minutes, until lightly golden brown and set in the center (see Note 3).

7. Cut into squares or allow guests to spoon out a serving. Serve immediately with hot sauce or salsa.

### MAKE-AHEAD GAME PLAN

The night before, make the batter. Keep it in the mixing bowl, cover, and refrigerate. Allow the refrigerated batter to sit out at room temperature for 15 minutes before pouring it into the greased casserole dish and baking. This will ensure that the center is fully baked before the top gets too browned.

### PAIRS WELL WITH

Easy Roasted Potatoes with Smoky Ketchup (page 152)

No-Chop Fancy Fruit Salad (page 188)

## SET IT AND FORGET IT
# SMOKED SALMON PLATTER

Between the muffins, cinnamon rolls, and coffee cakes, brunch can quickly turn into a sugar fest! So, I always like to include one or two protein-packed savory options to balance out all the sweetness. This also ensures that your guests feel as though they enjoyed "a meal" and don't go home with a screaming headache. This salmon platter is as easy as it gets because it's a hearty dish without any real cooking involved. True to its name, you just set it and forget it! It's really two recipes in one because your guests can mix and match the ingredients and get creative making salmon or avocado toasts. If you have a mandoline, this is a great time to use it: The radishes and cucumbers look extra beautiful when sliced thinly.

*SERVES 8*

### CREAM CHEESE SPREAD

16 ounces (454 g) whipped cream cheese

¼ cup (28 g) minced shallots

2 tablespoons (30 ml) capers, drained

2 tablespoons (30 ml) minced chives

1 tablespoon (15 ml) lemon zest

Freshly cracked black pepper, to taste

### PLATTER

1 dozen red radishes or Easter Egg radishes, thinly sliced (see Note 1)

1 medium English cucumber, thinly sliced

32 ounces (907 g) smoked salmon

Freshly cracked black pepper, to taste

One 0.5-ounce (14 g) package fresh dill

A small dish of fleur de sel salt

A small dish of red pepper flakes

2 large ripe avocados, cut into slices

2 lemons, sliced into wedges

2 medium tomatoes, cut into 8 to 10 slices

1 medium red onion, cut into 6 to 8 slices

1 dozen assorted bagels (onion, poppy seed, everything, and pumpernickel pair best with salmon)

8 to 10 slices rustic toast (sourdough, rye, or ciabatta bread)

1. **Make the spread:** Mix the cream cheese, shallots, capers, chives, lemon zest, and pepper with a spatula in a medium bowl. Cover and refrigerate until ready to serve.

2. **Make the platter:** Slice the radishes and cucumbers with a mandoline on the ⅟₁₆-inch (1.5 mm) setting or very carefully with a knife.

3. Take out a 20×15-inch (50×38 cm) rectangular board or a 19-inch (48 cm) round board.

4. Transfer the cream cheese spread into a serving bowl and place it in the center. Roll or ribbon the salmon on the board (see Note 2). Crack some pepper on top.

5. Chop about 2 tablespoons (30 ml) of the dill and then sprinkle on top. Add a few small dill fronds for garnish.

6. Place the fleur de sel and red pepper flakes in two individual pinch pots (see Note 3).

7. Nestle in the other ingredients, using your creativity to place them wherever you think looks best.

8. Add a small spreader to the bowl of cream cheese and a few small forks for serving the salmon and other ingredients.

9. Tuck in the bagels and toast if you have room, or place them in a basket lined with a napkin.

### NOTES

1. Easter Egg radishes are multicolored pastel radishes that appear in the spring. They look extra beautiful on this platter, but red radishes work, too.

2. Salmon can be oily; if you would like to protect your board, lay the salmon down on some tan parchment paper.

3. These seasonings are yummy for the avocado toast option (see Headnote).

### MAKE-AHEAD GAME PLAN

- One day ahead, prepare the cream cheese spread. Cover and refrigerate.

- One hour before, assemble the platter and refrigerate. Or refrigerate all the components separately and assemble them moments before guests arrive.

### PAIRS WELL WITH

Puffy Egg Bake (page 169)

Ham, Leek and Gruyère Strata (page 195)

# SHOW-STOPPING ALMOND CROISSANTS

The first time my husband told me almond croissants in France were made with the leftover croissants that didn't sell from the day before, I was like, *"wait, what?!"* But then he reminded me that nothing goes to waste in France, so of course, it all made perfect sense. Once I was back in the States, I wondered how I could make these delectable pastries at home, knowing we never have eight stale croissants just lying around. So, I developed a recipe you can make with fresh ones. These are fantastic for Christmas morning because you can prepare them the day before, and all you have to do is sneak downstairs and pop them in the oven. If you have in-laws coming for Christmas or anyone else you need to impress, this is the ticket. Once they take their first bite, it will be your mic-drop moment.

*SERVES 8*

8 store-bought croissants (see Note)

1⅓ cups (133 g) sliced raw almonds

½ cup (113 g) salted American butter, softened

½ cup (100 g) granulated sugar

2 large eggs

1 teaspoon (5 ml) pure almond extract

Pinch of kosher salt

¼ cup (35 g) all-purpose flour

**TOPPING**

⅓ cup (35 g) sliced raw almonds

1 tablespoon (8 g) powdered sugar

**NOTE**

Skip over the prepackaged croissants in the bread aisle of your grocery store; instead, head straight to the bakery section and spend the money on freshly baked croissants. Or better yet, go to your local French bakery and buy their plain croissants. My motto is "the better the plain croissant, the better the almond croissant."

1. Preheat the oven to 350°F (175°C). Place the oven rack in the lower third of the oven. Line a baking sheet with parchment paper.

2. Halve the croissants horizontally and place them, cut side up, on the baking sheet. This will dry them out a bit while you make the filling.

3. Place the almonds on the baking sheet. Bake for 8 minutes, until fragrant and golden brown. Set aside to cool and then transfer to a food processor. Pulse the almonds in the food processor until a coarse meal forms.

4. Beat together the butter, sugar, and ground almonds in the bowl of an electric mixer fitted with the paddle attachment. Add the eggs, almond extract, and salt. Beat to combine and then add the flour.

5. Spread 2 tablespoons (30 ml) filling on the bottom half of each croissant. Place the top half of the croissant on top.

6. Add another tablespoon (15 ml) filling to the top of each assembled croissant, spreading it into a thin layer. (It doesn't need to cover the croissant completely, just cover the curved top across the length of the croissant.) Add a sprinkle of raw almonds on top of each croissant. They will stick to the filling.

7. Bake for 16 to 18 minutes, until the almond filling is set and golden brown.

8. Let cool slightly and then dust with powdered sugar and serve immediately.

**MAKE-AHEAD GAME PLAN**

One day ahead, assemble the croissants completely on the parchment-lined baking sheet. Cover loosely with foil and refrigerate. Remove from the refrigerator, take off the foil, and bake in a 350°F (175°C) oven for 16 to 18 minutes. Let cool slightly and then dust with powdered sugar and serve immediately.

**PAIRS WELL WITH**

No-Chop Fancy Fruit Salad (page 188)

Puffy Egg Bake (page 169)

# BAKED BANANA FRENCH TOAST
## WITH RUM RAISIN SYRUP

French toast sounds like a delicious brunch idea, but serving individual portions to a crowd just isn't practical. That's why I love the idea of a baked French toast casserole, one that soaks overnight and can be popped in the oven the next day. It's the perfect "houseguest breakfast" anytime you have in-laws visiting or anyone else you need to impress. The bananas and rum raisin syrup make it feel extra fancy, but it couldn't be easier to make! You'll also love the flavor, which is a cross between decadent bread pudding and Bananas Foster. I love it hot right out of the oven and drizzled with the warm syrup, but my husband likes to eat it cold the next day!

### SERVES 8

1 pound (454 g) rustic French, Italian, or sourdough bread

8 large eggs

1½ cups (360 ml) heavy cream

1½ cups (360 ml) whole milk

¾ cup (120 g) light brown sugar

2 vanilla beans (see Note 1)

¼ teaspoon (1 g) kosher salt

Baking spray with flour

2 large very ripe bananas

**RUM RAISIN SYRUP**

One 12.5-ounce (370 ml) bottle pure maple syrup

⅓ cup (50 g) raisins

Three 2-inch (5 cm) orange peels, made with a potato peeler

1 cinnamon stick

¾ teaspoon (3.75 ml) imitation rum extract

#### NOTES

1. To save a little money (because vanilla beans can be pricy!), you can substitute the beans with 2 tablespoons (30 ml) vanilla extract.

2. It's better to wait to add the bananas until the next day; otherwise, they will turn brown and look a bit unsightly in the casserole.

1. Cut the bread into 1-inch (2.5 cm) cubes and set aside.

2. Whisk the eggs in a large bowl. Add the heavy cream, milk, and brown sugar and whisk to combine.

3. Split the vanilla beans down the middle and scrape the paste out with a knife. Add the paste to the mixture and then stir in the salt.

4. Toss the bread cubes into the mixture, stirring gently to submerge. The cubes should become heavy and completely drenched.

5. Cover the bowl with foil and refrigerate for at least 4 hours (overnight is even better for a custardy texture—and easier, too!).

6. Preheat the oven to 350°F (175°C). Place the oven rack in the lower third of the oven. Remove the bowl from the refrigerator to take the chill off.

7. Spray a 9×14-inch (23×36 cm) oven-safe casserole dish with baking spray.

8. Meanwhile, mash the bananas with a fork in a medium bowl. Then, fold them into the egg-bread mixture until combined (see Note 2).

9. Transfer the mixture to the casserole dish. Cover with foil and bake for 30 minutes.

10. **Meanwhile, make the syrup:** Heat a small saucepan over medium heat and add the syrup, raisins, orange peels, cinnamon stick, and rum extract. Simmer until bubbly, 2 to 3 minutes, and then reduce the heat to low to keep warm.

11. Uncover the casserole and bake for 15 minutes, until the cubes start to brown and set.

12. Place the casserole under the broiler for 1 to 2 minutes to crisp up the top and cook any cubes that still look wet. No liquid should be visible when you press the cubes with your fingertips.

13. Set aside to cool slightly. Dust the top with powdered sugar. To serve, cut into squares and drizzle the rum raisin syrup on top.

**MAKE-AHEAD GAME PLAN**

One day ahead, make the casserole filling, leaving the bananas out until just before baking. Refrigerate until ready to bake.

**PAIRS WELL WITH**

Set It and Forget It Smoked Salmon Platter (page 170)

No-Chop Fancy Fruit Salad (page 188)

# MELT-IN-YOUR-MOUTH
# BLUEBERRY MUFFINS

If a vanilla cupcake and a blueberry pancake got together and had a love child, it would be these light, fluffy, melt-in-your-mouth blueberry muffins. It leaves you wondering whether you should frost them or drench them in maple syrup. Whenever I invite my mother over for brunch, her response is always "Okay, but are you making those blueberry muffins?" This is a great muffin recipe for beginners because it's a two-bowl operation—no need to drag out the electric mixer!

*MAKES 12 MUFFINS*

2 large eggs

¾ cup (150 g) granulated sugar

½ cup (113 g) salted American butter, melted

¼ cup (60 ml) vegetable oil

½ cup (120 ml) water

1 teaspoon (5 ml) vanilla extract

1¾ cups (245 g) all-purpose flour

2 teaspoons (8 g) baking powder

½ teaspoon (3 g) kosher salt

1¼ cups (185 g) fresh blueberries, plus 36 blueberries (about ½ cup/75 g) for the top

### NOTE

For a crunchy, sugary muffin top, sprinkle 2 teaspoons (9 g) sugar on top of the muffins before baking.

1. Preheat the oven to 425°F (215°C). Place the oven rack in the lower third of the oven. Line a 12-cup muffin pan with parchment paper cupcake liners.

2. Whisk together the eggs, sugar, butter, vegetable oil, water, and vanilla in a large bowl.

3. Whisk together the flour, baking powder, and salt in a medium bowl.

4. Add the dry ingredients to the wet ingredients, in thirds, slowly whisking between each addition. Don't overmix, or you'll have a tough muffin. Gently stir in 1¼ cups (185 g) blueberries with a spatula.

5. Fill the muffin cups to the tops of the liners (see Note). Place three of the reserved berries on each muffin in a triangle shape (imagine two eyes and a nose on a teddy bear). The berries will burst and drizzle down the muffins in the final stages of baking, making them look extra inviting!

6. Bake for 18 to 20 minutes, until the muffins have risen and turned golden brown and the blueberries are bursting.

7. Let cool slightly for 3 to 4 minutes and then serve warm.

### MAKE-AHEAD GAME PLAN

These muffins are best made right before serving. Alternatively, you can also make them ahead and freeze them. Just allow them to cool and then place them in a resealable bag and freeze up to 2 weeks. To reheat, wrap them individually in a paper towel and microwave for 45 seconds to 1 minute, until warmed through.

### PAIRS WELL WITH

Hide-Away Granola (page 183)
Puffy Egg Bake (page 169)

# FOOLPROOF SPINACH QUICHE

A go-to quiche recipe should be in every entertainer's back pocket. It's a mainstay of fancy party food, and investing in perfecting this recipe will pay dividends at future brunches, showers, and potlucks. I've been making this quiche ever since we hosted our first housewarming party, and it's the recipe everyone always asks for on their way out. Now, I know this can be controversial, so brace yourself, but I don't blind bake the quiche crust because it can be hit-or-miss. Sometimes your crust can shrink despite all the refrigeration, and without the custard there to catch it, it's game over. Freezing the crust ahead of time and lining the bottom with cornstarch and cheese will keep the bottom crisp and avoid all that pesky blind baking business. A hot oven will make any crust slip a little bit, but don't worry: It will stop when it hits the level of the custard, and the two of them will set together in heavenly bliss. For the most impressive mile-high slices, I bake this quiche in a deep-dish fluted quiche pan. You can also use the pan for my Pumpkin Pie Tart on page 232.

# FOOLPROOF SPINACH QUICHE

*SERVES 8*

## CRUST

1¼ cups (175 g) all-purpose flour, plus more for dusting

½ teaspoon (3 g) kosher salt

½ cup (113 g) cold salted American butter, diced

1 large egg

2 tablespoons (30 ml) ice water

1 teaspoon (3 g) cornstarch

## SPINACH-ONION FILLING

1 tablespoon (14 g) salted American butter

½ cup (75 g) diced yellow onion

Kosher salt and freshly cracked black pepper, to taste

5.25 ounces (149 g) baby spinach

## EGG CUSTARD

10 large eggs

½ cup (120 ml) heavy cream

½ cup (120 ml) whole milk

1 teaspoon (6 g) kosher salt

Freshly cracked black pepper, to taste

⅛ teaspoon (0.625 ml) cayenne or ground nutmeg

1 cup (90 g) grated Gruyère, divided

## NOTE

The thick pre-shredded Gruyère/Swiss cheese from Trader Joe's works well for this recipe.

1. **Make the crust:** Combine the flour and salt in a food processor and pulse. Add the butter and pulse again.

2. Combine the egg and ice water in a small bowl and add to the food processor, pulsing until a dough ball forms. Remove the dough and roll into a ball on a floured surface.

3. Roll out the dough into a 14-inch (36 cm), ¼-inch-thick (6 mm) circle and fit it into the bottom and sides of a 9½ × 2-inch (24 × 5 cm) deep-dish quiche pan with a removable bottom. Use the back of your palm to fit the dough into all the crevices. Cut the excess dough off the top so the dough is flush with the top of the pan.

4. Place the pan in the freezer for 25 minutes, until the dough is frozen and does not bend to the touch.

5. Preheat the oven to 350°F (175°C).

6. **Make the filling:** Melt the butter in a large sauté pan over medium-high heat. Add the onions and sauté until soft and translucent, about 2 minutes. Season with a good pinch of salt and pepper. Add the spinach and cook until wilted, 1 to 2 minutes. Set aside to cool.

7. **Make the egg custard:** Whisk the eggs in a large bowl. Add the milk, heavy cream, salt, pepper, and cayenne. Whisk to combine.

8. Remove the spinach-onion mixture from the pan, give it a rough chop, and then add it to the egg mixture. Add (½ cup/45 g) Gruyère and mix to combine.

9. Remove the tart pan from the freezer and place it on a baking sheet. Add the cornstarch to the bottom of the crust and smooth it out to create an even layer. Tap the excess around the sides to coat. Tap any excess out of the pan.

10. Add the remaining Gruyère to the bottom of the crust in an even layer. Pour the filling on top.

11. Bake for 60 minutes, or until golden brown and puffed up. The middle should not be concave, and the quiche should jiggle slightly.

12. Let cool until the pan is cool enough to touch. Then, remove the fluted form from the bottom by holding the quiche in one hand at the bottom and pushing it through the fluted form.

13. Slice into eight wedges and serve on a cake stand or platter.

## MAKE-AHEAD GAME PLAN

- Two days ahead, make the dough. Refrigerate until ready to use.

- One day ahead, make the quiche. Let cool completely and cover with foil. Refrigerate in the pan. To reheat, place the covered quiche on a sheet pan in a preheated 300°F (150°C) oven for 25 minutes and then uncover and heat for 10 minutes.

## PAIRS WELL WITH

Tossed salad with 1, 2, 3 French Vinaigrette (page 181)

No-Chop Fancy Fruit Salad (page 188)

# 1, 2, 3 FRENCH VINAIGRETTE

It wasn't until I was well into my twenties, on a trip to France with my husband, that I saw someone make salad dressing from scratch. My mother-in-law took a large salad bowl, added a dollop of mustard and a splash of vinegar, and then ever so slowly drizzled a "mystery oil" from a huge bottle labeled "Huile de Pépin." Even with my rudimentary French at the time, I knew that "huile" meant oil, but I couldn't for the life of me make out what a "pépin" was. Little did I know, this would be the start of a love affair with grapeseed oil. When combined with Dijon mustard and vinegar, this oil has the power to make a creamy, pungent French vinaigrette that is better than anything you'll ever buy in a bottle. It's easy to commit to memory because of the ratios of 1, 2, and 3. For the classic French touch, don't forget the minced shallots!

*SERVES 4* *(Makes ¼ cup/60 ml)*

1 tablespoon (15 ml) Dijon mustard

2 teaspoons (10 ml) white wine or champagne vinegar

3 tablespoons (45 ml) grapeseed oil

½ small shallot, minced

Kosher salt and freshly cracked black pepper, to taste

Pinch of herbes de Provence

One 5-ounce (142 g) bag baby greens, for serving

1. Whisk together the mustard and vinegar in a large bowl until combined (see Note). Slowly drizzle in the oil, whisking all the while, until all the dressing is thick and creamy. Stir in the shallot and season with salt, pepper, and herbes de Provence.

2. To serve, add the greens and toss to coat.

### NOTE

Something I've learned from my French in-laws is how to prep a salad for serving. They mix up the dressing in the salad bowl so it's all ready to go. Then, all they have to do is toss it with the greens before serving. Mixing the dressing in a large bowl also gives you a bigger surface area to create the emulsion. When you add the oil, it combines more easily with the mustard and vinegar, preventing the emulsion from separating.

### MAKE-AHEAD GAME PLAN

Up to four days ahead, make this dressing and store it in the refrigerator, covered. It may thicken a bit with refrigeration, but you can thin it out with water in 1-teaspoon (5 ml) increments.

### PAIRS WELL WITH

No-Chop Fancy Fruit Salad (page 188)

Old-School Lasagna (page 120)

# HIDE-AWAY GRANOLA

This granola is best kept hidden away, tucked in a cupboard—because if it sits on your countertop too long, every time you pass through the kitchen, you'll grab another fistful of it and pop it in your mouth, until it's all gone. It has a highly addictive quality to it, coming from the candied crunchy oats, buttery spiced pecans, and—my favorite part—those chewy baked raisins. It's a fantastic addition to any brunch buffet and works well in a "parfait bar." Simply set out a selection of yogurt and berries to serve with the granola and let your guests build their own signature parfaits.

**SERVES 6 TO 8** *(Makes 4 cups/450 g)*

1 teaspoon (5 ml) vegetable oil

1 large egg white

¼ cup (60 ml) honey

2 tablespoons (20 g) brown sugar

1 teaspoon (5 ml) vanilla extract

½ teaspoon (2.5 ml) ground cinnamon

Pinch of kosher salt

2 cups (160 g) old-fashioned oats (see Note 1)

¾ cup (64 g) pecans

1 cup (150 g) raisins (see Note 2)

### NOTES

1. Be sure to buy old-fashioned oats. This recipe will not work with quick-cooking oats.

2. For a holiday twist, replace the raisins with dried cranberries and add a large pinch of ground cloves and 1 teaspoon (5 ml) orange zest to the egg white mixture.

1. Preheat the oven to 350°F (175°C). Place the oven rack in the lower third of the oven. Grease a large baking sheet with the vegetable oil.

2. Whisk together the egg white, honey, brown sugar, vanilla, cinnamon, and salt in a large bowl. Add the oats and toss with a rubber spatula to coat. Stir in the pecans and toss well to coat.

3. Transfer the mixture to the baking sheet, spreading it out in a single layer.

4. Bake for 12 to 13 minutes and then toss the granola with a metal spatula. Add the raisins and bake for 12 to 13 minutes more, until the granola is golden brown and fragrant.

5. Remove the granola and allow it to cool completely for 1 hour for the best candied texture. It will harden as it cools. If it's still sticky after 15 minutes of cooling, pop it back in a 350°F (175°C) oven for 5 minutes.

6. Store in an airtight container at room temperature for up to one week.

### MAKE-AHEAD GAME PLAN

Two to three days ahead, make the granola. Store in an airtight container at room temperature.

### PAIRS WELL WITH

Connecticut Christmas Bread (page 199)

Puffy Egg Bake (page 169)

# HEAVENLY BUTTERMILK BISCUITS

For this New Englander, making a flaky buttermilk biscuit has always been a bit intimidating. But after attending the High Point Furniture Market in High Point, North Carolina, many times with my parents, I've come to love a good Southern biscuit. In fact, we used to get up extra early each morning just to hit the local Biscuitville on our way to the furniture showrooms. This biscuit recipe is the easiest, most straightforward approach to achieving flaky, buttery bliss. They take minutes to prepare, rise mile high, and are the perfect complement to my Fall-Off-the-Bone Sticky Ribs (page 117) or my Puffy Egg Bake (page 169) for brunch. Just pull the biscuit apart and spoon in the egg bake for the ultimate breakfast sandwich!

*MAKES 9 BISCUITS*

2¼ cups (315 g) all-purpose flour, plus more for dusting

2½ teaspoons (10 g) baking powder

¾ teaspoon (5 g) kosher salt

½ cup (113 g) cold salted American butter, diced, plus 1 tablespoon (14 g), melted

1 cup (240 ml) cold buttermilk

### NOTES

1. Biscuit dough is not like bread dough; it does not need to be kneaded. The more you work it, the tougher your biscuits will be. So, manipulate it very gently. This will preserve its flakiness.

2. Folding the dough will create a flakier biscuit.

3. Do not twist the cutter to release the biscuit. Twisting will prevent the biscuit from rising and achieving its full flaky potential!

4. Cutting the biscuits in three stages will preserve the ½-inch (1 cm) thickness of the dough.

5. Baking the biscuits this way will allow them to rise equally as one mass while maintaining their soft interior texture.

1. Preheat the oven to 450°F (230°C). Line a baking sheet with parchment paper.

2. Whisk together the flour, baking powder, and salt in a large bowl.

3. Sprinkle the diced butter evenly over the flour mixture. Press the butter into the flour with your fingertips to form a coarse meal, working for 3 to 4 minutes.

4. Stir in the buttermilk with a Danish dough whisk or a wooden spoon to form a scraggly dough. Do not overmix or add any more buttermilk, or your biscuits will be rubbery.

5. Sprinkle 1 tablespoon (8 g) flour on a cutting board and smooth it out to cover.

6. Transfer the dough to the board. Gently form it into a ball, rolling it around the board to catch the flour, until it's no longer sticky (see Note 1).

7. Sprinkle a dusting of flour over your rolling pin and on the dough ball. Gently roll out the dough to a 10-inch-long (25 cm) rectangle. Fold the bottom half up to meet the top half. Rotate it one turn to the right and gently roll it out again to another 10-inch-long (25 cm) rectangle (see Note 2).

8. Fold the dough in half again and rotate it one turn to the right. Roll it out again to a loose ½-inch-thick (1 cm) square.

9. Dip a 2¾-inch (7 cm) metal biscuit cutter into a shallow bowl of flour to coat, and cut out six biscuits. Press the cutter down to cut the biscuits, lift it straight up, and then remove the scraps to release the biscuits (see Note 3).

10. Bring the scraps together and roll out to a 4-inch-long (10 cm) rectangle. Fold the bottom half up to the top half, and roll it out again. Cut out two biscuits, repeat the folding technique one more time, and cut out the last remaining biscuit (see Note 4).

11. Place the biscuits on the baking sheet, making sure they touch (see Note 5). Create three rows of three biscuits each.

12. Bake for 14 to 15 minutes, until risen and golden brown. Brush the biscuit tops with melted butter and serve.

### MAKE-AHEAD GAME PLAN

These biscuits are best enjoyed fresh and hot out of the oven, but you could bake them up to 2 hours ahead of time. Leave them at room temperature, loosely covered with a sheet of foil, and then place them in a preheated 300°F (150°C) oven for 10 to 15 minutes, until warmed through. Brush with the melted butter before serving.

### PAIRS WELL WITH

Fall-Off-the-Bone Sticky Ribs (page 117)

Puffy Egg Bake (page 169)

# BETTER THAN STORE-BOUGHT
# CHEDDAR SCONES

A store-bought scone and a homemade scone are worlds apart. Much like the family dog and the gray wolf, they may look alike, but that's where the similarity ends. A store-bought scone, with its typical dryness and bland flavor, could turn you off scones forever. But a homemade scone, served warm from your oven, with its flaky, buttery texture, will turn you into a scone baker for life. Serve these at a brunch with your favorite egg dish or with soups and salads for something a bit fancier than the predictable dinner roll.

*SERVES 8*

2 cups (280 g) all-purpose flour, plus more for dusting

2 teaspoons (8 g) baking powder

¾ teaspoon (5 g) kosher salt

½ teaspoon (2.5 ml) cayenne

10 tablespoons (150 g) cold salted American butter, diced

1 cup (100 g) shredded sharp cheddar

1 bunch scallions, thinly sliced into ¼-inch (6 mm) rings (about 1 cup/80 g)

⅔ cup (160 ml) heavy cream

1 large egg

¼ teaspoon (1 g) fleur de sel salt

Freshly cracked black pepper, to taste

## NOTE

The dough should be well chilled before hitting the oven, as this will preserve the scones' shape and prevent them from spreading out too much while baking.

1. Preheat the oven to 400°F (200°C). Place the oven rack in the lower third of the oven. Line a baking sheet with parchment paper to ensure soft-bottomed scones.

2. Whisk together the flour, baking powder, salt, and cayenne in a large bowl. Add the butter, working it into the flour with your fingertips to form a coarse meal. Add the cheese and scallions and toss together with your hands to combine.

3. Pour the heavy cream into a 2-cup (480 ml) measuring cup. Add the egg and whisk to combine. Create a well in the center of the flour mixture and pour the cream-egg mixture inside. (Do not wash out the measuring cup. Reserve the liquid that has collected on the sides and bottom: You'll use it to brush the tops of the scones before baking.)

4. Gently stir the mixture with a fork, combining the wet and dry ingredients to form a wet, sticky dough.

5. Turn the dough out onto a well-floured surface, adding more flour as needed to remove any stickiness. Form the dough into a ball and then press down gently to create a flat disc, 1½ inches (4 cm) thick.

6. Flour a chef's knife. Use it to square up the edges of the dough to create an 8-inch (20 cm) square. Cut the square in half vertically and then horizontally to create four equal squares.

7. Add more flour to the knife as needed to prevent sticking and then use the knife to tighten up the corners of each square, pressing the knife edge against the dough to form clean, neat edges. Cut each square in half diagonally to create triangles.

8. Transfer the triangles to the baking sheet. Brush the triangles with the leftover cream-egg mixture. Top with a sprinkle of fleur de sel and pepper.

9. Place the scones in the refrigerator, uncovered, for 15 minutes or in the freezer for 5 minutes to firm up (see Note).

10. Bake for 25 minutes, or until the scones are golden brown. Serve immediately.

## MAKE-AHEAD GAME PLAN

One day ahead, make, shape, and cut the scone dough. Brush with the cream-egg mixture and then cover and refrigerate. Just before baking, add the salt and pepper.

## PAIRS WELL WITH

A Little Bit Lighter Gazpacho (page 96)

Puffy Egg Bake (page 169)

# NO-CHOP FANCY FRUIT SALAD

Fruit salads are not all created equal. The worst of them are on display at your local brunch spot. You know the kind, served on the side of your omelet and typically loaded with unripe melon, sliced grapes, and, if you're lucky, a strawberry or two. But when hosting a brunch at home, we can do better! This recipe creates something far easier that doesn't involve scooping out melon and plucking off grapes. It's as easy as it gets because there's hardly any prep involved. Just rinse the berries, pop them in a bowl, add the pomegranate arils and mint, and you're done!

### SERVES 6 TO 8

12 ounces (340 g) fresh raspberries

12 ounces (340 g) fresh blueberries

12 ounces (340 g) fresh blackberries

4 ounces (113 g) pomegranate arils (see Note)

1 bunch fresh mint

#### NOTE

You can find pomegranate arils (seeds) at Trader Joe's or most major supermarkets in the refrigerated produce section. If you can't get ahold of these, you can buy a whole pomegranate and seed it yourself.

1. Rinse the berries and pat them dry with a paper towel.

2. Place the berries in a large, shallow serving bowl. Sprinkle the pomegranate arils on top.

3. Pluck the top leaves off the mint sprigs to garnish the bowl with 5 to 6 little mint sprigs. Or, if you don't mind getting out the knife, you can stack the mint leaves, roll them into a "cigar," and slice thin ribbons of mint to garnish.

#### MAKE-AHEAD GAME PLAN
Two hours ahead, assemble and refrigerate the fruit salad. Just before serving, add the fresh mint.

#### PAIRS WELL WITH
Baked Banana French Toast with Rum Raisin Syrup (page 174)

Hide-Away Granola (page 183)

# ULTIMATE BANANA BREAD

Banana bread is the type of recipe that warrants bragging rights. Ask anyone for the best banana bread recipe, and chances are, someone in their bloodline can claim it. Whether it's Mom, Dad, Grandma, or Aunt Susie, this person has cracked the code. Well, I'm throwing my hat into the ring with this one! It's moist, fluffy, and totally delicious, studded with buttery nuts and specks of bittersweet chocolate. It's been one of the top EWB fan favorites since my channel launched back in 2012, and with 1.6 million views and counting, it remains a cherished recipe in my archive.

***SERVES 6 TO 8*** *(Makes one 9½ × 5½-inch/24 × 14 cm loaf)*

Baking spray with flour

2½ cups (350 g) all-purpose flour

2 teaspoons (8 g) baking soda

½ teaspoon (3 g) kosher salt

4 large overripe bananas, gently mashed with a fork (about 1⅓ cups/300 g; see Note 1)

3 large eggs

¾ cup (180 ml) vegetable oil

½ cup (100 g) granulated sugar (see Note 2)

¼ cup (60 ml) water

1 tablespoon (15 ml) vanilla extract

½ cup (70 g) chopped Ghirardelli 60% cacao bittersweet chocolate

½ cup (60 g) chopped pecans or walnuts

## NOTES

1. No ripe bananas? No problem! You can "ripen" them in the oven. Preheat the oven to 300°F (150°C) and line a baking sheet with foil. Place the bananas on top and bake for 10 to 15 minutes, flipping halfway through, until the peels are black. Let cool and then scoop out the flesh and mash if needed.

2. I find that this recipe has enough sugar for my taste buds, especially if your bananas are very ripe and you are also adding the chocolate, but if you have a sweet tooth, increase the sugar to ¾ cup (150 g).

1. Preheat the oven to 350°F (175°C). Place the oven rack in the lower third of the oven.

2. Spray a 9½ × 5½ × 2½ inch (24 × 14 × 6.5 cm) loaf pan with baking spray.

3. Whisk together the flour, baking soda, and salt in a medium bowl. Mix the bananas, eggs, vegetable oil, sugar, water, and vanilla in a large bowl.

4. Gently add the dry ingredients to the wet ingredients, in thirds, mixing with a large wire whisk. Be careful not to overmix, or you will have tough bread. Stir in the chocolate and nuts.

5. Pour the batter into the loaf pan. Bake for 55 minutes, or until a toothpick comes out clean. If the bread starts to brown too much on top, cover it with foil and continue to bake until baked through.

6. Let cool before slicing into thick slices and serving.

### MAKE-AHEAD GAME PLAN

Two days ahead, make the bread. Leave it in the pan, cover, and refrigerate. When ready to serve, place it in a 300°F (150°C) oven to reheat and freshen up.

### PAIRS WELL WITH

No-Chop Fancy Fruit Salad (page 188)

Homemade Hot Chocolate (page 39)

# THE CINNAMON ROLL PROJECT

I call these cinnamon rolls a "project" because—let's face it—cinnamon rolls *are* a project. But if you want an otherworldly *Cinnamon Roll Experience*, you cannot cheat the steps: mixing, rising, rolling, baking, *and* dragging out the electric mixer for the frosting are all part of the process. These are not the "quick and easy" Christmas breakfast solution. (For that, turn to my Connecticut Christmas Bread on page 199.) Instead, make these rolls for Christmas brunch, when you have the morning to prep. I *promise* they are well worth the effort! Serve the frosting on the side to allow your guests to slather it on. But truth be told, these cinnamon rolls are so delicious and flavorful, some guests may prefer to go without the frosting and enjoy them "au naturel."

---

### *MAKES 12 ROLLS*

---

**ROLLS**

1 cup (240 ml) warm water (120°F to 130°F/50°C to 54°C)

⅓ cup (66 g) granulated sugar

One 0.25-ounce (7 g) packet dry active yeast (2¼ teaspoons/11.25 ml)

1 large egg

⅓ cup (80 ml) whole milk

6 tablespoons (84 g) salted American butter, melted, plus 1 tablespoon (14 g) for greasing

2 tablespoons (30 ml) orange zest (from 2 large oranges)

1 tablespoon (15 ml) vanilla extract

1 teaspoon (6 g) kosher salt

½ cup (75 g) raisins

¼ cup (60 ml) orange juice (from 2 oranges)

4 cups (560 g) all-purpose flour, plus more for dusting

**FILLING**

¼ cup plus 2 tablespoons (75 g) granulated sugar

¼ cup plus 2 tablespoons (60 g) light brown sugar

1 tablespoon (15 ml) ground cinnamon

4 tablespoons (56 g) salted American butter, melted and cooled

½ cup (60 g) finely chopped pecans

**FROSTING**

24 ounces (680 g) whipped cream cheese

1 cup (120 g) powdered sugar

1 tablespoon (15 ml) vanilla extract

1 to 2 tablespoons (15 to 30 ml) heavy cream (optional)

1. **Make the rolls:** Whisk the water, sugar, and yeast in a large bowl. Let sit for 5 minutes, until cloudy and foamy.

2. Add the egg, milk, 6 tablespoons (90 ml) melted butter, orange zest, vanilla, and salt to the yeast mixture and whisk to combine.

3. Place the raisins in a small bowl. Pour the orange juice over the raisins and soak them for 5 to 8 minutes until plump. Then drain the raisins, discard the juice, and add the raisins to the mixture.

4. Add the flour to the wet ingredients, in thirds, mixing with a wooden spoon or a Danish dough whisk to form a sticky dough.

5. Turn the dough out onto a floured surface and knead for 15 to 20 turns, until it's a more workable dough. Grease a large bowl with the remaining butter and then form the dough into a ball and place it into the bowl. Cover the bowl with plastic wrap and let the dough rise at room temperature for 1 hour, until doubled in size.

6. **Meanwhile, make the filling:** Whisk together the granulated sugar, brown sugar, and cinnamon in a small bowl.

7. Preheat the oven to 350°F (175°C). Line a 9×13-inch (23×33 cm) oven-safe casserole dish with a 12×16-inch (30×41 cm) sheet of parchment paper; it should hang over the sides for easy removal of the buns once baked.

8. Remove the dough from the bowl and place it on a well-floured surface, rolling it around in the flour until the dough is easy to handle and no longer wet.

9. Roll it out to a rough 15×16-inch (38×41 cm) rectangle. Pour the 4 tablespoons (60 ml) cooled melted butter on the dough. Then, sprinkle the sugar mixture on top, rubbing it gently into the dough to coat well. Sprinkle the pecans evenly on top.

10. Starting from the long end of the rectangle, roll the dough away from you and tightly into a log. Give it one last roll so it ends up seam side down.

11. Slice the log into twelve 1¼-inch rolls (3 cm) and fit them into the baking dish in four rows, three to a row.

12. Bake for 35 to 40 minutes, until golden brown and well risen.

13. **Meanwhile, make the frosting.** Beat together the cream cheese and powdered sugar in the bowl of an electric mixer until smooth. Add the vanilla. If the frosting is too thick, add the heavy cream in 1-tablespoon (15 ml) increments to reach your desired consistency.

14. Transfer the frosting to a small bowl and serve it on the side.

**MAKE-AHEAD GAME PLAN**

• One day ahead, make the frosting. Cover and refrigerate, and bring to room temperature 30 minutes before serving. Make the filling. Cover and store at room temperature.

**PAIRS WELL WITH**

No-Chop Fancy Fruit Salad (page 188)

Puffy Egg Bake (page 169)

# HAM, LEEK, AND GRUYÈRE STRATA

This strata might just be the king of all brunch dishes. It's filled with the hopes and dreams all brunches are made of—toasty bread, cheesy eggs, salty ham—and best of all, it can be made the night before. In fact, it's even better that way! All you have to do the next day is bake and serve. Assembling the strata ahead of time allows the bread to soak up all the egg filling, which leads to a soft, custardy texture that is somewhere between a quiche and a soufflé. It looks beautiful when baked in a large gratin pan, allowing everyone to get a little bit of the crispy, cheesy topping, but a casserole dish works well, too. Pop it in the oven right as guests arrive, and it will be done as soon as you offer them a second mimosa.

*SERVES 6 TO 8*

1 tablespoon (14 g) salted American butter

1 tablespoon (15 ml) olive oil

3 large leeks, white parts only, sliced into half-moons (about 1¾ cups/125 g)

8 large eggs

Kosher salt and freshly cracked black pepper, to taste

1½ cups (360 ml) heavy cream

1½ cups (360 ml) whole milk

⅓ cup (80 ml) dry white wine (chardonnay or sauvignon blanc)

2 tablespoons (30 ml) Dijon mustard

3 tablespoons (45 ml) minced chives, divided

1 pound (454 g) rustic French, Italian, or sourdough bread, cut into 1-inch (2.5 cm) cubes

6 ounces (170 g) Black Forest ham, chopped

1¼ cups (119 g) shredded Gruyère (see Note)

## NOTE

The thick pre-shredded Gruyère/Swiss cheese from Trader Joe's works well for this recipe.

1. Grease an 11×14-inch (28×36 cm) gratin dish or 9×14-inch (23×36 cm) oven-safe casserole dish with the butter. Heat the olive oil in a large nonstick skillet over medium-high heat.

2. Sauté the leeks in the oil until soft, fragrant, and golden brown, 3 to 5 minutes. Set aside to cool.

3. Whisk together the eggs, salt, and pepper in a large bowl. Add the heavy cream, milk, wine, mustard, and 2 tablespoons (30 ml) chives.

4. Add the bread cubes and toss gently in the egg mixture until well coated and saturated. Stir in the ham, ½ cup (48 g) Gruyère, and the leeks.

5. Transfer the mixture to the prepared dish and top with the remaining cheese. Cover and refrigerate for at least 4 hours (overnight is even better).

6. Preheat the oven to 375°F (190°C). Place the oven rack in the lower third of the oven. Remove the strata from the refrigerator while the oven preheats.

7. Bake, covered, for 40 minutes. Uncover and bake for 15 to 20 minutes, until the bread cubes are golden brown and the cheese is bubbling. No egg liquid should be visible when you press gently on the strata with your fingertips.

8. Garnish with pepper and the remaining chives.

## MAKE-AHEAD GAME PLAN

The night before, prepare the casserole. I highly recommend this to give the bread cubes time to soak. The strata's texture will be softer and creamier.

## PAIRS WELL WITH

Tossed green salad with 1, 2, 3 French Vinaigrette (page 181)

DIY Bloody Mary Bar (page 31)

# CLASSIC COFFEE CAKE
## WITH DOUBLE CRUMB TOPPING

When I was growing up on the East Coast, this type of brunch cake was known as a "coffee cake" despite not having any coffee *in* the cake. It was a cake you served *with* coffee. As I got older, I noticed that West Coasters would call it a crumb cake. But in my mind, it will always be a coffee cake. This recipe reminds me of those little coffee cakes we used to buy at the gas station as kids, but way better! At our house, there's always a debate about which is better: the crunchy sweet crumb topping or the fluffy cake. I go heavy on the topping so that it's an equal match since they are both so good!

*MAKES 9 SQUARES*

### CRUMB TOPPING

2 cups (280 g) all-purpose flour

½ cup (100 g) granulated sugar

½ cup (80 g) light brown sugar

2½ teaspoons (12.5 ml) ground cinnamon

2 teaspoons (8 g) baking powder

½ teaspoon (2.5 ml) ground allspice

Pinch of kosher salt

1 cup (226 g) salted American butter, melted

2 teaspoons (10 ml) vanilla extract

1 tablespoon (8 g) powdered sugar

### CAKE

½ cup (113 g) salted American butter, room temperature

¾ cup (150 g) granulated sugar

2 large eggs

1 tablespoon (15 ml) vanilla extract

2 cups (280 g) all-purpose flour

2 teaspoons (8 g) baking powder

½ teaspoon (3 g) kosher salt

½ cup (120 ml) whole milk

#### NOTE

It will look like a ton of crumbs! But as it bakes, it will settle into a compacted 1-inch (2.5 cm) layer.

1. Preheat the oven to 350°F (175°C). Place the oven rack in the lower third of the oven.

2. Line a 9-inch (23 cm) square baking pan with parchment paper. Cut two sheets of parchment to the width of the pan, leaving 4-inch (10 cm) overhangs that rise over two sides of the pan in opposing directions.

3. **Make the topping:** Whisk together the flour, granulated sugar, brown sugar, cinnamon, baking powder, allspice, and salt in a large bowl. Add the butter and vanilla, whisk with a fork, and then mix with your fingertips until small crumbs form.

4. **Make the cake:** Beat together the butter and sugar in the bowl of an electric mixer until soft and fluffy. Add the eggs one at a time and beat well, scraping down the bowl in between each addition. Beat in the vanilla.

5. Whisk together the flour, baking powder, and salt in a small bowl. Add the flour mixture to the butter-sugar mixture in thirds, alternating with the milk, scraping down the bowl as needed, until a batter forms.

6. Transfer the batter to the baking pan. Spread it out to the corners and the sides with an offset spatula and then smooth it out to form an even layer.

7. Sprinkle the crumb topping all over the batter to cover, forming an even layer (see Note).

8. Bake for 25 to 30 minutes, until the cake is golden brown and risen and a toothpick comes out clean.

9. Let cool for 10 to 15 minutes. Remove the cake from the pan by lifting up the parchment paper overhangs. Dust with powdered sugar, cut into nine squares, and serve.

**MAKE-AHEAD GAME PLAN**
- One day ahead, make the crumb topping. Cover and refrigerate.
- Two hours ahead, make the cake. Cover lightly and keep at room temperature until ready to serve.

**PAIRS WELL WITH**
No-Chop Fancy Fruit Salad (page 188)

Puffy Egg Bake (page 169)

# CONNECTICUT CHRISTMAS BREAD

When I was growing up in New England, my parents had a fascination with all things colonial at Christmas. This meant the house was always festooned with natural decorations sourced from our yard. It resembled something out of Colonial Williamsburg. My siblings and I were envious of the multicolored lights and tinsel that hung on our friends' trees because at our house, it was a different story. You'd find evergreens and berries tucked on top of portraits, cranberry popcorn garland strung on the tree, and, of course, a huge pile of orange and clove pomander balls in the front hall. It took us hours to create those balls after our parents convinced us it would be a fun weekend project. I still wince when I see a whole clove in my spice cabinet, remembering the pain in our thumbs! But this is why I love this recipe so much: It's a Connecticut Christmas rolled into one totally delicious snack bread. The bread is light and fluffy and extra moist, and you'll love the delicate flavor coming from the orange zest and ground cloves. I make it every Christmas morning in Los Angeles when I'm homesick for the snowy woods of New England.

**SERVES 6 TO 8** *(Makes one 9½ × 5½-inch/24 × 14 cm loaf)*

Baking spray with flour

3 large eggs

1¼ cups (250 g) granulated sugar

12 tablespoons (169 g) salted American butter, melted and cooled

½ cup (120 ml) water

¼ cup (60 ml) vegetable oil

2 tablespoons (30 ml) coarsely grated orange zest (from 2 large navel oranges)

1 teaspoon (5 ml) vanilla extract

2⅓ cups (326 g) all-purpose flour

2 teaspoons (8 g) baking powder

1 teaspoon (5 ml) ground cloves

1 teaspoon (6 g) kosher salt

1½ cups (175 g) fresh cranberries, rinsed and dried

½ cup (68 g) walnuts, chopped

1. Preheat the oven to 350°F (175°C). Place the oven rack in the lower third of the oven. Spray a 9½ × 5½ × 2½-inch (24×14×6.5 cm) loaf pan with baking spray.

2. Whisk together the eggs, sugar, butter, water, vegetable oil, orange zest, and vanilla in a large bowl.

3. Whisk together the flour, baking powder, cloves, and salt in a medium bowl.

4. Slowly add the dry ingredients, in thirds, to the wet ingredients, whisking until just combined. Stir in the cranberries and walnuts.

5. Transfer the batter to the loaf pan, and smooth it out with a spatula.

6. Bake for 55 to 60 minutes, until a skewer comes out clean. If the bread is becoming too browned before the center is fully baked, cover it loosely with a sheet of foil.

7. Let cool for 15 minutes before slicing and serving.

**MAKE-AHEAD GAME PLAN**

This bread is best enjoyed the day it's made. But if you want to make it a day ahead, bake it, keep it in the pan, cover, and refrigerate. To reheat (and freshen up!), place the covered pan in a preheated 300°F (150°C) oven for 20 minutes and then bake uncovered for 5 minutes.

**PAIRS WELL WITH**

Puffy Egg Bake (page 169)

Set it and Forget it Smoked Salmon (page 170)

# DESSERTS

# DANGEROUSLY DELICIOUS
# CHOCOLATE CHIP COOKIES

Let's face it: Everyone should know how to make a fantastic chocolate chip cookie. But the older I get, the more my taste buds have changed. The chocolate chip cookies of my youth just don't seem to cut it anymore. These days, I crave a cookie that is less sweet. It must also be chewy on the inside *and* crispy on the outside. To achieve the best flavor and texture, I brown the butter first. *I know, I know,* it's a trend most people wish would die off. But trust me: Browning the butter is worth doing because it gives these cookies a subtle caramel flavor. And the chunks of bittersweet chocolate feel a bit more grown-up than traditional semisweet chocolate chips. These cookies are dangerously delicious! You do not want to be left unsupervised with them because you cannot eat just one. Okay, you've been warned. Now, bake responsibly!

---

*MAKES 9 COOKIES*

---

½ cup (113 g) salted American butter

½ cup (100 g) granulated sugar

½ cup (80 g) light brown sugar

1 large egg

2 teaspoons (10 ml) vanilla extract

1¼ cups (175 g) all-purpose flour

1 teaspoon (4 g) baking soda

½ teaspoon (3 g) kosher salt

4 ounces (113 g) Ghirardelli 60% cacao bittersweet chocolate, roughly chopped (see Note 1)

Sprinkle of fleur de sel salt (optional)

1. Preheat the oven to 350°F (175°C). Place the oven rack in the lower third of the oven. Line two baking sheets with parchment paper.

2. Melt the butter in a nonstick skillet over medium-high heat until foamy. Then, swirl it around the pan until it starts to turn amber in color, then translucent, then a rich brown, 4 to 5 minutes.

3. Transfer the brown butter to a small heat-safe Pyrex pitcher and let it come to room temperature, 30 to 40 minutes (see Note 2).

4. Combine the granulated sugar, brown sugar, and brown butter in the bowl of an electric mixer. Be sure to add any sediment that has collected in the bottom of the pitcher—that's where all the flavor is. Beat on high to form a sandy texture, 2 to 3 minutes.

5. Add the egg and beat until a smooth texture forms, 3 to 4 minutes. Scrape down the bowl as needed. Stir in the vanilla.

6. Whisk together the flour, baking soda, and salt in a medium bowl. Add the dry ingredients, in thirds, to the wet ingredients, scraping down the bowl in between each addition, until combined. Add the chocolate and beat until just combined.

7. Using a 2-ounce (60 ml) cookie scoop (see Note 3), portion out six dough balls on one sheet and three on the other, scraping the scoop against the bowl to get a flat bottom. This will ensure that your dough balls are the same size and will bake at the same rate. Leave room in between for the cookies to spread.

8. Bake one tray at a time for 12 to 13 minutes, until the cookies are puffed up, golden brown, and beginning to crack slightly.

9. Let cool for 5 minutes on the baking sheet. The residual heat from the pan will help the cookies set. Sprinkle with the fleur de sel if desired and then transfer to a cooling rack before serving (see Note 4).

## NOTES

1. Not all chocolate melts alike. You'll get the best flavor and melt from the Ghirardelli 60% cacao chocolate.

2. This is key! It cannot be the least bit warm, or it will melt the sugar too much and you will have a thinner cookie.

3. For smaller cookies, use a 1-ounce (30 ml) cookie scoop to make twenty 3-inch (7.5 cm) cookies. Bake these for 8 to 9 minutes.

4. These cookies are great on their own, but they also make fantastic ice cream sandwiches! Sandwich a scoop of vanilla ice cream between two cookies. Press down to flatten. Then, place them on a baking sheet, cover with foil, and freeze until ready to serve.

## MAKE-AHEAD GAME PLAN

Up to one month ahead, make the cookies and freeze. Thaw at room temperature or pop in the microwave for 10 to 15 seconds until warmed through.

## PAIRS WELL WITH

Easy Gourmet Burgers (page 137)

All-Occasion Cut Sugar Cookies (page 221)

# BETTER THAN BOX-MIX
# BROWNIE SUNDAES

Mention the phrase "box-mix brownies," and a few attributes come to mind: a shiny and crackly top, a moist and fudgy interior, and a soft and chewy exterior. But the one thing I find missing is a deep chocolate flavor. This recipe combines the best of both worlds: the texture and appearance of a box-mix brownie and the deep chocolate flavor that comes with a homemade one! While it may be hard to beat the convenience of a box mix, this recipe comes close because it can all be mixed up in one pot. No mixing bowls, sifters, or stand mixers involved! Serve these brownies on their own, or add a scoop of vanilla ice cream and a drizzle of my hot fudge sauce for the ultimate brownie sundae.

*MAKES 9 BROWNIE SUNDAES*

## BROWNIES

1 cup (226 g) salted American butter

8 ounces (227 g) Ghirardelli 60% cacao bittersweet chocolate, broken into pieces

2 cups (400 g) granulated sugar

4 large eggs

1½ teaspoons (7.5 ml) vanilla extract

½ teaspoon (3 g) kosher salt

1¼ cups (175 g) all-purpose flour

Vanilla ice cream, for serving

## HOT FUDGE SAUCE

One 12-ounce (340 g) package semisweet chocolate chips

⅔ cup (160 ml) heavy cream

1 tablespoon (15 ml) honey

1 teaspoon (5 ml) vanilla extract

1. Preheat the oven to 350°F (175°C). Place the oven rack in the lower third of the oven. Line a 9-inch (23 cm) square baking pan with parchment paper cut to the size of the bottom of the pan, with 4-inch (10 cm) overhangs that rise over two sides of the pan in opposing directions.

2. **Make the brownies:** Heat the butter in a medium saucepan over medium-low heat until a thin layer of melted butter coats the bottom. Add the chocolate (see Note 1) and whisk until the chocolate and butter are completely melted.

3. Add the sugar and whisk to combine. Add the eggs, one at a time, whisking very well in between each addition. Add the vanilla and salt and then add the flour and whisk to combine.

4. Stir the batter with a rubber spatula to make sure no melted chocolate has stuck to the bottom and all the ingredients are incorporated. Transfer the batter to the prepared pan, smoothing out into an even layer with a spatula. Tap the pan on the counter to remove any air bubbles.

5. Bake for 28 to 30 minutes, until a toothpick comes out clean. For the best flavor and texture, let cool for 1 hour (see Note 2).

6. **Make the sauce:** Heat the chocolate chips and heavy cream in a medium saucepan over medium-high heat. Whisk until the chocolate chips are melted and the sauce is smooth and shiny, 2 to 3 minutes. Add the honey and vanilla and whisk to combine.

7. Slice the brownies into nine squares and serve with ice cream and hot fudge on top.

## NOTES

1. The layer of melted butter will prevent the chocolate from scorching.

2. I know this is torture. But the brownie interior needs to cool and set to achieve its lovely chewy yet fudgy texture.

## MAKE-AHEAD GAME PLAN

- Two days ahead, make the sauce. Transfer it to a 2-cup (480 ml) heat-safe Pyrex pitcher. To reheat, microwave on high in 15-second intervals until hot and liquified.

- One day ahead, make the brownies. They are even better—and chewier—when made in advance. Cover and store at room temperature until ready to serve.

## PAIRS WELL WITH

Easy Gourmet Burgers (page 137)

Perfect Lemon Bars (page 236)

# FULLY LOADED CARROT CAKE

For me, carrot cake must be "fully loaded" or the deal is off. It must have fresh fruit (pineapple) and dried fruit (raisins); it needs buttery nuts (pecans) and shredded coconut (unsweetened). It must be extra moist and not too sweet. And most of all, the frosting should play a supporting role to the shining star, the cake. I know it's a lot to ask, but carrot cake, in my opinion, can go really wrong—usually in the form of a dried-out, flavorless cake, masked with overly sweet frosting. It's a classic springtime dessert that deserves a straightforward, easy approach. I've spent years perfecting this recipe, and this cake is it! It's extra moist and perfectly spiced, and the frosting is lightly sweetened, with a luscious, billowy texture. It's a fan favorite in the EWB archive, and if you haven't tried it, you are in for a treat!

# FULLY LOADED CARROT CAKE

*SERVES 8 TO 10*

## CAKE
Baking spray with flour

4 large eggs

1 cup (240 ml) vegetable oil

¾ cup (150 g) granulated sugar

¾ cup (120 g) brown sugar

8 ounces (227 g) crushed pineapple, undrained (see Note 1)

2 teaspoons (10 ml) vanilla extract

2 cups (280 g) all-purpose flour

2 teaspoons (8 g) baking powder

1½ teaspoons (6 g) baking soda

2 teaspoons (10 ml) ground cinnamon

½ teaspoon (3 g) kosher salt

2 cups/334 g grated carrots (2–3 large carrots; see Note 2)

1 cup (150 g) raisins

½ cup (48 g) unsweetened shredded coconut

⅓ cup (60 g) finely chopped pecans

## FROSTING
16 ounces (454 g) whipped cream cheese, room temperature

⅔ cup (80 g) powdered sugar

1 cup (240 ml) heavy cream

1 teaspoon (5 ml) vanilla

## GARNISH
⅓ cup (60 g) finely chopped pecans

1 tablespoon (15 ml) grated carrots

1. Preheat the oven to 350°F (175°C). Place the oven rack in the lower third of the oven. Spray two 9-inch (23 cm) round cake pans with baking spray and line the bottom of the pans with parchment paper (see Note 3).

2. **Make the cake:** Whisk together the eggs, vegetable oil, granulated sugar, and brown sugar in a large bowl. Add the pineapple and vanilla and whisk to combine.

3. Whisk together the flour, baking powder, baking soda, cinnamon, and salt in a medium bowl. Slowly add the dry ingredients to the wet ingredients, in thirds, whisking until combined. Add the carrots, raisins, coconut, and pecans, and stir to combine.

4. Pour the batter equally into the prepared pans. Bake for 25 to 30 minutes, until a toothpick comes out clean. Let cool completely.

5. **Make the frosting:** Beat the cream cheese and powdered sugar in the bowl of an electric mixer with the paddle attachment until smooth, scraping down the bowl as needed.

6. Add the heavy cream and vanilla and beat on high for 5 to 7 minutes, until the mixture is smooth and the volume has increased by one-third.

7. Remove the first cake from the pan: With one hand on the top of the cake and the other hand on the bottom of the pan, flip the cake upside down. Place the cake on the cake stand, flat side up. Frost the top of the cake only (see Note 4). Add the second cake layer (flat side up) and frost the top only, leaving the sides bare.

8. **Add the garnish:** Sprinkle pecans around the edge of the cake and then add the grated carrots in the center.

9. Refrigerate the cake, uncovered, for at least 1 to 2 hours to set. Slice and serve.

## NOTES

1. Use an 8-ounce (227 g) can of pineapple, and don't drain it. The juice is the exact amount you need to add moisture to the cake.

2. Avoid buying pre-grated carrots; they are too coarse and thick for this recipe. It's better to grate them yourself with the largest holes of a box grater.

3. Spraying the pans and lining the bottoms may seem like a pesky thing to do, but this cake is so moist that it's necessary. Otherwise, half your cake will stick to the bottom of the pan when you try to release it.

4. Frosting the flat side will make the cake easier to frost.

## MAKE-AHEAD GAME PLAN

- One day ahead, make the cake and keep it refrigerated.

- At least 45 minutes before serving, remove the cake from the refrigerator to allow it to come to room temperature. This improves the texture of the frosting and the flavor of the cake.

## PAIRS WELL WITH

Easy Grilled Salmon with Mango Salsa (page 127)

Sheet-Pan Lamb with Caramelized Shallots and Provençal Tomatoes (page 110)

# LEMON-SCENTED
# STRAWBERRY SHORTCAKES

Strawberry shortcakes are an elegant dessert to serve a crowd. They are as beautiful as they are delicious, and when strawberries are in season, there's no better move. The delicate shortcake is light and moist and requires no rolling out or cutting. An ice cream scoop is all you need! This dessert is flavored with both lemon zest and limoncello, which are the perfect complements to the ripe strawberries and luscious homemade whipped cream. And if you gather a group of helpers, putting it together is also fun! Form a short assembly line, with each person helping to move the process along so it doesn't become too cumbersome for the host. It's a fun bonding exercise that will make your guests feel like they all had a hand in making the dessert.

*SERVES 8*

## SHORTCAKES

1¾ cups (245 g) all-purpose flour

2 tablespoons (25 g) granulated sugar

2¼ teaspoons (9 g) baking powder

½ teaspoon (3 g) kosher salt

2 tablespoons (30 ml) lemon zest

½ cup (113 g) cold salted American butter, diced

1 large egg

1 cup (240 ml) heavy cream

1 teaspoon (5 ml) pure lemon extract

1 teaspoon (5 g) turbinado sugar

2 tablespoons (16 g) powdered sugar, for dusting

## STRAWBERRIES

1 pound (454 g) strawberries, hulled and quartered

2 tablespoons (25 g) granulated sugar

1 tablespoon (15 ml) limoncello liqueur (see Note)

## WHIPPED CREAM

1½ cups (360 ml) heavy cream

2 tablespoons (16 g) powdered sugar

1½ teaspoons (7.5 ml) vanilla extract

1. Preheat the oven to 400°F (200°C). Place the oven rack in the lower third of the oven. Line a baking sheet with parchment paper.

2. **Make the shortcakes:** Whisk the flour, sugar, baking powder, and salt in a large bowl. Then, whisk in the lemon zest.

3. Add the butter, working it into the flour with your hands to create a coarse meal. You should end up with small, pea-sized butter bits.

4. Whisk the egg, heavy cream, and lemon extract in a medium bowl. Make a small well in the center of the flour mixture. Pour the cream mixture into the well and work the dough with a fork to form a sticky, scraggly dough.

5. Use a 2-ounce (60 ml) ice cream scoop to scoop out eight mounds of dough and place them on the baking sheet. Sprinkle each mound with turbinado sugar and then put the baking sheet in the freezer for 10 minutes to firm up the butter. (Otherwise, the shortcakes will spread too much.)

6. Remove from the freezer and bake for 17 to 18 minutes, until risen, golden brown, and set.

7. **Meanwhile, make the strawberries:** Toss the strawberries and sugar in a medium bowl. Add the limoncello and toss to combine. Cover and refrigerate for at least 1 hour or up to 4 hours before serving.

8. **Make the whipped cream:** Place the heavy cream, sugar, and vanilla in the bowl of a stand mixer fitted with the whisk attachment and whip until soft peaks form, about 2 minutes.

9. To assemble, slice off the upper third of each shortcake and set aside. Spoon a layer of whipped cream (about ¼ cup/60 ml) onto the base of the shortcake, top with 1 to 2 tablespoons (30 to 60 ml) strawberries, and then finish with the top of the shortcake.

10. Dust with powdered sugar and serve.

## NOTE

It may seem silly to buy a whole bottle of limoncello to use only such a small amount. But it really does add that special something to the strawberries. The bottle will last for at least a year in the freezer, and you can use this strawberry recipe on top of panna cotta or vanilla ice cream, too!

## MAKE-AHEAD GAME PLAN

- One day ahead, make the whipped cream. Cover and refrigerate until ready to serve.

- Eight hours ahead, bake the shortcakes. Let cool on the baking sheet and then cover loosely with a sheet of foil. Uncover and place the baking sheet in a 300°F (150°C) oven for 15 minutes to allow the shortcakes to regain their flaky texture.

- Four hours ahead, prepare the strawberries. Cover and refrigerate until ready to serve.

## PAIRS WELL WITH

Better BBQ Chicken (page 133)

Easy Grilled Salmon with Mango Salsa (page 127)

# CHOCOLATE BOTTOM
# BANANA CREAM PIE

Banana and chocolate are great "flavor mates," and in this recipe, the chocolate adds more than just flavor. It serves as a type of "bodyguard" for your crust, warding off any soggy bottom syndrome. This has always been my issue with banana cream pie: The bananas and custard can make your crust soft and mushy! But not with this recipe. The chocolate gets poured over the cooled crust. Once it hardens, it turns into a delicious chocolate layer, much like a candy bar, which keeps the crust below nice and crisp. It also forms a protective barrier against the moisture of the bananas and creamy custard. The result is four distinct layers of delicious flavors and textures that make every little bite indulgent. It's best made a day ahead; then, all you have to do is slice and serve!

*SERVES 8*

### GRAHAM CRACKER CRUST

Baking spray with flour

13 Nabisco Honey Maid Graham Crackers (196 g)

1 tablespoon (13 g) granulated sugar

½ cup (113 g) salted American butter, melted

½ cup (85 g) semisweet chocolate chips

### FILLING

2 ripe, but not overly ripe, large bananas (see Note 1)

5 large egg yolks

⅓ cup (45 g) cornstarch

Pinch of kosher salt

1½ cups (360 ml) whole milk

½ cup (120 ml) heavy cream

½ cup (100 g) granulated sugar

1 vanilla bean, scraped

2 tablespoons (28 g) salted American butter

### TOPPING

1 cup (240 ml) heavy cream

1 tablespoon (8 g) powdered sugar

½ teaspoon (2.5 ml) vanilla extract

1 thick bittersweet chocolate bar

1. Preheat the oven to 375°F (190°C). Spray a 9-inch (23 cm) pie plate with baking spray, distributing it evenly with a pastry brush.

2. **Make the crust:** Add the graham crackers and sugar to a food processor and pulse to form a coarse meal. With the machine running, slowly add the melted butter to form a wet crumb.

3. Transfer the crumb to the pie plate and "fist-bump" the crumbs up the sides, working your way around until the crust covers all sides. Place the pie plate on a baking sheet and bake for 5 to 6 minutes, until the crust is set and golden brown.

4. Place the chocolate chips in a small heat-safe Pyrex pitcher and melt them in the microwave on high in 30-second increments, stirring with a fork between each increment.

5. Pour the chocolate into the pie crust. Then, pick up the pie plate and swirl it around to distribute the chocolate into a thin, even layer (or smooth with an offset spatula). Refrigerate for 20 minutes to set the chocolate.

6. **Make the filling:** Cut the bananas into ¼-inch (6 mm) slices and place them on top of the chocolate layer, covering up all of the chocolate.

7. Whisk together the egg yolks, cornstarch, and salt in a large bowl to form a paste.

8. Bring the milk, heavy cream, sugar, and vanilla bean paste to a simmer in a medium saucepan. Whisk until the sugar has dissolved and the mixture is hot, 1 to 2 minutes. Slowly pour it into the egg yolk mixture, whisking all the while, until combined.

9. Clean out the pan and place a fine mesh sieve over it. Pour the egg yolk–cream mixture over the sieve to catch any solids. This will create a smoother custard. Discard the solids.

10. Cook the custard over medium-high heat, whisking slowly, 3 to 4 minutes. It will thicken gradually and then suddenly develop a pudding-like consistency. Remove from the heat once it reaches 190°F (88°C) (see Note 2).

11. Whisk the butter into the custard. Let cool slightly for 3 to 4 minutes, whisking as it cools to avoid lumps. Pour the custard on top of the bananas and let cool for 15 minutes.

12. **Meanwhile, make the topping:** Place the heavy cream, powdered sugar, and vanilla in the bowl of an electric mixer and whip on high until stiff peaks form, about 2 minutes.

13. Transfer the whipped cream to a pastry bag fitted with a star tip and pipe decorative swirls on top of the custard to cover it completely. Garnish the top with chocolate

shavings, made by shaving the chocolate bar with a potato peeler.

14. Refrigerate, uncovered, for at least 3 hours or overnight. Slice into wedges and serve.

## NOTES

1. The bananas shouldn't be too ripe, or they will look unsightly in the pie and make your custard runny.

2. Use a candy or meat thermometer to determine the temperature of the custard. It will be thick but not set at this point; it will set in the refrigerator. Don't overcook it, or it will become lumpy.

## MAKE-AHEAD GAME PLAN

One day ahead, make the pie. Any earlier, the bananas will start to turn brown.

## PAIRS WELL WITH

Pan-Seared Salmon with Lemon Butter Caper Sauce (page 113)

Sheet-Pan Lamb with Caramelized Shallots and Provençal Tomatoes (page 110)

# ALL-YOU-CAN-EAT
# CHOCOLATE MOUSSE

One of my favorite things to witness in a French bistro is the large tureens of chocolate mousse, served up with a big silver spoon. There is something so decadent and generous about it. This is exactly how I like to serve it at home, in a large-footed compote right at the table, doling out seconds to anyone who asks. My husband has shared stories about a concept in France called *"mousse au chocolat à volonté"* essentially all-you-can-eat chocolate mousse, which sounds *really decadent*! And the French think our habit of refillable soda is a problem?!

***SERVES 6 TO 8*** (*Makes 8 cups/1.4 kg*)

## CHOCOLATE MOUSSE

¼ cup (50 g) granulated sugar

2 large eggs, room temperature, lightly beaten

1 tablespoon (15 ml) vanilla extract

2 tablespoons (28 g) salted American butter

2 cups (340 g) Nestlé Dark Chocolate Morsels chocolate chips (see Note 1)

5 large egg whites

1 teaspoon (5 ml) cream of tartar

## WHIPPED CREAM

2 cups (480 ml) heavy cream

1 tablespoon (8 g) powdered sugar

1 teaspoon (5 ml) vanilla extract

## GARNISH

2 ounces (57 g) thick dark chocolate bar

1. **Make the mousse:** In three separate bowls, measure out the granulated sugar, beaten eggs, and 1 tablespoon (15 ml) vanilla. You can also add the egg whites and cream of tartar to the bowl of an electric mixer, but do not whip yet (see Note 2).

2. Place the butter in a large microwave-safe bowl and then put the chocolate chips on top. That way, the chocolate will melt into the butter and not scorch. Microwave on high, in 30-second increments, until melted, whisking in between each increment, about 2 minutes and 30 seconds total.

3. Add the sugar and whisk until dissolved. Add the vanilla, whisk to combine, and then add the eggs and whisk until smooth.

4. Using the whisk attachment of your electric mixer, whip the egg whites and cream of tartar on high until stiff peaks form, 2 to 3 minutes.

5. Using a rubber spatula, fold the egg whites, in thirds, into the chocolate mixture, until combined. Be sure to reach under the surface to fully integrate the heavier chocolate mixture with the egg whites.

6. **Make the whipped cream:** Clean out the mixer bowl and add the heavy cream, powdered sugar, and vanilla. Whip with the whisk attachment until stiff peaks form, about 2 minutes. Reserve 1 cup (120 g) whipped cream for garnish and then gently fold the remaining cream into the chocolate mixture.

7. Transfer to a large serving bowl, and top with the reserved whipped cream. Holding the chocolate bar over the whipped cream, peel some chocolate shavings on top with a potato peeler.

8. Refrigerate, uncovered, for at least 4 hours before serving (overnight is even better).

## NOTES

1. Nestlé Dark Chocolate Morsels provide the best dark chocolate flavor for this recipe, and they melt easily in the microwave. Don't be tempted to use semisweet chocolate chips; they will make the mousse too sweet.

2. It's best to have everything pre-measured so you can mix up the chocolate base quickly. This way, the chocolate won't seize up.

## MAKE-AHEAD GAME PLAN

One day ahead, make the mousse. Keep uncovered and refrigerated.

## PAIRS WELL WITH

Fennel-Crusted Pork Loin with Spiced Parsnips and Apples (page 134)

Rosemary Beef Tenderloin with Horseradish Cream (page 143)

# NEW YORK–STYLE CHEESECAKE
## WITH STRAWBERRY SAUCE

Everyone needs a fantastic cheesecake recipe, and you cannot go wrong with an over-the-top cheesecake. I hate water baths almost as much as I hate blind baking, and I've gone on record a few times with cheesecake recipes that can skirt this issue. But for a New York–style cheesecake, truly the king of cheesecakes, there's no way around the water bath (believe me, I've tried!). It's worth every pesky step! So, soldier on, my friends: Follow these steps exactly, and you will be rewarded with a cheesecake that will be the envy of anyone you serve it to. The syrupy strawberry sauce is the pièce de résistance!

# NEW YORK–STYLE CHEESECAKE
## WITH STRAWBERRY SAUCE

*SERVES 8 (Makes one 9-inch/23 cm cheesecake and 1½ cups/360 ml sauce)*

### CRUST

Baking spray with flour

13 Nabisco Honey Maid Graham Crackers (196 g)

1 tablespoon (13 g) granulated sugar

7 tablespoons (98 g) salted American butter, melted

### FILLING

32 ounces (907 g) cream cheese, room temperature

1¼ cups (250 g) granulated sugar

3 large eggs

¾ cup (180 g) full-fat sour cream

1 vanilla bean, scraped

¼ teaspoon (1 g) kosher salt

¼ cup (35 g) all-purpose flour

### STRAWBERRY SAUCE

1 tablespoon (10 g) cornstarch

⅓ cup (80 ml) plus 1 tablespoon (15 ml) water, divided

24 ounces (680 g) strawberries, hulled and halved

⅓ cup (66 g) granulated sugar

2 tablespoons (30 ml) lemon zest

### NOTES

1. Do not skip this two-part cooling process! It will prevent cracks in your cheesecake.

2. To get nice, clean edges, wipe off the knife in between slices.

1. Preheat the oven to 325°F (165°C). Spray a 9-inch (23 cm) springform pan with baking spray.

2. **Make the crust:** Process the graham crackers in a food processor to form a fine crumb. Add the sugar and pulse. Add the butter, pulsing to form wet crumbs.

3. Place the crumbs in the pan and shake the pan to level them out. Press them down to create an even layer. Bake for 10 minutes and then let cool.

4. **Meanwhile, make the filling:** Place the cream cheese and sugar in the bowl of a stand mixer. Beat on high until smooth and creamy, 1 to 2 minutes. Add the eggs, one at a time, beating in between each addition and scraping down the bowl as needed. Add the sour cream and beat until combined. Then, beat in the vanilla bean paste and salt. Gently beat in the flour until combined. Remove the bowl from the mixer and, using a wire whisk, whisk the mixture to remove any lumps at the bottom or sides of the bowl.

5. Set a kettle or two pots with at least 12 cups (2.8 L) water to boil.

6. Wrap the outside of the cheesecake pan in foil to prevent leaks. Place two sheets of foil (12×23 inches/30×58 cm each) on top of each other in opposing directions to form a cross. Place the pan in the center and wrap it with the foil all the way up the sides.

7. Pour the cream cheese mixture into the cooled crust. Shake the pan gently to level out the batter and smooth out the top if needed with an offset spatula.

8. Place a 13×16-inch (33×41 cm) roasting pan in the oven. Place the cheesecake pan into the roasting pan. Slowly pour the boiling water into a corner of the roasting pan. (This will prevent the water from splattering on your cheesecake.) The water should reach halfway up the cheesecake pan.

9. Bake for 55 to 60 minutes, until most of the cheesecake is set with a center that jiggles very slightly. Turn off the oven, prop the door open, and allow the cheesecake to cool and set in the oven for 30 minutes (see Note 1).

10. Remove the cheesecake pan from the water bath and let cool at room temperature for 30 minutes. Refrigerate, uncovered, for at least 4 hours (overnight is even better).

11. **Make the sauce:** Whisk together the cornstarch and 1 tablespoon (15 ml) water in a small bowl to form a slurry.

12. Add the strawberries, sugar, and ⅓ cup (80 ml) water to a medium pot. Cover and simmer for 3 to 5 minutes, until the strawberries are very tender and a bubbly syrup has formed. Gently press the strawberries down with a fork to create a chunky sauce.

13. Slowly pour the slurry into the strawberry mixture, whisking until thickened. Turn off the heat, stir in the lemon zest, and let cool. Transfer the sauce to an airtight container and refrigerate until ready to serve.

14. To serve, run a warm, sharp knife around the perimeter of the cheesecake to loosen the sides. Release the springform pan. Slice into wedges and top with the strawberry sauce (see Note 2).

## MAKE-AHEAD GAME PLAN

- Two days ahead, make the strawberry sauce. Cover and refrigerate until ready to serve.

- One day ahead, make the cheesecake. Refrigerate until ready to serve.

## PAIRS WELL WITH

Easy Grilled Salmon with Mango Salsa (page 127)

Sheet-Pan Lamb with Caramelized Shallots and Provençal Tomatoes (page 110)

# ALL-OCCASION CUT SUGAR COOKIES

There is no cookie recipe more versatile than the cut sugar cookie. You can turn them into treats for Christmas, Valentine's Day, Easter, and more! All you need is this delicious, buttery cookie recipe and your choice of cutter. For decoration, you can dip sections of the cookies in melted white or dark chocolate and top with crushed candy canes or sprinkles. But my kids always loved to pile on the icing and let their creativity flow! For this, I highly recommend the store-bought Wilton Cookie Icing that comes in a variety of colors and dries hard. Using premade icing means you don't have to create your own royal icing and put it into different bowls with food coloring or break out the pastry bags, which just spells disaster for the underage set (yes, I'm speaking from experience). The store-bought bottles are also easy to hold and even easier to clean up. Seriously, you'll thank me later!

***SERVES 10-12*** (*Makes 2 to 3 dozen cookies, depending upon size of cutter*)

1 cup (226 g) salted American butter, softened

1 cup (200 g) granulated sugar

1 large egg

1½ teaspoons (7.5 ml) vanilla extract (see Note 1)

3 cups (420 g) all-purpose flour, plus more for dusting

¼ teaspoon (1 g) baking powder

¾ teaspoon (5 g) kosher salt

**TOPPINGS** (OPTIONAL)

1 cup (170 g) semisweet chocolate chips, melted

1 cup (170 g) white chocolate chips, melted

Sprinkles of choice

Crushed candy canes (see Note 2)

Wilton Cookie Icing

1. Beat the butter and sugar together in a stand mixer until light and fluffy. Add the egg and vanilla and beat to combine.

2. Whisk together the flour, baking powder, and salt in a large bowl.

3. Add the dry ingredients, in thirds, to the butter mixture, scraping down the bowl as needed, until a dough forms.

4. Divide the dough into two balls, flatten them into discs, and wrap each in plastic wrap. Refrigerate the dough for at least 2 hours and up to 3 days. After that, you can freeze the dough for up to 1 month. Thaw in the refrigerator overnight before using.

5. Preheat the oven to 350°F (175°C). Place the oven rack in the lower third of the oven. Line a baking sheet with parchment paper.

6. Roll the dough out onto a floured surface to ⅛-inch (3 mm) thickness. Cut out the cookies with your cookie cutter of choice and transfer them to the baking sheet (see Note 3).

7. If the cookie dough has sat out too long and is soft, place the tray in the freezer for 5 minutes to firm up before baking. This will help your cookies retain their shape.

8. Bake for 8 to 10 minutes, depending on the size of the cookies, until set and slightly golden brown. Let cool.

9. For chocolate-dipped cookies, place the chocolate chips or white chocolate chips in a microwave-safe shallow bowl and melt on high in 15-second intervals. Stir with a fork to combine. Once the chocolate is completely melted, dip the section of the cookie you want to cover and then place it on parchment paper. Repeat with the remaining cookies.

10. For iced cookies, follow the instructions on the back of the icing bottle.

11. Top with sprinkles or crushed candy canes and let them dry on the parchment paper.

**NOTES**

1. For almond-flavored cookies, reduce the vanilla to ½ teaspoon (2.5 ml) and add 2 teaspoons (10 ml) almond extract.

2. The easiest way to crush candy canes is to unwrap them, place them in a resealable plastic bag, and gently whack the bag with a hammer or a French-style rolling pin.

3. If you are making cookies of different shapes and sizes, make sure to bake similar cookies together to help them cook at the same rate.

**MAKE-AHEAD GAME PLAN**

At the start of the holiday season, you can make several batches of this dough, separate it into smaller quantities, and freeze it for up to 1 month. When you're ready to decorate, all you have to do is thaw the dough in the fridge the night before, cut, and bake.

**PAIRS WELL WITH**

Homemade Hot Chocolate (page 39)

Soft and Chewy Gingerbread Men (page 247)

# ROASTED PEACH COBBLER
## WITH LIGHT AND FLUFFY BISCUITS

I love a great peach cobbler as much as the next person, but I hate how most recipes have you start by making an X in the peaches and submerging them in hot water to remove their skins. In the middle of a summer heat wave, this is the last thing I feel like doing! So, I tried roasting the peaches with the skin on instead, and a funny thing happened: The cobbler was ten times more delicious! There is natural pectin in peach skins, which makes the roasted peaches perfectly syrupy. You can also get away with using peaches that are just slightly underripe because the roasting deepens their flavor and softens their texture. The peach skins give this dessert a beautiful rosy glow, too. And without all that pesky blanching, ice bathing, and peeling, you'll have more time to spend at the beach, which is where I want to be in August—don't you? Serve this with high-quality vanilla ice cream: This is the time to spring for the good stuff.

---

*SERVES 8 TO 10*

4½ pounds (2 kg) peaches, pitted and sliced (unpeeled)

¼ cup (50 g) granulated sugar

¼ cup (50 g) turbinado sugar (see Note)

1 tablespoon (8 g) all-purpose flour

1 teaspoon (5 ml) ground cinnamon

½ teaspoon (2.5 ml) ground nutmeg

½ teaspoon (3 g) kosher salt

¼ cup (60 ml) fresh lemon juice (from about 2 lemons)

¼ cup (60 ml) room temperature water

3 tablespoons (42 g) salted American butter, cubed

**BISCUIT TOPPING**

2½ cups (350 g) all-purpose flour

2 tablespoons (25 g) granulated sugar

2½ teaspoons (10 g) baking powder

1 teaspoon (6 g) kosher salt

1 cup (226 g) cold salted American butter, diced

1 large egg

1 cup (240 ml) heavy cream

Sprinkle of turbinado sugar

**FOR SERVING**

Good-quality vanilla ice cream (Häagen-Dazs Vanilla Bean is my favorite)

1. Preheat the oven to 450°F (230°C). Place the oven rack in the lower third of the oven.

2. Place the peaches in a large bowl. Toss with the granulated sugar, turbinado sugar, flour, cinnamon, nutmeg, salt, lemon juice, and water. Spoon the mixture into a 9×12-inch (23×30 cm) oven-safe casserole dish. Top with the butter cubes.

3. Roast for 30 minutes, tossing halfway through, until the peaches are bubbling and a bit syrupy. Set aside to cool slightly and then wipe the edges with a damp cloth to clean up the casserole a bit. (This will create a prettier presentation.) Reduce the oven temperature to 400°F (200°C).

4. **Meanwhile, make the topping:** Whisk together the flour, sugar, baking powder, and salt in a large bowl.

5. Add the butter, working it into the flour with your hands, to form a coarse meal with pea-sized pieces of butter.

6. Whisk together the egg and heavy cream in a small bowl until smooth. Add this mixture to the flour mixture and stir with a fork to create a sticky dough. If the dough looks too dry, add up to ¼ cup (60 ml) more of heavy cream.

7. Using a 2-ounce (60 ml) ice cream scoop, dollop the dough on top of the warm peaches, leaving a little room in between each one to allow them to spread and to see the peaches underneath. You should have 10 to 12 biscuits. Sprinkle some turbinado sugar on top of each biscuit.

8. Bake for 22 to 25 minutes, until the biscuits puff up, turn golden brown, and begin to crack slightly on top.

9. Spoon the cobbler into shallow bowls and serve with a scoop of vanilla ice cream.

### NOTE

Turbinado sugar can be found in stores under the brand name Sugar in the Raw. It's partially refined sugar that still retains some of its molasses, adding a delicious, subtle caramel flavor to the cobbler. If you can't find it, you can use brown sugar instead.

### MAKE-AHEAD GAME PLAN

- One day ahead, roast the peaches. Cover and refrigerate.
- Right before serving, whip up the biscuits, place them on top, and bake as directed for the best results.
- Alternatively, you can prebake the cobbler 2 hours before serving, leave it at room temperature, and then reheat it in a preheated 300°F (150°C) oven for 15 to 20 minutes.

### PAIRS WELL WITH

Fall-Off-the-Bone Sticky Ribs (page 117)

Grilled Dijon Chicken with Charred Lemons (page 123)

# GO-TO CHOCOLATE BUNDT CAKE

A great chocolate Bundt cake is like a little black dress: It goes everywhere. Need a cake for a potluck? Look no further. Holiday office party? Gotcha covered. I've even seen it cause a frenzy at a school bake sale! Best of all, it's at your service when, heaven forbid, disaster strikes and the more elaborate dessert you were planning, well, flops. Fear not, this cake has got your back and is ready to deliver *big* time! You'll wonder why you didn't start here in the first place. It's rich and chocolaty and as moist as a well-made muffin. It needs nothing more than an unrestrained dollop of my homemade whipped cream. It feeds a crowd, and if you choose the fanciest Bundt pan you can find, it decorates itself! Et voilà! You've *won* dessert!

### SERVES 8 TO 10 (MAKES ONE 10-INCH/25 CM CAKE)

Baking spray with flour

1 cup (100 g) unsweetened cocoa powder

2 ounces (57 g) bittersweet chocolate (Ghirardelli 60% to 70% cacao), broken into pieces

1 cup (240 ml) boiling water

2 cups (400 g) granulated sugar (see Note 1)

1 cup (240 ml) vegetable oil

3 large eggs

2 large egg yolks

1 tablespoon (15 ml) vanilla extract (yes, a full tablespoon)

1¼ cups (175 g) all-purpose flour

1 teaspoon (4 g) baking soda

1 teaspoon (6 g) kosher salt

Powdered sugar, for dusting (optional)

#### FOR WHIPPED CREAM

2 cups (480 ml) heavy cream

2 tablespoons (14 g) powdered sugar

1 teaspoon (5 ml) vanilla extract

1. Preheat the oven to 350°F (175°C). Spray a 12-cup (10 inches/25 cm with a 2.8 L capacity) Bundt pan with baking spray. Use a pastry brush to distribute it into all the crevices.

2. Add the cocoa powder, chocolate, and boiling water to a large heat-safe bowl. Let sit for 5 minutes to melt the chocolate and "bloom" the cocoa powder (see Note 2). Whisk to combine. Whisk in the sugar until it dissolves and the mixture is smooth. Then, slowly whisk in the vegetable oil.

3. Add the eggs one at a time, whisking after each addition (see Note 3). Add the egg yolks, one at a time, whisking after each addition, until the mixture is thick. Whisk in the vanilla extract and then set aside.

4. Whisk together the flour, baking soda, and salt in a medium bowl. Add the dry ingredients, in thirds, to the wet ingredients, whisking in between each addition, until just combined. Do not overmix.

5. Pour the batter into the prepared Bundt pan. Bake for 40 to 45 minutes, until a long skewer comes out clean.

6. Let cool for at least 30 minutes before attempting to flip the cake out of the pan. Lightly cover with foil and then keep in the pan at room temperature until ready to serve.

7. **Make the whipped cream:** Place all the ingredients in the bowl of an electric mixer and whip on high until soft peaks form, 1 to 5 minutes depending upon mixer. Cover and refrigerate until ready to serve.

8. To serve, loosen the cake around the edges with a small paring knife. Place a serving platter or cake stand on top of the Bundt pan. Flip the whole thing over, gently wiggle the pan to loosen the cake, and remove the pan. If desired, dust with powdered sugar. Slice and serve with a dollop of whipped cream.

### NOTES

1. Two cups (400 g) may seem like a lot of sugar, but keep in mind that we're adding one full cup (100 g) of *unsweetened* cocoa powder! So, the cake needs this amount of sugar to be palatable.

2. Adding hot water to cocoa powder ("blooming" it) will bring out the best chocolate flavor.

3. This takes a while since eggs and oil don't naturally combine. Spend the time to make sure they are fully combined before adding the flour; otherwise, your cake will be oily.

### MAKE-AHEAD GAME PLAN

- One day ahead, make the cake. Cover the pan and keep at room temperature until ready to serve. Make the whipped cream. Cover and refrigerate until ready to serve.

### PAIRS WELL WITH

Make-Ahead Beef Stew (page 130)

Hot fudge sauce from Better than Box-Mix Brownie Sundaes (page 204)

# SYRUPY BLUEBERRY PIE
## WITH FLAKY DOUBLE CRUST

I never realized how tricky blueberry pie can be. Add too much thickener, and you'll lose that syrupy goodness; not enough thickener, and you'll have a watery mess. After I was about five fails in, I discovered the secret to success: It's best to use both cornstarch and flour as thickeners. They each have their own superpower: Cornstarch delivers on the syrupiness, and flour delivers on the structure. The other secret is to precook some of the filling on the stovetop. This will give the syrup a head start! Now, here's the power tip: As painstaking as it sounds, you must allow this pie to cool completely for 2 hours for the filling to set before slicing into it. So, plan ahead! You'll be rewarded with a flaky crust and a syrupy filling, the dreams summer pies are made of! Serve with high-quality vanilla ice cream.

# SYRUPY BLUEBERRY PIE
## WITH FLAKY DOUBLE CRUST

*SERVES 8* *(Makes one 9-inch/23 cm pie)*

### CRUST

2½ cups (350 g) all-purpose flour, plus more for dusting

3 tablespoons (38 g) granulated sugar

½ teaspoon (3 g) kosher salt

1 cup (226 g) salted American butter, diced

½ cup (120 ml) ice water

1 large egg

1 tablespoon (15 ml) water, room temperature

½ teaspoon (2.5 g) turbinado sugar

### FILLING

¼ cup (40 g) plus 1 tablespoon (10 g) cornstarch, divided

¼ cup (60 ml) plus 2 tablespoons (30 ml) very cold water, divided

36 ounces (1 kg) blueberries, divided

1 cup (200 g) granulated sugar, divided

2 tablespoons (30 ml) lemon zest

3 tablespoons (45 ml) lemon juice (from about 1½ lemons)

1 teaspoon (5 ml) ground cinnamon

⅓ cup (46 g) all-purpose flour

1 tablespoon (14 g) salted American butter, diced

### FOR SERVING

Good-quality vanilla ice cream (Häagen-Dazs Vanilla Bean is my favorite)

1. **Make the crust:** Place the flour, granulated sugar, and salt in a food processor and pulse until combined. Add the butter, about 1 tablespoon (14 g) at a time, and pulse to form a coarse meal.

2. Add the ice water in a slow stream through the feed tube, and pulse just enough to form a scraggly dough. Don't overwork the dough, or it will lose its flakiness.

3. Turn the dough out onto a floured surface, form it into a ball, and then cut it in half to make two balls. Flatten the balls into discs and then wrap in plastic wrap and refrigerate for at least 1 hour or overnight.

4. **Make the filling:** Whisk together 2 tablespoons (20 g) cornstarch and 2 tablespoons (30 ml) very cold water in a small bowl to form a slurry.

5. Heat 12 ounces (340 g) blueberries, ¼ cup (60 ml) very cold water, and ¼ cup (50 g) granulated sugar in a medium pot over medium-high heat. Cover and simmer for 3 minutes, until the blueberries are tender and a foamy syrup forms.

6. Whisk in the slurry until thickened. Transfer to a large bowl to cool.

7. Combine the remaining blueberries, remaining sugar, 2 tablespoons (20 g) cornstarch, and the lemon zest, lemon juice, and cinnamon in a large bowl. Add the flour and toss gently to coat. Stir in the blueberry filling with a rubber spatula.

8. Roll out the first dough disc on a floured surface into a 14-inch (36 cm) circle. Drape the dough over the rolling pin to fit it into a 9-inch (23 cm) pie plate, allowing for a 2-inch (5 cm) overhang of dough.

9. Add 1 tablespoon (10 g) cornstarch to the bottom of the crust, distributing it evenly with a pastry brush on the bottom and sides.

10. Add the berry mixture, and level out the mound with a spatula (do not flatten; just shape it). Distribute the diced butter equally across the mound.

11. Roll out the second dough disc to a 14-inch (36 cm) circle and then place it on top of the filling.

12. Press the overhangs of dough together and trim off the excess with kitchen shears so that there's an even 1-inch (2.5 cm) overhang all the way around. Press the two layers together again to seal. Then, tuck the dough under to rest on the pie pan rim all the way around.

13. With your right pointer finger on the inside of the pie pan and your left thumb and pointer finger on the outside of the pan, press the perimeter of the dough to create fluted crimping all the way around.

14. Make an egg wash by mixing the egg and room-temperature water in a small bowl. Brush the top of the pie and the crust with the egg wash. Place the pie in the freezer for 20 minutes to firm up the dough.

15. Meanwhile, preheat the oven to 375°F (190°C). Line a baking sheet with foil.

16. **Create the steam vents:** Cut two vertical 2-inch (5 cm) and two horizontal 2-inch (5 cm) steam vents in the center of the pie in the shape of a decorative starburst.

Cut smaller 1-inch (2.5 cm) incisions in between those vents. Wipe the knife clean after each incision. They will widen in the oven and reveal the blueberry filling.

17. Sprinkle the top of the pie with the turbinado sugar. Place on the baking sheet.

18. Bake for 60 to 70 minutes, until the pie is golden brown and the filling is bubbling through the steam vents.

19. Let cool for 2 hours at room temperature before slicing. This will allow the filling to set. Serve with a scoop of vanilla ice cream.

**MAKE-AHEAD GAME PLAN**
- Two days ahead, make the pie dough. Wrap in wax paper and refrigerate until ready to use.
- One day ahead, cook the blueberry filling. Cover and refrigerate until ready to use.

**PAIRS WELL WITH**
Better BBQ Chicken (page 133)
Easy Gourmet Burgers (page 137)

# JUST A SCOOP OF TIRAMISU

Tiramisu is one of the world's most delicious desserts. But it might also be the world's messiest dessert to serve at home: Just try cutting it into neat squares and graciously placing it on a plate. For this reason, I had relegated tiramisu to a restaurant dessert until I spent a few weeks in Italy. There, I saw it served in so many ingenious ways, and my favorite was a large scoop sensually placed in a footed glass bowl. I felt liberated. Of course that's the best way to serve it! And what could be easier? This dessert is best made the day before to allow the filling to set and chill. When it's time to serve, do the scooping in the kitchen, and present your guests with individual servings in footed glass bowls. Footed ice cream dishes, martini glasses, or champagne coupes work nicely, too! Don't forget the grated chocolate on top for an elegant garnish.

*SERVES 8*

## WHIPPED CREAM MIXTURE

2 cups (480 ml) heavy cream

¾ cup (90 g) powdered sugar

1 tablespoon (15 ml) vanilla extract

8 ounces (227 g) mascarpone, room temperature

## EGG MIXTURE

5 large egg yolks, room temperature (see Note 1)

¼ cup (50 g) granulated sugar

## FOR ASSEMBLY

24 Matilde Vicenzi ladyfingers (see Note 2)

1¾ cups (420 ml) strong coffee, completely cooled

2 tablespoons (30 ml) Myers's Dark Rum (see Note 3)

2 ounces (57 g) bittersweet dark chocolate, chopped, plus 1 ounce (28 g), grated

2 tablespoons (12 g) unsweetened cocoa powder, divided

1. **Make the whipped cream:** Place the heavy cream, sugar, and vanilla in the bowl of a stand mixer fitted with the whisk attachment and whip until soft peaks form, about 2 minutes.

2. Place the mascarpone in a large bowl. Using a rubber spatula, gradually fold in the whipped cream.

3. **Make the egg mixture:** Whip the egg yolks and granulated sugar in a large bowl for at least 5 minutes on high, or until the mixture has doubled in volume and is light pale yellow.

4. Gently fold the egg mixture, in thirds, into the whipped cream-mascarpone mixture, until combined and voluminous.

5. **Prepare the assembly station:** Pour the coffee and rum into a shallow bowl, and have 1 ounce (28 g) chopped chocolate ready to go. Take out a 9×9×2-inch (23×23×5cm) casserole dish.

6. Start with 12 ladyfingers. Dip one ladyfinger into the coffee-rum mixture for 1 second on each side (no longer or it will disintegrate!). Place the ladyfinger in the casserole dish. Repeat this process until all 12 have been dipped and transferred, creating two rows of six ladyfingers and leaving about ¼ inch (6 mm) between each one.

7. Add half of the filling, smoothing it out to completely cover the ladyfingers.

8. Using a fine-mesh sieve, dust 1 tablespoon (6 g) cocoa powder all over the filling. Then, add the 1 ounce (28 g) chopped chocolate.

9. Repeat steps 6 and 7 with the remaining ladyfingers and filling.

10. Cover and refrigerate for at least 2 hours (overnight is even better).

11. Just before serving, add the remaining cocoa powder and 1 ounce (28 g) chopped chocolate. Scoop the tiramisu into footed glass bowls, grate the remaining 1 ounce (28 g) chocolate on top of each portion, and serve.

## NOTES

1. To replace the raw eggs with pasteurized eggs, use 1 cup (240 ml) Lucerne Dairy Farms Liquid Egg Product. Beat for 10 to 15 minutes. It won't be as voluminous, but it will still be good!

2. Use whole ladyfingers (not ones that are split down the middle) They should be dry and hard, not soft and cakey. Matilde Vicenzi is my favorite brand; it is worth seeking out, even if you have to get them online. The package includes 24 ladyfingers, the exact amount you need for this recipe.

3. For a nonalcoholic version, substitute the rum with 2 teaspoons (10 ml) imitation rum extract.

## MAKE-AHEAD GAME PLAN

One day ahead, make and assemble the tiramisu, leaving the final layer of cocoa powder off (otherwise, the condensation will make it unsightly). Just before serving, dust with cocoa powder and garnish each serving with the grated chocolate.

## PAIRS WELL WITH

Frenzy-Free Chicken Pot Pie (page 114)

Old-School Lasagna (page 120)

# PUMPKIN PIE TART

Pumpkin pie spice is a classic American fall spice blend, and I love to use it in just about everything *except* pumpkin pie. Wait, what? I know it sounds strange, but let's be honest, there isn't much going on with pumpkin pie. Its two best features are the spice and the texture, so it pays to get both right. I like to create my own spice blend that heightens the flavors of the ginger and cloves. This gives you a more flavorful pie that is less basic and a bit more gourmet. I also bake it in a tall tart pan to upgrade the presentation and to provide taller slices. And for the texture? My motto is "low and slow is the way to go!" Blast the heat at 450°F (230°C) to set the crust and then continue baking at 325°F (165°C). This will create a luscious, creamy filling without any cracks!

---

*SERVES 8*

---

### CRUST

1¼ cups (175 g) all-purpose flour, plus more for dusting

2 tablespoons (16 g) powdered sugar

¼ teaspoon (1 g) kosher salt

½ cup (113 g) salted American butter, diced

1 large egg yolk

2 tablespoons (30 ml) very cold water

1 teaspoon (3 g) cornstarch

### FILLING

Two 15-ounce (425 g) cans Libby's 100% Pure Pumpkin puree (see Note)

1½ teaspoons (7.5 ml) ground ginger

1 teaspoon (5 ml) ground cinnamon

½ teaspoon (2.5 ml) ground cloves

½ teaspoon (3 g) kosher salt

Two 14-ounce (397 g) cans sweetened condensed milk

2 large eggs

### WHIPPED CREAM

1 cup (240 ml) heavy cream

1 tablespoon (8 g) powdered sugar

½ teaspoon (2.5 ml) vanilla extract

### FOR SERVING

Ground nutmeg

1. **Make the crust:** Add the flour, sugar, and salt to a food processor. Pulse to combine. Add the diced butter, about 1 tablespoon (14 g) at a time, pulsing in between each addition, to form a coarse meal.

2. Whisk together the egg yolk and cold water in a small bowl. Then, add to the flour mixture in a steady drizzle, pulsing just until a scraggly dough forms. (Do not over-pulse, or you will have a tough crust.)

3. Turn the dough out onto a floured surface. Form it into a ball and then flatten it into a disk. Wrap the dough in wax paper and refrigerate for at least 1 hour (overnight is even better).

4. Roll the dough out to a 16-inch (41 cm), ¼-inch-thick (6 mm) circle and fit it into the bottom and sides of a 9½×2-inch (24×5 cm) tart pan with a removable bottom. Use the back of your palm to fit the dough into all the crevices. Cut the excess dough off the top so the dough is flush with the top of the pan.

5. Place in the freezer for 25 minutes, until the dough is frozen and does not bend to the touch.

6. Preheat the oven to 450°F (230°C).

7. **Meanwhile, make the filling:** Whisk the pumpkin puree in a large bowl to loosen it and then sift in the ginger, cinnamon, cloves, and salt (to avoid clumps). Add the sweetened condensed milk and whisk to combine. Add the eggs, one at a time, whisking together until smooth.

8. Remove the pan from the freezer, add the cornstarch to the bottom of the crust, and distribute well with a pastry brush. Place the pan on a baking sheet.

9. Pour the filling into the pan and bake for 10 minutes, until the crust begins to set. Reduce the oven temperature to 325°F (165°C) and bake for another 45 to 50 minutes, until the center jiggles slightly. Turn the oven off and prop the door open to allow the tart to cool in the oven for 15 minutes.

10. Remove the pan from the oven and let cool for 45 minutes at room temperature. Refrigerate, uncovered, for at least 4 hours (overnight is even better).

11. **Make the whipped cream:** Place the heavy cream, sugar, and vanilla in the bowl of a stand mixer fitted with the whisk attachment and whip until soft peaks form, about 2 minutes. Transfer to a serving bowl and cover and refrigerate until ready to serve.

12. Before serving, gently pat the tart with a paper towel to absorb any condensation. Slice into wedges and serve with a dollop of whipped cream and a sprinkle of nutmeg.

### NOTE

This is not pumpkin pie filling, which is already sweetened and spiced. I prefer Libby's because it is a thick puree without a lot of water. This will create a creamier filling that will set better after baking.

### MAKE-AHEAD GAME PLAN

- Two days ahead, make the tart dough. Refrigerate until ready to use. (Do not freeze.)
- One day ahead, make the tart. Refrigerate, uncovered, in the pan until ready to serve. Make the whipped cream. Cover and refrigerate until ready to serve.

### PAIRS WELL WITH

Beginner's Roast Turkey (and Gravy) (page 140)

Fennel-Crusted Pork Loin with Spiced Parsnips and Apples (page 134)

# PERFECT LEMON BARS

Oh, lemon bars, how you have mocked me in the past with your cracked, overly sweet filling and soggy crust! Well, today I can finally say I have the last word. After hours of testing, I achieved what I believe to be the most perfect lemon bar. The filling is balanced, with subtle sweetness from the sugar that doesn't upstage the real star of the show: the lemon. The secret is to cook the filling and bake the crust separately, then combine the two, and refrigerate. This will give you a set filling with a crispy, crumbly crust that melts in your mouth. And the secret ingredient for preventing cracks? A little bit of gelatin, which ensures a velvety, smooth surface that also delivers on clean slices. I don't dare add any powdered sugar on top for fear of tipping the sweetness scale. But you can if you wish (some traditions are hard to break). If you ask me, a dollop of homemade whipped cream and a little lemon zest are all you need.

# PERFECT LEMON BARS

*MAKES 9 BARS*

## SHORTBREAD CRUST

¾ cup (169 g) salted American butter, softened

½ cup (60 g) powdered sugar

1 teaspoon (5 ml) vanilla extract

¼ teaspoon (1 g) kosher salt

1½ cups (210 g) all-purpose flour, plus more for dusting

## LEMON FILLING

6 large egg yolks

⅓ cup (45 g) cornstarch

¼ teaspoon (1 g) kosher salt

1½ cups (360 ml) water

¾ cup (150 g) granulated sugar

One 0.25-ounce (7 g) envelope Knox powdered gelatin

2 tablespoons (28 g) salted American butter

⅓ cup (80 ml) fresh lemon juice (from about 2 lemons)

2 tablespoons (30 ml) lemon zest

## WHIPPED CREAM

1 cup (240 ml) heavy cream

1 tablespoon (8 g) powdered sugar

½ teaspoon (2.5 ml) vanilla extract

## GARNISH

Zest of 1 lemon

1. **Make the crust:** Add the butter and sugar to the bowl of a stand mixer. Beat slowly to incorporate the sugar and then increase the speed to high for 2 to 4 minutes, until combined.

2. Add the vanilla and salt. Beat them together and then scrape down the bowl. Add the flour in thirds, beating in between each addition and scraping down the bowl as needed. Continue to beat for 2 to 3 minutes, until small and then larger balls of dough form. Stop, scrape down the bowl, form the dough into one ball, and flatten it into a disc. Wrap the disc in parchment paper and refrigerate for 1 hour.

3. Preheat the oven to 325°F (165°C). Line a 9-inch (23 cm) square baking pan with parchment paper cut to the width of the pan, leaving 4-inch (10 cm) overhangs that rise over two sides of the pan in opposing directions.

4. Roll out the shortbread dough on a floured surface. Then, fit it into the pan, pressing down to make an even surface. Prick the dough with a fork all over to allow for steam to escape.

5. Bake for 25 minutes, or until golden brown, set, and risen. Set aside to cool.

6. **Meanwhile, make the filling:** Whisk together the egg yolks, cornstarch, and salt in a large heat-safe bowl until combined.

7. Heat the water, sugar, and gelatin in a medium saucepan over medium-high heat. Simmer just until the sugar and gelatin dissolve, 1 to 2 minutes.

8. Slowly add the hot mixture to the egg mixture in a slow stream, whisking all the while to incorporate without scrambling the eggs. Pour the custard mixture through a fine-mesh sieve into a large clean pot.

9. Cook over medium-high heat until the custard thickens to a pourable curd and reaches a temperature between 190°F and 195°F (88°C and 91°C), 3 to 4 minutes. Remove from the heat.

10. Add the butter and whisk until melted. Then, add the lemon juice and zest and whisk to combine. Pour the filling into the cooled crust, but do not scrape the bottom of the pan (see Note). Gently shake the pan to level out the filling.

11. Let cool for 15 minutes at room temperature and then place in the refrigerator, uncovered, for at least 3 hours.

12. **Make the whipped cream:** Place the heavy cream, sugar, and vanilla in the bowl of a stand mixer fitted with the whisk attachment and whip until soft peaks form, about 2 minutes.

13. Remove the lemon bars from the pan by pulling up on the parchment paper. Slice into squares. Add a dollop of whipped cream to each square and sprinkle some freshly grated lemon zest on top.

### NOTE

Whatever sticks to the bottom of the pan should stay there, since it has formed clumps. It's worth the loss of a little bit of lemon curd for a velvety, smooth filling.

### MAKE-AHEAD GAME PLAN

One day ahead, make the lemon bars and refrigerate, uncovered. Make the whipped cream, cover, and refrigerate.

### PAIRS WELL WITH

Sheet-Pan Lamb with Caramelized Shallots and Provençal Tomatoes (page 110)

Better than Box-Mix Brownie Sundaes (page 204)

# NONNIE'S SOUR CREAM POUND CAKE

You can always tell what a family values by the gifts they give. One of the most thoughtful gifts my mother received as a new bride was a little green box filled with recipes from my dad's family. Fifty years later, the card with the most stains and splatters is the sour cream pound cake recipe by my Nonnie (a term of endearment for "nonna," which is Italian for grandmother). By the looks of this recipe card, it was one of my mom's favorites. Apparently, it was also a favorite of local restaurant owners too! According to family lore, my grandfather, who sold large commercial mixers to restaurants in the tristate area, would demonstrate the mixers by using Nonnie's pound cake recipe. Restaurant owners were so blown away by how delicious the cake was, it easily sold the mixer! It's moist, fluffy, and full of vanilla flavor. It can stand on its own as a snack cake, or you can serve it for dessert with fresh berries and a dollop of the whipped cream from my Go-To Chocolate Bundt Cake Recipe (page 225).

**SERVES 6-8** *(Makes one 9½ × 5½-inch/24 × 14 cm loaf)*

1 cup (240 g) full-fat sour cream, room temperature

1 cup (226 g) salted American butter, room temperature

4 large eggs, room temperature (see Note 1)

Baking spray with flour

1¼ cups (250 g) granulated sugar

1 tablespoon (15 ml) vanilla extract

1¾ cups (245 g) all-purpose flour

2 teaspoons (8 g) baking powder

½ teaspoon (3 g) kosher salt

### FOR SERVING (OPTIONAL)

2 cups (280 g) mixed berries

Whipped cream (see page 236)

1. Let the sour cream, butter, and eggs rest at room temperature for 45 minutes. This will allow them to combine better.

2. Preheat the oven to 350°F (175°C). Place the oven rack in the lower third of the oven.

3. Spray a 9½×5½×2½-inch (24×14×6 cm) loaf pan with baking spray, distributing it evenly with a pastry brush.

4. Beat together the butter and sugar in the bowl of a stand mixer until fluffy, 5 to 8 minutes. Add the eggs one at a time, beating in between each addition and scraping down the bowl (see Note 2). Beat in the vanilla.

5. Whisk together the flour, baking powder, and salt in a large bowl. Mixing on slow speed, add the dry ingredients, in thirds, to the wet ingredients, alternating with the sour cream, in thirds, until both are used up and the mixture is just combined. Scrape down the bowl as needed.

6. Transfer the batter to the loaf pan, and smooth it out with a spatula. Bake for 60 to 65 minutes, until a toothpick comes out clean.

7. Let cool completely. Then, remove the loaf from the pan and cut into 1-inch (2.5 cm) slices.

8. Serve, topped with berries and whipped cream, if desired.

## NOTES

1. If you forget to take the eggs out of the fridge before starting, you can submerge them in a bowl of warm water for 5 minutes to bring them up to room temperature.

2. It pays to scrape down the bowl frequently. Streaky pound cake happens when the ingredients are not at room temperature or the bowl hasn't been scraped down enough.

## MAKE-AHEAD GAME PLAN

Eight hours ahead, make the cake. It's best enjoyed the day it's made.

## PAIRS WELL WITH

Better BBQ Chicken (page 133)

Hot fudge sauce from Better than Box-Mix Brownie Sundaes (page 204)

# KEY LIME PIE

When I was a new bride, I was known for bringing desserts to my parent's holiday gatherings. It was the one thing I could manage with my fifty-hour-a-week job in TV production. One Easter, I made a key lime pie with a store-bought graham cracker crust and was shocked to learn how easy it was. Just three ingredients? Was that really all there was to it? It was totally delicious, and ever since then, it's my go-to springtime dessert when time is tight. I've since upgraded to a homemade graham cracker crust that doesn't take that much more effort, but if you decide to go with the store-bought crust, I get it. You can get creative with the whipped cream topping by using your favorite pastry tip and piping designs. Or go the rustic route and place one big dollop in the center. If you happen to live in a citrus-growing region, a few citrus blossoms on top are a nice touch!

---

*SERVES 8 (Makes one 9-inch/23 cm pie)*

---

## GRAHAM CRACKER CRUST

Baking spray with flour

13 Nabisco Honey Maid Graham Crackers (196 g)

1 tablespoon (13 g) sugar

½ cup (113 g) salted American butter, melted

## FILLING

4 large egg yolks

Two 14-ounce (397 g) cans sweetened condensed milk

1 cup (240 ml) fresh key lime juice (from about 1 pound/454 g key limes; see Note)

## TOPPING

1 cup (240 ml) heavy cream

1 tablespoon (8 g) powdered sugar

½ teaspoon (2.5 ml) vanilla extract

2 key limes

### NOTE

If you can't find key limes, use ¾ cup (180 ml) lime juice, since limes are more sour than key limes. But do not, for any reason, use bottled key lime juice. The flavor is awful!

1. **Make the crust:** Preheat the oven to 350°F (175°C). Spray a 9-inch (23 cm) pie plate with baking spray, distributing it evenly with a pastry brush.

2. Add the graham crackers and sugar to a food processor and pulse to form a coarse meal. With the machine running, slowly add the melted butter to form a wet crumb.

3. Transfer the crumb mixture to the pie plate and "fist-bump" the crumbs up the sides of the pan, working your way around to form a crust on all sides. Flatten out the bottom with your hands to form an even layer.

4. Place the pan on a baking sheet and bake for 5 to 6 minutes, until the crust is set and golden brown. Set aside to cool.

5. **Make the filling:** Whisk together the egg yolks and condensed milk in a large bowl. Slowly whisk in the lime juice. Pour the filling into the cooled crust and bake for 30 minutes, until the custard is set and not jiggly.

6. Let cool for 30 minutes at room temperature and then refrigerate, uncovered, for at least 1 hour.

7. **Make the whipped cream topping:** Place the heavy cream, sugar, and vanilla in the bowl of a stand mixer fitted with the whisk attachment and whip until soft peaks form, about 2 minutes.

8. Pipe the whipped cream on top or place one big dollop in the center. Garnish with lime zest from one key lime and 4 or 5 slices of lime from the other key lime.

9. Refrigerate, uncovered, for at least 4 hours (overnight is even better). Key lime pie is best when it is very chilled.

### MAKE-AHEAD GAME PLAN

One day ahead, make the pie. Refrigerate, uncovered, until ready to serve.

### PAIRS WELL WITH

Easy Grilled Salmon with Mango Salsa (page 127)

Sheet-Pan Lamb with Caramelized Shallots and Provençal Tomatoes (page 110)

# RICH CHOCOLATE BIRTHDAY CAKE

In a world full of store-bought sheet cakes, the homemade birthday cake reigns supreme! Is there anything more sincere than making a frosted cake for someone you love (especially one that creates a sink full of dishes)? But not to worry, this recipe is as easy as it gets! It's light, moist, and chocolaty. Store-bought cakes may look tempting, but they often lack the rich flavor that makes homemade cakes truly special! This cake delivers big on the chocolate; from the cake to the silky-smooth frosting, it's *the* birthday cake for any chocoholic in your life.

# RICH CHOCOLATE BIRTHDAY CAKE

***SERVES 8*** *(Makes one 9-inch/23 cm two-layer cake)*

## CAKE

Baking spray with flour

1 cup (100 g) unsweetened
  cocoa powder

½ cup (85 g) Nestlé Dark
  Chocolate Morsels chocolate
  chips

1 cup (240 ml) boiling water

2¼ cups (450 g) granulated
  sugar

1 cup (240 ml) vegetable oil

4 large eggs, room temperature

1 tablespoon (15 ml) vanilla
  extract

1½ teaspoons (9 g) kosher salt

1½ cups (210 g) all-purpose flour

1 teaspoon (4 g) baking soda

## FROSTING

1 pound (454 g) dark chocolate,
  chopped (see Note 1)

2 cups (452 g) salted American
  butter, softened

¾ cup (95 g) powdered sugar

2 teaspoons (10 ml) vanilla
  extract

Pinch of kosher salt

1. Preheat the oven to 350°F (175°C). Place the oven rack in the lower third of the oven.

2. **Make the cake:** Spray two 9-inch (23 cm) round cake pans with baking spray, distributing it evenly with a pastry brush. Line each pan with a parchment paper round, and brush the rounds with the leftover baking spray on the brush.

3. Mix the cocoa powder and chocolate chips in a large bowl. Pour in the boiling water and let sit for 10 minutes. Whisk until the chocolate is melted and the mixture is smooth. Immediately whisk in the sugar so it dissolves from the heat.

4. Slowly add the vegetable oil, whisking a little bit at a time to incorporate. Don't rush this step! Add the eggs one at a time, whisking in between each addition. Whisk in the vanilla and salt.

5. Sift the flour and baking soda into a medium bowl. Then, add to the chocolate mixture in thirds, whisking gently in between each addition. Distribute the batter equally between the pans (see Note 2).

6. Bake for 22 to 25 minutes, until the cakes have risen and a toothpick comes out clean. Let cool completely in the pans.

7. **Make the frosting:** Place the chocolate in a large microwave-safe bowl. Microwave on high in 30-second intervals, whisking in between each interval, until melted, about 3½ minutes. Let cool for at least 20 minutes.

8. Meanwhile, beat the butter and powdered sugar in the bowl of an electric mixer until it's light and fluffy, about 5 minutes. Add the vanilla and salt. Then, add the melted chocolate and beat until fluffy and smooth.

9. Place a tablespoon (15 ml) of frosting in the center of a 12-inch (30 cm) cake stand to help stabilize the cake.

10. Remove the first cake from the pan: With one hand on the top of the cake and the other hand on the bottom of the pan, flip the cake upside down. Place the cake on the cake stand, flat side up (see Note 3).

11. Tuck a few 4×2-inch (10×5 cm) parchment paper strips under the cake to protect the cake stand from the frosting. (You'll remove these after you're done frosting.)

12. Place a few large dollops of frosting (about 1 cup/240 ml) on the first layer, and use an offset spatula to spread the frosting evenly. Remove the second cake from the pan and then stack it on top, flat side up. Put a few more dollops of frosting (about 1 cup/240 ml) on the top layer and smooth it out.

13. Use the remaining frosting to cover the sides, turning the cake stand as you go. If any crumbs get kicked up, place the cake in the freezer to harden and then try again. Once the cake is completely covered with frosting, create some decorative swoops with an offset spatula.

14. Refrigerate, uncovered, until ready to serve. Remove from the refrigerator 20 minutes before serving to allow the cake to come to room temperature.

## NOTES

1. Trader Joe's Pound Plus Dark Chocolate works great in this recipe! It's a scant bit more than a pound, but you can use the whole thing if you don't have a kitchen scale to measure out 1 pound (454 g) exactly. It will just make the cake a touch more chocolaty!

2. If you have a kitchen scale, you can create really even layers by measuring the batter. Weigh each pan, zero out the scale, and then pour 1 pound and 7 ounces (652 g) batter in each pan.

3. Don't level off the cake with a knife because this cake is too delicate and will crumble. Instead, flip it so the dome is on the bottom and the flat side is up. It's way easier and will give you flat-topped layers.

## MAKE-AHEAD GAME PLAN

One day ahead, bake and frost the cake. Refrigerate, uncovered, until ready to serve.

## PAIRS WELL WITH

Frenzy-Free Chicken Pot Pie (page 114)

Grilled Dijon Chicken with Charred Lemons (page 123)

# SOFT AND CHEWY GINGERBREAD MEN

When it comes to Christmas cookies, I go all in on the classics—and gingerbread is at the top of my list. These cookies are equally good straight out of the oven or the following day, when the flavors are even more pronounced. I love this recipe for the balance of spices it provides. It has just enough ginger to live up to its name, and the allspice and cloves pack a holiday punch! It's the kind of cookie we all crave at Christmastime, and having this go-to recipe will add years of enjoyment to your holiday gatherings. It also makes great gifts for neighbors, teachers, or friends. Skip the typical raisins in favor of currants; they work much better for a 4-inch (10 cm) cookie.

*SERVES 10 TO 12* (Makes 3 dozen cookies)

1 cup (226 g) salted American butter

¾ cup (150 g) granulated sugar

¾ cup (180 ml) molasses

1 teaspoon (5 ml) vanilla extract

3 cups (420 g) all-purpose flour, plus more for dusting

1 tablespoon (15 ml) ground cinnamon

1 teaspoon (4 g) baking soda

1 teaspoon (5 ml) ground ginger

¼ teaspoon (1.25 ml) ground allspice

⅛ teaspoon (0.625 ml) ground cloves

Pinch of kosher salt

½ cup (75 g) dried black currants

## NOTES

1. You can try other shapes, too. I like to make mittens using the currants to create a decorative trim or small stars with currants in the centers. Just be sure to bake like shapes together so they bake at the same rate. Cookies that are half the size will take less baking time. Start at 5 minutes for a 2-inch (5 cm) cookie and increase the time as needed until they are puffed up and set.

2. For a chewy cookie, bake for 8 minutes; for a crispier cookie, bake for the full 10 minutes.

1. Beat together the butter and sugar in a stand mixer until fluffy. Add the molasses and vanilla, and beat until well combined.

2. Whisk together the flour, baking soda, cinnamon, ginger, allspice, cloves, and salt in a large bowl. Slowly add the dry ingredients to the wet ingredients and beat just until combined.

3. Roll the dough into a large ball, cut it in half, and flatten it into two discs. Wrap well in plastic wrap and refrigerate for at least 2 hours (overnight is even better).

4. Preheat the oven to 350°F (175°C). Place the oven rack in the lower third of the oven. Line a baking sheet with parchment paper.

5. Roll out the dough on a well-floured surface to about ⅛ inch (3 mm) thick.

6. Cut out the gingerbread men with a 4-inch (10 cm) gingerbread man cookie cutter (see Note 1) and then transfer them to the baking sheet.

7. Press two currants into the cut gingerbread men to form the eyes and use three currants for buttons on the chest.

8. Bake for 8 to 10 minutes (see Note 2), until slightly puffed and set. Transfer to a cooling rack and let cool completely before serving or packaging.

## MAKE-AHEAD GAME PLAN

At the start of the holiday season, you can make several batches of this dough, separate it into smaller quantities, and freeze it for up to 1 month. When you need a host gift, all you have to do is thaw the dough in the fridge the night before, cut, and bake.

## PAIRS WELL WITH

Homemade Hot Chocolate (page 39)

All-Occasion Cut Sugar Cookies (page 221)

# MENU PLANS

# FALL DINNER PARTY

SERVES 4 TO 6

Sweet and Spicy Candied Pecans
*(page 69)*

Stuffed Mushroom Caps
*(page 49)*

Butternut Squash Soup with Raisin Bread Croutons
*(page 79)*

Fennel-Crusted Pork Loin with Spiced Parsnips and Apples
*(page 134)*

Roasted Broccoli with Garlic and Parmesan
*(page 147)*

Go-To Chocolate Bundt Cake and Homemade Whipped Cream
*(page 225)*

## TWO DAYS BEFORE

- Read through all the recipes.
- Do the shopping.
- Make the butternut squash soup, except for the croutons. Let cool completely and then cover and refrigerate.

## THE DAY BEFORE

- Bake the pecans and then allow them to dry and harden. Transfer to an airtight container and store at room temperature.
- Make the whipped cream, cover, and refrigerate.
- Make the croutons for the soup. Let cool completely. Then, cover loosely with foil and store at room temperature.

## THE DAY OF

- Bake the chocolate cake. Let cool completely, keep it in the pan, and cover loosely with foil.
- Prepare the mushroom caps all the way through step 5. Cover loosely and refrigerate.
- Cut the broccoli into florets, cover, and refrigerate.
- Thirty minutes before guests arrive, preheat the oven to 350°F (175°C) and then bake the mushroom caps for 12 to 15 minutes.
- Prep the pork through step 1. Place in a Pyrex casserole, cover, and refrigerate.
- Peel and slice the parsnips. Cover and refrigerate.
- Two hours before serving, remove the pork from the refrigerator and let it come up to room temperature for 30 minutes.
- Preheat the oven to 400°F (200°C).
- Slice the apples and toss it with the parsnips, olive oil, and spices.
- Sear the pork in the roasting pan. Add the apples and parsnips and then place in the oven to roast.
- Thirty minutes later, reheat the soup and keep it on a low simmer.
- Meanwhile, toss the broccoli in the oil and seasonings and place it on two baking sheets.
- Transfer the pork to a carving board. Cover with foil to keep warm. Leave the apples and parsnips in the roasting pan.
- Increase the oven temperature to 450°F (230°C) for the broccoli. While the pork is resting, roast the broccoli for 20 minutes. Remove the broccoli from the oven and keep it on the baking sheets (residual heat will keep it warm). It's okay to serve the broccoli at room temperature, too.
- Reduce the oven temperature to 425°F (215°C). Serve and enjoy the soup!
- Have a buddy clear the soup bowls while you transfer the parsnips and apples to a baking sheet (they'll caramelize more quickly this way). Place in the oven for 10 to 15 minutes to reheat.
- Meanwhile, make the gravy in the roasting pan.
- Carve the pork and serve with the apples and parsnips.
- Flip the cake out of its pan onto a cake stand, dust with powdered sugar, and serve with whipped cream.

# CLASSIC THANKSGIVING

SERVES 8 TO 10

**Beginner's Roast Turkey (and Gravy)**
*(page 140)*

**Homemade Cranberry Sauce**
*(page 141)*

**Make-Ahead Thanksgiving Stuffing**
*(page 163)*

**Sweet Potato Casserole with Toasted Marshmallows**
*(page 164)*

**Fresh Green Bean Casserole**
**(For Those Who Don't Like Green Bean Casserole)**
*(page 159)*

**Pumpkin Pie Tart**
*(page 232)*

## TWO DAYS BEFORE

- Read through all the recipes.
- Do the shopping.
- Slice the bread for the stuffing into cubes. Keep them in a container with the cover open just slightly to let the air in. You want them to dry out.
- Chop the vegetables for the stuffing. Cover and refrigerate.
- Make the cranberry sauce. It's even better made ahead; the flavors will marry. Cover and refrigerate.
- Make the dough for the pumpkin tart. Wrap in plastic wrap and refrigerate.

## THE DAY BEFORE

- Assemble and bake the stuffing. Let cool completely and then cover with foil and refrigerate.
- Make the sweet potato casserole filling, transfer it to a baking dish, and let cool. Do not put the marshmallows on yet. Cover with foil and refrigerate.
- Make the green bean casserole. Let cool, but don't add the onions yet. Cover and refrigerate.
- Make the pumpkin pie tart. Let cool completely and then refrigerate, uncovered.
- Make the whipped cream. Cover and refrigerate.

## THE DAY OF

- Prepare the turkey 3 to 4 hours before serving. Ideally, the turkey should rest for at least 20 minutes before serving, but you could keep it resting for up to an hour. It will still be warm because it's such a large piece of meat, and the hot gravy will also bring the temperature up. I serve turkey between warm and room temperature because you need that extra time to make the gravy and heat up the side dishes.
- Increase the oven temperature to 350°F (175°C) to reheat the side dishes simultaneously.
- Place an oven rack in the middle position. Put the sweet potato casserole, covered, on the top rack. Bake for 35 to 40 minutes, until heated through.
- Meanwhile, place the crispy onions on top of the green bean casserole, cover, and bake on the lower rack (left side) for 20 to 25 minutes, until the sauce begins to bubble.
- Place the stuffing on the lower rack (right side) and bake, covered, for 20 to 25 minutes, until warmed through.
- As the side dishes are heating up, get a trusted guest to carve the turkey (decide who this person will be in advance!) while you make the gravy.
- Uncover the green bean casserole and the stuffing and bake for 5 minutes, until the onions on the casserole are glistening and the bread cubes on the stuffing crisp up. Remove the stuffing and the green bean casserole from the oven.
- Remove the sweet potato casserole from the oven, top with the marshmallows, and place under the broiler to toast the marshmallows, 1 to 2 minutes. You must *stand there* and watch them! They will burn if left unattended.
- While you "stand watch," have a buddy remove the cranberry sauce from the refrigerator and place it in a bowl.
- Transfer the gravy to a gravy boat and serve with the turkey.
- After the meal, while plates are being cleared, remove the pumpkin tart from the refrigerator to take the chill off. Transfer the whipped cream to a serving bowl.
- Slice the tart and serve with a dollop of cream and a pinch of nutmeg on top.

# CHRISTMAS
# BREAKFAST

## SERVES 6 TO 8

**Sweet and Spiced Mulled Cider**
*(page 32)*

**Connecticut Christmas Bread**
*(page 199)*

**Puffy Egg Bake**
*(page 169)*

**Easy Roasted Potatoes with Smoky Ketchup**
*(page 152) x 2*

**Hide-Away Granola parfaits**
*(see page 183)*

**No-Chop Fancy Fruit Salad**
*(page 188)*

### TWO DAYS BEFORE

- Read through all the recipes.
- Do the shopping.
- Make the granola. Let cool completely. Then, transfer to an airtight container and leave at room temperature.
- Make the smoky ketchup. Cover and refrigerate.

### THE DAY BEFORE

- Prep the egg bake through step 5, but keep it in the mixing bowl. Cover and refrigerate.
- Bake the Christmas bread. Let cool completely. Keep in the pan, cover loosely with foil, and store at room temperature.

### THE DAY OF

- Preheat the oven to 300°F (150°C).
- Reheat the Christmas bread, covered, for 20 minutes. Then, uncover and bake for 5 minutes. Set aside to cool.
- Increase the temperature to 350°F (175°C) for the potatoes and egg bake.
- Prep the potatoes. Place them on two baking sheets in the oven on the middle rack. Set the timer for 20 minutes.
- Remove the egg bake batter from the refrigerator. Transfer to a greased casserole dish and let come to room temperature.
- Make the mulled cider and serve it with the Christmas bread to start.
- When the potato timer goes off, transfer them to the bottom rack and adjust the middle rack to the lowest setting. Bake the egg bake on the middle rack for 30 minutes.
- Meanwhile, make the fruit salad.
- Assemble the parfaits, either in individual glasses (martini glasses work well) or as a DIY bar with a bowl of granola, a bowl of vanilla yogurt, and the fruit salad laid out.
- Transfer the potatoes to a serving bowl and serve with the smoky ketchup.
- Serve the egg bake.

# CHRISTMAS DINNER

SERVES 6 TO 8

**Sparkling Christmas Punch**
*(page 44)*

**Baked Brie with Fig Jam, Rosemary, and Walnuts**
*(page 66) × 2*

**Rosemary Beef Tenderloin with Horseradish Cream**
*(page 143)*

**Roasted Ratatouille**
*(page 151) × 2*

**Crispy Hasselback Potatoes**
*(page 160) × 2*

**All-You-Can-Eat Chocolate Mousse**
*(page 215)*

## TWO DAYS BEFORE

- Read through all the recipes.
- Do the shopping.
- Season the beef, cover, and refrigerate.
- Make the ratatouille. Transfer to a microwave-safe bowl (for easy reheating). Cover and refrigerate.

## THE DAY BEFORE

- Make the chocolate mousse. Garnish with whipped cream and chocolate shavings. Refrigerate, uncovered.
- Make the horseradish cream. Cover and refrigerate.

## THE DAY OF

- I recommend making two baked Bries, if it's the only appetizer you'll be serving. Prep the Bries by placing them on a plate along with the toppings. Cover and refrigerate.
- Two hours before guests arrive, toast the baguette slices. Keep loosely covered at room temperature.
- Thirty minutes before guests arrive, preheat the oven to 375°F (190°C).
- Prepare the punch. Add the garnishes, but don't add the champagne until guests arrive.
- Place the Bries in mini skillets or oven-safe casserole dishes. Bake them in the oven for 12 to 15 minutes.
- Prep your heat-safe Brie platter (a cutting board with a fabric trivet or decorative folded tea towel works well). Add the baguette toasts and grapes.
- Prep the potatoes through seasoning with salt and pepper in step 6. Place them on a sheet pan so they are ready to go. Increase the oven temperature to 425°F (215°C).
- As soon as the guests arrive, add the champagne to the punch. Place the Brie on the platter and serve.
- Place the potatoes in the oven on the middle rack and set the timer for 35 minutes. Remove the beef from the refrigerator and let it come up to room temperature.
- When the potato timer goes off, brush them with the melted butter and place them on the bottom rack, leaving the middle rack free for the beef.
- Sear the beef in the roasting pan.
- Place the beef in the oven on the middle rack and reduce the temperature to 425°F (215°C). Roast the beef for 15 to 20 minutes, brushing the potatoes with butter at the 15-minute mark and then check the beef for doneness at the same time.
- Continue to roast the beef until a meat thermometer registers 140°F (60°C) for medium in the thickest part of the meat. The potatoes can roast a bit longer if needed while the beef rests before carving.
- While the beef is resting, reheat the ratatouille in the microwave on high in 1-minute intervals, stirring with a fork after each interval. Transfer to a serving bowl.
- Carve the beef and serve with the horseradish cream, potatoes, and ratatouille.
- Serve the chocolate mousse at the table, portioning it out into footed bowls.

# EASTER LUNCH

SERVES 6 TO 8

**Strawberry Margarita Smoothies**
*(page 35) × 2*

**Crudité Platter with Green Goddess Dip**
*(page 50)*

**Creamy Asparagus Soup with Crème Fraîche**
*(page 88) × 2*

**Easy Grilled Salmon with Mango Salsa**
*(page 127) × 2*

**Summer Corn Confetti Salad**
*(page 95)*

**Key Lime Pie**
*(page 240)*

## TWO DAYS BEFORE

- Read through all the recipes.
- Do the shopping.
- Make the asparagus soup. Cover and refrigerate.

## THE DAY BEFORE

- Make the key lime pie. Refrigerate, uncovered.
- Make the green goddess dip. Cover and refrigerate.
- Prepare the corn salad through step 4. Do not add the herbs or the dressing until ready to serve.
- Prepare the vegetables for the crudité. Arrange them on a platter and cover with a clean, damp dish towel or damp paper towels. Refrigerate.

## THE DAY OF

- Two hours ahead, season the fish. Cover and refrigerate.
- One hour ahead, prep the fruit and onion for the salsa. Cover and refrigerate.
- Thirty minutes before guests arrive, place the dip on the platter with the crudité.
- Whisk together the dressing for the corn salad. Cover and keep at room temperature.
- Ten minutes before guests arrive, place the margarita ingredients in the blender. Do not blend until guests arrive. Prep the garnishes.
- Serve the margaritas with the crudité platter.
- Thirty minutes before you plan to serve lunch, grease and preheat an outdoor grill.
- Reheat the soup and serve.
- Ask a buddy to clear the soup bowls while you grill the fish. Remove the fish from the grill and set aside.
- Add the herbs and dressing to the corn salad, toss, and then transfer to a serving bowl.
- Add the cilantro, lime zest, and lime juice to the salsa.
- Plate the fish, add the salsa, and garnish with the cilantro sprigs, lime, and radish. Serve the fish with the corn salad.
- Remove the pie from the refrigerator. Slice and serve.

# MOTHER'S DAY BRUNCH

---

SERVES 6 TO 8

---

DIY Bloody Mary Bar
*(page 31) × 2*

Southern Cheese Straws (The Yankee Version)
*(page 62)*

Ham, Leek, and Gruyère Strata
*(page 195)*

Tossed salad with 1, 2, 3 French Vinaigrette
*(page 181) × 2*

Set It and Forget It Smoked Salmon Platter
*(page 170)*

Perfect Lemon Bars
*(page 236)*

## TWO DAYS BEFORE

- Read through all the recipes.
- Do the shopping (except for the bagels).
- Make the shortbread dough for the lemon bars. Wrap in plastic and refrigerate.
- Bake the cheese straws and let cool completely. Place in a resealable plastic bag and freeze.

## THE DAY BEFORE

- Bake the lemon bars. Let cool completely and then refrigerate, uncovered.
- Make the whipped cream. Cover and refrigerate.
- Prep the strata mixture through step 5. Cover with foil and refrigerate overnight.
- Make the cream cheese spread for the salmon platter. Cover and refrigerate.
- Make the vinaigrette. Cover and refrigerate.
- Mix up the Bloody Mary mix and refrigerate. Place the garnishes in bowls, cover, and refrigerate.

## THE DAY OF

- Purchase the bagels in the morning; you'll have a better selection if you get them early. Keep them tightly wrapped in their bag.
- Two hours before guests arrive, arrange the salmon platter. Cover and refrigerate.
- Thirty minutes before guests arrive, set up the Bloody Mary bar.
- Preheat the oven to 300°F (150°C). Place the frozen cheese straws on a baking sheet and bake for 5 to 7 minutes, until warmed through. Plate to serve at room temperature.
- Preheat oven to 375°F (190°C). Remove the strata from the refrigerator to take the chill off while the oven preheats.
- Once guests arrive, serve the drinks and cheese straws.
- Bake the strata, covered, for 40 minutes, and then uncovered for 15 to 20 minutes. Garnish the strata with black pepper and chives.
- Slice the bagels and toss the salad with the dressing.
- Serve the salad and the strata along with the salmon board and bagels.
- Slice the lemon bars, add a dollop of whip cream, a grate of lemon zest and serve.

# SUMMER BBQ

SERVES 6 TO 8

**Fresh and Fruity White Wine Sangria**
*(page 36) × 2*

**Leave-It-Chunky Guacamole**
*(page 73) × 2*

**Better BBQ Chicken**
*(page 133)*

**Horseradish Potato Salad with Caramelized Shallots**
*(page 84) × 2*

**Grilled Panzanella Salad**
*(page 92) × 2*

**Ice cream sandwiches made with Dangerously Delicious
Chocolate Chip Cookies**
*(page 203)*

## TWO DAYS BEFORE

- Read through all the recipes.
- Do the shopping. Remember to buy vanilla ice cream for the cookie sandwiches.
- Cook the potatoes and let them cool. Keep them whole, cover, and refrigerate.

## THE DAY BEFORE

- Make the BBQ sauce. Let cool and then transfer to a 2-cup (480 ml) glass measuring cup. Cover and refrigerate.
- Make the dressing for the potato salad. Cover and refrigerate.
- Make the cookies. Use a 1-ounce (30 ml) scoop to make smaller cookie sandwiches (I recommend this, since they are pretty rich) or double the recipe to use a 2-ounce (60 ml) scoop and make larger cookie sandwiches.
- Let the cookies cool completely. Meanwhile, remove the ice cream from the freezer to soften. Assemble the ice cream sandwiches and freeze.
- Make the melon balls and melon ball garnish for the sangria. Cover and refrigerate.
- Make the shallots for the potato salad. Let cool and then cover and refrigerate.

## THE DAY OF

- Grill the bread for the panzanella and leave at room temperature. Cover loosely with foil only when the bread is completely cooled (otherwise, your bread will get soggy).
- Two hours before guests arrive, make the sangria. Refrigerate until ready to serve.
- Two hours before, make the panzanella salad vinaigrette and slice the tomatoes. Place the tomatoes in a serving bowl. Cover both and leave at room temperature.
- Two hours before, chop the tomatoes and onions for the guacamole. Cover and refrigerate.
- Fifteen minutes before guests arrive, make the guacamole. Transfer to a serving bowl and place on a platter with the tortilla chips. Serve with the sangria.
- Forty-five minutes before you plan to serve, heat an outdoor grill to medium-high heat. Preheat the oven to 350°F (175°C).
- Grill the chicken, adding the sauce as directed. Then, transfer to the oven and bake for 10 to 15 minutes.
- While the chicken is in the oven, slice the potatoes and toss them with the dressing. Then, transfer to a serving bowl and garnish with the shallots.
- Cut the grilled bread into cubes, add to the tomatoes, and toss with the vinaigrette.
- Transfer the chicken to a platter and serve with the salads.
- Remove the ice cream sandwiches from the freezer. If serving large sandwiches, slice them in half with a large chef's knife so they are easier to eat.

# SUMMER DINNER PARTY

SERVES 6 TO 8

**Bellini Cocktails**
*(page 43)*

**Deconstructed Cherry Tomato Bruschetta**
*(page 61)*

**Grilled Dijon Chicken with Charred Lemons**
*(page 123)*

**Philippe's Pesto Orzo Salad**
*(page 87)*

**Cool as a Cucumber Salad with Crème Fraîche, Dill, and Mint**
*(page 99)*

**Lemon-Scented Strawberry Shortcakes**
*(page 211)*

## TWO DAYS BEFORE

- Read through all the recipes.
- Do the shopping.

## THE DAY BEFORE

- In the morning, make the marinade and marinate the chicken. Cover and refrigerate.
- Make the pesto salad. Cover and refrigerate.
- Slice the vegetables for the cucumber salad. Cover and refrigerate.
- Make the whipped cream. Cover and refrigerate.

## THE DAY OF

- Make the strawberry shortcakes. Let cool on the baking sheet. Then, cover loosely with foil and store at room temperature.
- Four hours ahead, prepare the strawberries. Cover and refrigerate.
- Two hours ahead, make the cucumber salad through step 3. Wait to add the herbs and seasonings until just before serving.
- Forty-five minutes before guests arrive, prepare the tomatoes for the bruschetta. Grill the bread and keep at room temperature.
- Make the bellini puree in the blender. Do not mix with the prosecco until guests arrive.
- Serve the bruschetta with the bellini.
- Thirty minutes before serving dinner, heat an outdoor grill to medium-high. Remove the chicken from the refrigerator. Prep the lemons.
- Grill the chicken and lemons. Transfer to a serving platter and garnish.
- Serve the chicken with the salads.
- Preheat the oven to 300°F (150°C) and then clear the dinner plates.
- Uncover the shortcakes and reheat for 5 minutes. Assemble and serve.

# INDEX

# ACKNOWLEDGMENTS

To my followers across every platform: This book never would have been written without you. Your comments and words of encouragement over the years have kept me going in ways you will never know. I'm truly grateful for every single one of you. You made this book happen.

To my parents, the consummate entertainers: This book is filled with memories and ideas that were born in your home, a place of enormous love, festivity and celebration that continues to inspire me to this day.

To my sister, Meg: Thank you for being my earliest coconspirator in all things fabulous. Our early dinner parties in our first apartment set me on this course! And to my brother, Joe: You brought the fun to every family gathering as soon as you walked in the door, and your presence is deeply missed.

To Joie, Orlando, Eddie, and Luke and a long list of dear family friends: The recipes in this book are a testament to all the good times we've shared around the table.

To all my sweet aunts and uncles and amazing cousins: Thank you for being my number one fans and for sharing my recipes with your friends, book clubs, neighbors, and clients. Word of mouth is the best compliment there is!

A big heartfelt thanks to my agent, Sally Ekus, for not giving up on me. I'm so grateful for your talents and expertise and, more importantly, for your patience as I navigated this whole book-proposal-publishing process. And to Frances Baca for designing one heck of a proposal. We did it!

To my editor, Olivia Peluso, my favorite English teacher! Thank you for smoothing out my words, making my instructions easier to follow, and putting those ingredients in the right order. I couldn't have done it without your guidance! I'm so grateful you saw potential in me and rolled the dice on this book.

To Jessica Lee, for your beautiful book design, good taste, and problem-solving. I'm so grateful for your ability to address a challenge with the beauty of design.

To Michael Wayne, CEO of Kin Community: Thank you for giving the Entertaining with Beth brand its wings and taking a chance on me. And, more importantly, for pushing me in ways that allowed me to grow professionally even when I didn't want to be pushed! It made all the difference.

A big heartfelt thanks to the EWB production crew: Cody, Goro, Tristan, Tyler, Geoff, Adrian, Nick, and Clelia, I never could have done it without you guys! Thank you for showing up at the crack of dawn, even on Sundays, to shoot my videos. For staying late to get just one more shot, putting up with all my five-plus-recipe shoot days, and packing up all the food and taking it home. I could never have gone this far without each of your talents!

To Ed Rudolph: Your photographs in this book capture the exact way these recipes taste! I'm in awe of your talents. Thank you for showing up each day on a grueling schedule, as fresh as you were on day one. And to your assistants, Justin and David: Thank you both for your fun, positive personalities and for tasting and enjoying all the food!

To Marah Abel: Thank you for reading my mind. Your food styling in this book was better than anything I had in my head. You have the true soul of an artist! And to Jason Strohl: Thank you for taking such care with my recipes, laughing at my headnotes, and being the best grillmaster there is!

To Jennifer Barguiarena: Thank you for your beautiful eye and for giving these photos additional life and personality with your beautiful props!

To Sofia Suarez: Thank you for the hours and hours of help in the kitchen. The onion chopping, the pan scrubbing, and all the countless groceries you helped me organize made this process way less daunting. And to Ben Weiner for retesting all the recipes; I really appreciated all of your notes, tips, and suggestions! And the pictures were fun, too!

To Karine and the whole team at Sézane: Thank you for the beautiful clothes that grace these pages. They added the exact spirit I was after.

To all of my French family and friends: Thank you for introducing me to a love of French food and culture. Your inspiration continually seeps into my recipes and style of entertaining.

And lastly, to my husband, Philippe: Thank you for the countless hours of taking the kids out on Sundays so I could shoot my videos, tasting a recipe just one more time when I knew you couldn't stomach another bite, welcoming countless crews into our home, and, most importantly, believing in my potential before I could ever see it for myself. *Je t'aime toujours.*

## ABOUT THE AUTHOR

Beth Le Manach has been cooking and entertaining for over thirty years. Her cooking philosophy is "minimal effort for maximum impact," which translates into simple recipes elegant enough for entertaining but also easy enough for a weeknight meal. Beth's recipe videos are posted weekly on her YouTube channel, Entertaining with Beth, and on all major social media platforms.